VISIONS OF HOPE

VISIONS OF HOPE

Emerging Theologians and the Future of the Church

Edited by

Kevin J. Ahern

ORBIS BOOKS

Maryknoll, New York 10545

Founded in 1970, Orbis Books endeavors to publish works that enlighten the mind, nourish the spirit, and challenge the conscience. The publishing arm of the Maryknoll Fathers and Brothers, Orbis seeks to explore the global dimensions of the Christian faith and mission, to invite dialogue with diverse cultures and religious traditions, and to serve the cause of reconciliation and peace. The books published reflect the views of their authors and do not represent the official position of the Maryknoll Society. To learn more about Maryknoll and Orbis Books, please visit our website at www.maryknollsociety.org.

Copyright © 2013 by Kevin J. Ahern.

Published by Orbis Books, Maryknoll, New York 10545–0302.
Manufactured in the United States of America.
Manuscript editing and typesetting by Joan Weber Laflamme.

Library of Congress Cataloging-in-Publication Data

Visions of hope : emerging theologians and the future of the church / edited by Kevin J. Ahern.
    p. cm.
  ISBN 978–1–62698–016–7 (pbk.)
  1. Church. 2. Catholic Church—Doctrines. 3. Church renewal—Catholic Church. 4. Catholic Church—History—1965– I. Ahern, Kevin.
BX1746.V56 2013
282.09'051—dc23

                2012037227

Contents

The Documents of the Second Vatican Council   vii

I. Introduction: Looking to the Future with Hope   1
Kevin J. Ahern

Is Vatican II Still Relevant?   7
Massimo Faggioli

II. Liturgy in the Twenty-First Century   21
Benjamin Durheim

Our Fragile Flesh: Sacramental Hospitality Toward
Persons with Intellectual Disabilities and Its Implications
for Theology   25
Elizabeth L. Antus

Mystical "Body": An Ecclesiology Informed by
Judith Butler   39
Gina Ingiosi

III. Ministry for the Future   49
Nathaniel Hibner

"Pastors" and "the Other Faithful" (LG, 32): The
Sexual-Abuse Scandal and the Emergence
of Authority Relationships in the Church   53
Anselma Dolcich-Ashley

The Structure and Structures of Ministry: Shaping the
Future   69
Peter Folan, SJ

Renewing the Permanent Diaconate   85
Sofia Seguel Ñancucheo

IV. **The Future of Dialogue** 97
Christopher Conway

Interreligious Dialogue in a Post–***Nostra Aetate*** Church:
The Tension Between Mutuality and Evangelization 99
Heather Miller Rubens

Consensus Ecclesiarum Viewed in the Light of *Elementa
Ecclesiae* and *Sensus Fidelium* 109
Sandra Arenas

Dialogue for Peacebuilding in the Light of
Human Rights 123
Charles Ochero Cornelio

V. **The Enduring Ethical Vision of *Gaudium et Spes:* Catholic
Moral Engagement in the Twenty-First Century** 129
Michael P. Jaycox

The Ethical Potential of Communal Movements for
Catholic Social Thought: The Trinitarian Anthropology
of the Focolare Movement 133
Ellen Van Stichel

The Future of Catholic Public Theology: Mediating the
Church and the World in Pluralistic Societies 151
Gonzalo Villagrán, SJ

What Does *Gaudium et Spes* Have to Say toward
Contemporary Issues of Racism? 167
Krista Stevens

VI. **The Future of Ecclesiology** 177
Stephen Okey

The Local Church in Dialogue: Toward an Orthopraxis
of Reception 181
Amanda C. Osheim

The Local and Universal Churches: Expressing
Catholicity Through Their Reciprocity 191
B. Kevin Brown

The Documents of the Second Vatican Council

SC   *Sacrosanctum Concilium, Constitution on the Sacred Liturgy* (1963)

IM   *Inter Mirifica, Decree on the Means of Social Communication* (1963)

LG   *Lumen Gentium, Dogmatic Constitution on the Church* (1964)

OE   *Orientalium Ecclesiarum, Decree on the Catholic Churches of the Eastern Rite* (1964)

UR   *Unitatis Redintegratio, Decree on Ecumenism* (1964)

CD   *Christus Dominus, Decree Concerning the Pastoral Office of Bishops in the Church* (1965)

PC   *Perfectae Caritatis, Decree on Renewal of Religious Life* (1965)

OT   *Optatam Totius, Decree on Priestly Training* (1965)

GE   *Gravissimum Educationis, Declaration on Christian Education* (1965)

NA   *Nostra Aetate, Declaration on the Relation of the Church to Non-Christian Religions* (1965)

DV   *Dei Verbum, Dogmatic Constitution on Divine Revelation* (1965)

AA   *Apostolicam Actuositatem, Decree on the Apostolate of the Laity* (1965)

DH   *Dignitatis Humanae, Declaration on Religious Freedom* (1965)

AG   *Ad Gentes, Decree on the Mission Activity of the Church* (1965)

PO   *Presbyterorum Ordinis, Decree on the Ministry and Life of Priests* (1965)

GS   *Gaudium et Spes, Pastoral Constitution on the Church in the Modern World* (1965)

Unless otherwise noted, quotations from the texts of the Second Vatican Council are taken from *Vatican Council II: The Basic Sixteen Documents: Constitutions, Decrees, Declarations*. 2nd ed. Edited by Austin Flannery. Northport, NY: Costello, 1996. All official Vatican documents also are available on the vatican.va website.

I.

INTRODUCTION

Looking to the Future with Hope

KEVIN J. AHERN

*The conciliar decrees are not the end of a jour-
ney, but rather a point of departure for new des-
tinations. The spirit and the renewing breath of
the Council have yet to penetrate the life of the
Church to its depths. The seeds of life planted by
the Council in the soil of the Church have yet to
come to their full maturity.*

—POPE PAUL VI[1]

In the five decades since Blessed John XXIII opened the Second Vatican Council our world has witnessed profound social and cultural
changes. While it has brought benefits to many people, the complex
phenomenon of globalization has not been purely positive. On the
one hand, technological developments in medicine, science, and social
communications engender new hopes as people and cultures become
increasingly interconnected across the world. On the other, new inequalities, conflicts, and afflictions divide and polarize people at local
and global levels.[2] In the four decades since the end of Vatican II, for
example, the global gap between the rich and the poor, according to a
recent United Nations report, has "widened to a gulf," with over one
billion people living in extreme poverty.[3]

As *Gaudium et Spes* reminds us, the church cannot be detached from these social and cultural dynamics (GS, 1). Sharing in the hopes and afflictions of humanity, the Catholic Church faces new possibilities and challenges in today's world.[4] The "renewing breath" of the council initiated a process that has given life to many important pastoral developments across the world: new roles for the laity, a deeper appreciation of scripture, and more frequent reception of the Eucharist. Additionally, the council spurred practices of interreligious dialogue, projects of solidarity and justice with the poor, ecumenism, and the development of a vibrant local church in Africa, Asia, and Latin America.

Despite the variety of positive theological insights and movements that has taken root in the church since Vatican II, the ecclesial community faces a number of unresolved questions today. In traditionally Catholic regions of Europe, for example, the number of practicing Catholics—especially among young adults—has dropped significantly in the face of powerful cultural trends. In North America, Ireland, and elsewhere, the clergy sexual-abuse crisis continues to shock and alienate people from the church. At the same time, theological and pastoral debates concerning sexual ethics, the relationship of the church and the world, the role of women, and liturgical reform polarize Catholics and Christian communities. While these conflicts often reflect polarizing trends within the broader society, other conflicts are centered on differing theological interpretations of Vatican II.[5]

In light of these complex challenges, many are asking, "What is the future of the church?" Born after the seeds of the council were planted, young theologians and church leaders are in a unique position to offer hopeful responses to this question. As the first generations of theologians who did not directly experience the council and its pastoral reforms, "Generation X" and "Millennial" theologians offer fresh insights into the significance of the council's teaching and its relevancy for the future. This book brings together the "visions" of twenty-two theologians from seven countries who gathered in March 2012 for the Emerging Theologians conference sponsored by the International Catholic Movement for Intellectual and Cultural Affairs (Pax Romana–ICMICA) and the Boston College Theology Graduate Student Association.

THE NEED FOR CONVERSATION AND DIALOGUE

Writing shortly after the close of Vatican II, Cardinal Leo Joseph Suenens, one of the major figures of the council, lamented the "lack of dialogue among theologians" from different "theological schools" that existed before and during the council. Looking to the future, Suenens called for greater cooperation and communication among different universities as an important need in the church.[6] In many ways this volume, with contributions from young scholars at twelve different theological faculties and institutions in the United States and Europe, responds to Suenens's challenge.[7] At a time when theology is becoming increasingly specialized, and in many places polarized, this project aims to contribute to wider conversations within the church and the academy by sharing the perspectives of young scholars from different subfields of theology.

IS VATICAN II STILL RELEVANT?

While there are certainly theological differences among the young scholars featured in this volume, all agree that the Second Vatican Council remains relevant for the present and future life of the church. This book stands in contrast to those prevailing perceptions of young adults as uninterested in what happened at Vatican II. It is my experience that young adult Catholics *are* interested in what happened at the council and its insights on key features of Christian faith such as the Eucharist, social justice, the role of the laity, and dialogue with other faiths.

We begin this volume with an insightful analysis by Massimo Faggioli on why the council remains relevant today. Given the often-heated debates surrounding the lasting impact of the council, Faggioli examines the relationships between the teachings of Vatican II about the internal life of the church on liturgy, ministry, and ecclesiology with its teachings on external issues such as ethics and dialogue. No vision for the future of the church, he argues, can ignore the insights of Vatican II and the integral connection between the *ad intra* and *ad extra* dimensions of Catholic theology. We are, as he writes, "at a point of no return." We simply cannot go back to a pre–Vatican II church.

Faggioli's historical and integrated analysis helps to situate the following five sections of this book: liturgy, ministry, dialogue, ethics, and ecclesiology. In each section young scholars specializing in these areas look to the future while grounding themselves in conciliar texts and the needs of the present. As Faggioli's analysis reminds us, the specific thematic considerations in the following sections should not be seen in isolation from one another. Rather, as the authors demonstrate, there are clear connections among morality, the sacraments, church structures, spirituality, and Christian daily life.

Young theologians, as this volume illustrates, offer important insights on the role of the council and its relevancy for the future of the church. The composition of this project, where the majority of authors are lay men and lay women, itself reflects the legacy and relevance of the council. It is our hope that this collection of essays will further the much-needed dialogue on issues of importance for the church in the world today.

IN GRATITUDE

The Emerging Theologians organizing committee is very grateful for the support of all those who helped to make this publication possible. First and foremost, we would like to thank the contributors to this volume and the more than sixty young scholars who participated in our conference in March 2012. Their hopeful presence is a gift for our church and the theological academy. We look forward to continuing this network of young theologians in the future. We are particularly grateful to our keynote speaker, Massimo Faggioli, and his respondent, María Teresa Dávila. We also would like to extend our thanks to the many insightful emerging theologians who took time from their busy schedules to review the papers proposed for this volume, including Douglas Ballas, Daniel Cosacchi, Maria Cruz, Nichole Flores, Brian Green, Katherine Greiner, Suzanne Mulligan, Elizabeth Osborne, Andrew Staron, David Scholl, John Slattery, Stuart Squires, and Raymond Ward.

Second, we would like to thank those from Pax Romana–ICMICA and Boston College who supported the organization of the Emerging Theologians conference. Thank you especially to the Boston College Theology Department, School of Theology and Ministry, Graduate School of Arts and Sciences, and Center for the Church in the Twenty-First Century. President William Leahy, SJ, Mark Massa, SJ, David Quigley, Catherine Cornille, James Keenan, SJ, Erik Goldschmidt, Karen Kiefer, Megan McCabe, and many other Boston College faculty, administrators, students, and staff were extremely generous in their support of our initiative.

Finally, we are especially grateful to all of those at Orbis Books, in particular Robert Ellsberg and Michael Leach, who have long supported the research and writing of young scholars. We deeply appreciate the important contribution of Orbis Books to theological scholarship and life of the church as a whole.

NOTES

1. Letter of Pope Paul VI to the International Theological Congress of Rome, September 21, 1966. Quoted in Leon-Joseph Suenens, "Introduction: Co-Responsibility: Dominating Idea of the Council and Its Pastoral Consequences," in *Renewal of Religious Structures: Proceedings of the Congress on the Theology of the Renewal of the Church Centenary of Canada, 1867–1967*, vol. 2, ed. L. K. Shook (New York: Herder and Herder, 1968), 8.

2. See Vincent J. Miller, "Where Is the Church? Globalization and Catholicity," *Theological Studies* 69, no. 2 (June 2008): 412–32.

3. United Nations Development Programme, *Human Development Report 2010: The Real Wealth of Nations: Pathways to Human Development* (New York: Palgrave Macmillan, 2010), 42.

4. For an overview of these possibilities and challenges, see John L. Allen, *The Future Church: How Ten Trends Are Revolutionizing the Catholic Church* (New York: Doubleday, 2009); Richard R. Gaillardetz, *Ecclesiology for a Global Church: A People Called and Sent* (Maryknoll, NY: Orbis Books, 2008); Bradford E. Hinze, *Practices of Dialogue in the Roman Catholic Church: Aims and Obstacles, Lessons and Laments* (New York: Continuum, 2006); and Gerard Mannion, *Ecclesiology and Postmodernity: Questions for the Church in Our Time* (Collegeville, MN: Liturgical Press, 2007).

5. See Massimo Faggioli, *Vatican II: The Battle for Meaning* (New York: Paulist Press, 2012).

6. Suenens, "Introduction," 17.

7. Boston College, Boston College School of Theology and Ministry, the Catholic University of Leuven, the University of Dayton, Fordham University, Institute for Christian and Jewish Studies, the International Movement of Catholic Students, Loras College, Loyola Marymount University, the University of Notre Dame, the University of St. Thomas, and the Pontifical Gregorian University.

Is Vatican II Still Relevant?

MASSIMO FAGGIOLI

Is the Second Vatican Council still relevant after fifty years? This is not a rhetorical question. The church and the world have changed since the opening of the council on October 12, 1962. For many other councils in the history of the Catholic Church, that same exact question—Is the ecumenical council of fifty years ago still relevant?—would have received a negative answer (to put it mildly). Let us imagine a gathering of theologians in 1562 (during the Council of Trent) trying to understand the relevancy of the Fifth Lateran Council (1512–17), which had ended in Rome in the same year of the "95 theses" of Martin Luther—a council that never detected the signs of corruption and "theological unrest."

On the other hand, there are other councils that proved—fifty years after their completion—their relevancy and their role in the life of the church and of theology.[1] The ecumenical councils of the fourth and fifth century, like the Council of Trent, showed their importance in the decades and generations following their conclusions.

This reveals to us three facts. First, *there are different kinds of councils*, even among ecumenical councils. There are councils with lasting impact and councils with ephemeral life (or, as then Cardinal Ratzinger put it a few years ago, "failed councils").[2]

Vatican II clearly does not belong in the category of the failed councils: no one in 1562 was talking about the Fifth Lateran Council that began fifty years before. Today, the role of Vatican II in today's Catholicism is completely different. Vatican II is not only remembered and studied, but it has become part of the everyday life of Catholics and serves as a compass for the church and for Catholic theology.[3]

A second fact is that *Vatican II had, in its first fifty years of life, an interesting and complex history of reception*, rooted in a theological debate that encompassed all cultural and geographical latitudes of world Catholicism. The debate on the reception of Vatican II survived not only the generation of bishops and theologians who were at the council, but it also survived very difficult and important moments in the relationship among the magisterium, theologians, people of God, and the wider world: the encyclical *Humanae Vitae* in 1968, Paul VI's disappointments of the mid-1970s, the new *Code of Canon Law* in 1983, the Extraordinary Synod of 1985, the Great Jubilee of the year 2000, and the 2005 election of Pope Benedict XVI, the first pope who was not a council father. All these eventful and consequential moments never managed to overshadow the council or put it in the broader context of the theological *Zeitgeist* of the "Sixties." The message of Vatican II has not become tame or a distant reference, at least for theologians.

A third fact that we can see is that *all the most important events in the history of Catholic theology in the last fifty years are firmly rooted in the council's message.* The new push for evangelization in the 1970s, the ecumenical and interreligious outreach of John Paul II, the new protagonism of lay theologians, the vitality of Catholic theology facing new challenges—all these would be unthinkable without Vatican II: the final documents and the event, the letter and the spirit of the council.

Vatican II is still relevant because it has produced a change that is now clearly, in its fundamental core, irreversible—or reversible only at an unimaginable cost. The amount and the quality of change have now gone beyond anyone's ability to turn back the clock. Much still needs to be accomplished. But even those who try to appeal to nostalgia of various kinds know that too much has already been accomplished. To use a metaphor taken from the world of aviation, Catholicism is today at a "point of no return": the church is no longer capable of returning to the airfield it took off from, that is, the "long nineteenth century" of Catholicism.[4]

The church of Vatican II is surely not immune from infidelity to the message of the council or from attacks trying to make Catholicism a kind of "nature refuge" for conservative ideologies of different kinds. This is clearly a very delicate moment. We are not sure of what kind of Catholicism we will have in fifty years. But we are sure that it will not look like the Catholicism of fifty years ago.

VATICAN II: *AD INTRA* AND *AD EXTRA*

Vatican II is a special kind of ecumenical council because it started, from the very beginning, as a council aimed at dealing with ecclesiology, and in particular with ecclesiological issues both *ad intra* and *ad extra*.[5] Some of the core issues of Vatican II—liturgy and ecclesiology—are part of both the *ad intra* and the *ad extra* dimensions of the council. The impossibility of turning back is clear if we examine the closely connected theological dimensions of *ad intra* and *ad extra*, especially in the field of liturgy and ecclesiology, but also for their impact on the rest of the conciliar teaching.

Liturgy Ad Intra and Ad Extra

The liturgical reform is the most visible and important fruit of Vatican II. No wonder this aspect of the council has been under attack from various fronts especially over the past decade. The connection between theological *ressourcement* and the liturgy is key to understanding the liturgical reform and its importance for the life of Vatican II. The anti–Vatican II "new liturgical movement" (active especially on the Internet) is nostalgic, but not moved by pure nostalgia: its theological and ecclesiological consequences reach far beyond nostalgia.

The advocates of the anti–Vatican II new liturgical movement are indeed right as they identify *Sacrosanctum Concilium* as the main target, since the liturgical constitution of Vatican II is a powerful moment of *ressourcement* in the theology of the council and the most anti-traditionalist document of the council. The principle of *ressourcement* affected *Sacrosanctum Concilium* like no other conciliar document. It is hard to find in the corpus of the documents passages more expressive of the very essence of the church and driven by the idea of *ressourcement*.[6]

For the *ad intra* dimension, the liturgical reform as intended by *Sacrosanctum Concilium* aimed at the rediscovery of the centrality of scripture and the Eucharist. It is the most direct way to grasp Vatican II's ecclesiology. *Sacrosanctum Concilium* is aware that "the life of the Church cannot be reduced to the sole eucharistic moment" (SC, 9–10), and that liturgy has its role in the church as a "theologia prima," as "locus theologicus," and as "culmen et fons." The liturgical constitution sponsored a new awareness within the Roman Catholic Church that *things change*.

That is why both the liturgical reform of Vatican II and the most recent calls for a "reform of the reform" touch the whole essence of Vatican II. Changing worship sets off a rethinking of ecclesiology in a more profound and long-lasting way than the definition of the church in *Lumen Gentium*. Liturgy is not worship of a dominating power but the celebration of the grace of God, of God's free given gift to us in Jesus Christ.

In its dimension *ad extra* the eucharistic ecclesiology of *Sacrosanctum Concilium* provides the grounds for the basic direction of Vatican II, that is, *rapprochement* inside and outside the church. *Rapprochement*—a term used many times by the pioneer of ecumenism and liturgist Lambert Beauduin[7]—is not part of the corpus of Vatican II in a material way, but it belongs fully to the aims of Vatican II.

The council's liturgical reform plays a significant role in developing (during Vatican II) and performing (after Vatican II) this key feature of the council, in a way that is no less important than the other "rapprochement manifestos" of Vatican II, such as the decree on ecumenism *Unitatis Redintegratio*, the declaration *Nostra Aetate*, and the pastoral constitution *Gaudium et Spes*.

The main rapprochement carried out by *Sacrosanctum Concilium* consists in a reconciled and unifying vision of the church, of Christian life, of the existential condition of the faithful in the world.[8] Far from being a purely esthetic option, the theological starting point of the liturgical reform aimed at resetting the relationship among Christian liturgy, the spiritual needs of the faithful, and Catholic theological reading of the modern world in its historical and social dimensions.

Ressourcement, eucharistic ecclesiology, and rapprochement require a drive for a full implementation of Vatican II and provide an unambiguous appraisal of the issue of Vatican II's continuity *and* discontinuity and the role of liturgical reform in the church of the twenty-first century. Any attempt to undermine the liturgical reform of Vatican II reveals a clearly reductionist view of the council and its epoch-making changes.

Ecclesiology Ad Intra *and* Ad Extra

Liturgy and ecclesiology are closely connected in the theological balance of Vatican II. The liturgical reform anticipated and called for a church reform that was centered more on the Eucharist and the gospel of Jesus Christ than on an understanding of the institution based in the juridical structure of the Roman Empire. The ecclesiological constitution *Lumen Gentium* did not receive fully the ecclesiology of the liturgical constitution, and its most delicate focus is in the third chapter about the bishops and the papacy—a section that has very few connections with a eucharistic ecclesiology.

In this sense the *ad intra* dimension of the ecclesiology of Vatican II is still a building site. There have been failed attempts of Vatican II to reform the institution *ad intra*. For example, the rejection of the proposal of a Central Board of Bishops *(Consilium Centrale Episcoporum)* acting with the pope in Rome between 1963 and 1965; the rejection of the proposals for a reform of the appointment of the bishops; the controversial reform on the retirement age for bishops at seventy-five; the creation of Paul VI's Synod of Bishops in the summer 1965, in order to prevent the council from proposing its own design for a synod; the restrictions imposed on the new forms of collegiality and synodality in the local church (the role of the priests) and at the universal level (the role of the bishops).[9]

But *Lumen Gentium*, together with the decree on the bishops, *Christus Dominus*, restored a fundamental balance within Catholic ecclesiology: between the juridical and communional dimension of the church; between the idea of *societas* and the idea of "people of God," between universal ecclesiology and ecclesiology of the local church; opened a path toward new ways to live communion and collegiality in the church; and reframed the debate on ministry in light of the gospel and not in light of the social functions performed by the church in medieval and early modern history.[10]

The new ecclesiological self-understanding of the Catholic Church is inextricably connected to the relationship of the church *ad extra*. The fundamental passage of the "subsistits in" in *Lumen Gentium* no. 8 about the relationship between the Catholic Church and the Church of Christ gives new shape to the debate about the "members" of the church and the historical fact of the fragmentation of Christianity in different churches since the very beginning of Christianity, thus calling Christians to a new unity.[11]

The same ecclesiological constitution reframed the issue of the relationship with non-Christians and nonbelievers. *Lumen Gentium* nos. 15–16 emphasized new (and now even more visible) forms of communion beyond the criteria offered by Cardinal Robert Bellarmine after the Council of Trent (communion in prayer and communion in martyrdom).

The decree on ecumenism, *Unitatis Redintegratio*, built new bridges with other churches, at the same time achieving very important theological results, such as the "hierarchy of truths"—now a fundamental and essential tool for the self-understanding of Catholicism.

The pastoral constitution *Gaudium et Spes* put an end to the long history of mutual mistrust between the Catholic Church and the modern world. It moved the church toward the ability to assess the "signs of our times" thanks to a new aptitude to understand itself historically, a church born and developed and living in human history, affected by historical change in its human features not less than other human institutions.

The declaration *Nostra Aetate* represented the first step in knowing and understanding the "religious other," starting from the very source of otherness, the relationship between Judaism and Christianity.

All of these teachings *ad extra* have now become integral parts of the theological identity of Catholicism as expressed in public gestures of church leaders. The "magisterium through gestures" of John XXIII, Paul VI, and John Paul II still needs a proper theological and magisterial reception. Theology needs to be written in order to preserve the meaning of those gestures and to show that they were interpreting the *sensus fidei* of the whole church. But these gestures would have never been possible without the seeds planted by the council.

THE FUNDAMENTAL CHANGES:
FROM *AD EXTRA* TO *AD INTRA*

A few key examples of liturgy and ecclesiology show the intimate relationship between *ad intra* and *ad extra* in the teaching of the council. Liturgy and ecclesiology represent two major fields of debate in the history of the interpretation of Vatican II. Their relevance is in the fact that the contents of the documents on liturgy and ecclesiology are inextricably connected.

Understanding or misunderstanding the liturgical and ecclesiological content of Vatican II implies understanding or misunderstanding Vatican II as such. Much of what the council documents have in common—and much of their relevance—goes beyond their technical labeling; they express the fundamental fact that Vatican II talks not only to the church but to humanity and humankind as such. This is the real meaning of a pastoral council.[12] The value of Vatican II lies in the first steps of removing barriers and boundaries between the Catholic Church as a culture, a theology, a system, and the world.

1) *Sacrosanctum Concilium* reframed Catholicism not around its historically determined social and political patterns but around the Eucharist; *Lumen Gentium* no. 8 unlocked the juridical and theological identification between "Church of Christ" and "Catholic Church." On this basis, the declaration of religious liberty *Dignitatis Humanae* was the beginning of the end of fifteen hundred years of *Staatskirchentum*—national established churches according to the ideal of medieval "Christendom."

2) *Sacrosanctum Concilium* rephrased the importance of liturgy under the emphasis of liturgical pluralism; *Lumen Gentium* acknowledged the constraints of history and of canon law on the Catholic self-understanding of the church.

On this very basis, the decrees on ecumenism and on the Eastern Catholic Churches marked the beginning of the end of one thousand years of division between Western and Eastern Christianity (*Orientalium Ecclesiarum*, 14–18; *Unitatis Redintegratio*, 13–17). This meant not only the end of theological hatred and enmity, but also the end of a mono-cultural church, a church whose European culture had become a *hypostasis* for the self-understanding of Catholicism.

In *Unitatis Redintegratio* we have the importance of the positive significance of different liturgical traditions: the riches of the Eastern spiritual traditions, and the traditions of religious orders. Customs and traditions do not preclude the "unity of the church" but rather enrich the church. Vatican II put an end to "confessionalization" as a way to enforce socially different and competing theological views based on the clashes sparked by the Reformation, four centuries earlier. One example of these types of issues of faith as the primary vision of the church is the Bellarminian idea of the church as a "perfect society." Vatican II rejected a "confessionalized" understanding of faith. In *Dei Verbum* there is a post-Tridentine explanation of the importance of scripture and tradition in the definition of the faith.

3) Following John XXIII's opening speech of the council, *Gaudet Mater Ecclesia*, the liturgical constitution *Sacrosanctum Concilium* argued in the very beginning of the constitution for a new unity between church and humanity (SC, 1). *Lumen Gentium* developed an ecclesiology not only in light of the Gospel of Jesus Christ, but also in light of the new needs of a church evolving in history. The pastoral constitution *Gaudium et Spes* signaled the end of almost two hundred years of hatred of modernity and modern culture.

The ecclesiology of *Lumen Gentium* and the pastoral constitution opens a new understanding not only of the church itself but also of the role of its members and of ministry in the world. In *Gaudium et Spes* we see the human dignity in the context of today's situation, the community of humankind and its activities, its work. Given the changes reflected in human development in recent decades, in view of the globalization of social and economic conditions, Vatican II made the necessary choices to engage the church in this unfolding modernity.

4) *Sacrosanctum Concilium* recentered Catholic worship around Jesus Christ and the Eucharist (SC, 7); *Lumen Gentium* argued for a new understanding of non-Catholics and nonbelievers (LG, 15–16).

Nostra Aetate showed the key role of Judaism for a deeper understanding of non-Christian religions for what they are, that is, not an accident of history but a fundamental fact of the human condition.

THE RELEVANCE OF VATICAN II IN THE CHURCH OF TODAY

All these changes in Catholic theology—we can call them *discontinuities*—showed that there is an intimate connection between changes *ad extra* and *ad intra*. As a whole these changes represent—no less than the moments of continuities of Vatican II with *the great tradition* of the church—moments of conversion of Catholic theology in a fundamental reorientation of the church around the Gospel.[13]

One possible difference in the appreciation, between 1962 and now at the beginning of the twenty-first century, is how we understand the value of the *ad extra* dimension for the *ad intra* of Vatican II. What the church says *ad extra*—about non-Catholics, about Jews, about non-Christians, about modernity—has now become impossible to separate from the church's core identity *ad intra*, that is, from what the church believes and proclaims about itself.

This intimate connection becomes more evident if we consider that one of the visions of hope of Vatican II comes from the fact that the council does not have in mind a determined *social or political or cultural or ideological* definition of Catholicism. That was key to making the church able to receive and absorb the huge changes occurring in our world in these last fifty years.

In the relationship between the *ad intra* and *ad extra* dimensions of Catholic theology, these last fifty years have almost been divided in two parts by the interreligious gathering of Assisi in 1986, almost twenty-five years after the opening of Vatican II. In the twenty-five years between Assisi 1986 and now—with 9/11 in between—we now understand better the signs of hope coming from Vatican II. Only the church of *Nostra Aetate*, of *Dignitatis Humanae*, of *Gaudium et Spes*, of *Lumen Gentium* can make theological sense of these last fifty years.

The theological unfeasibility of going back *cannot* reassure us about the inevitability of conciliar theology. On the contrary, the hopes of Vatican II need to be cultivated, developed, and transmitted to the next generation of Christians, theologians, clergy, and to each and every person in contact with Catholicism today.

Fifty years after the event of Vatican II we find ourselves in that crucial moment of passage between the short run and the long run; the "clash of narratives" about the council encounters here the perennial law of the reception of the councils of the church. Recalling the worrisome memorandum sent between 1600 and 1612 by Robert Bellarmine to Pope Clement VIII on the progress of the reforms decided by the Council of Trent (between 1545 and 1563), Giuseppe Alberigo had estimated that it took at least fifty years for the reception of Trent to begin.[14]

In the last few years younger generations of Catholic theologians have been credited by theological pundits with a detached or even skeptical view of Vatican II that symbolizes polarization, culture wars, and division in the church—something they allegedly feel the need to distance themselves from, as if the common ground they seek could only be a ground as distant as possible from Vatican II.

My experience could not be more different from this misperception. Whether liberal or conservative, Catholic and non-Catholic students of every theological and spiritual orientation know well that longing for and aspiring to revive the period before Vatican II is a dream nourished only by people who do not live the real, day-to-day reality of the church. Ecumenism, religious freedom, and the rejection of anti-Semitism cannot be reduced to partisan issues. The post-9/11 world has revealed the prophetic value of documents like *Nostra Aetate*, whose theological necessity had vastly outgrown the narrow boundaries of its short text. To belittle Vatican II is to belittle these achievements as well, while disparaging these achievements means disparaging the very theology of Vatican II that brought about this opening of the church *ad extra*, but also the reflection of the church *ad intra*.

The election of pope Benedict XVI in 2005 and the reopening of the debate about Vatican II are two "signs of the times" for the church of the early twenty-first century, which represents simultaneously a time of progress and regress. For Catholics, the council is not a foil in the self-identification of their ways of being Catholic, but a real reference and a given condition of existence, especially for Catholicism outside the geopolitical and cultural boundaries of the North Atlantic regions.

Richard John Neuhaus's statement about Vatican II in 1987, "The contest over the interpretations of Vatican II constitutes a critical battlefront in our society's continuing cultural wars,"[15] must also be read in reverse: the substantial and undeniable ability of the Catholic Church to remain together in the Western hemisphere and in the rest of the world—despite the wars (cultural and otherwise)—owes much to Vatican II and its interpretations. Behind the very identity of the church and its relationship with the modern world there is a specific (if sometimes unconscious or indirect) interpretation of Vatican II.

In the first decades of the post–Vatican II period the debate on Vatican II lived through major moments of discussion and dispute.[16] The 1970s saw the beginning of the entrenching of different positions along a fault line in the interpretation of Vatican II within Catholic theology, and the birth of a schismatic group (the Lefebvrites) whose existence found motivation only in their rejection of Vatican II and in particular new orientations of the church *ad extra*.

The *Code of Canon Law* of 1983 and the final results of the Extraordinary Synod of Bishops of 1985 steered the hermeneutics of Vatican II toward a more cautious interpretation of the relationship between *letter* and *spirit* of the council and inaugurated John Paul II's complex reception of Vatican II.

A few months after his election Pope Benedict XVI's speech on December 22, 2005, conveyed a clear message about the much-anticipated shift in the doctrinal policy about Vatican II of the former Cardinal Prefect of the Congregation for the Doctrine of Faith. That speech celebrated the passage of Joseph Ratzinger's take on Vatican II from the level of an individual theologian, if not a powerful cardinal, to the level of the Roman pontiff's official interpretation of the council.

The everlasting political and institutional constraints of the "office of Peter" have clearly shown Benedict XVI the difficulty of turning back from the language and orientation of Vatican II. Not for the first time in history the unintended consequences of a major historical event had an effect outside the boundaries of the institution as well, thus creating an external framework for the interpretation of Vatican II that is not less visible and tangible than the hermeneutical balance struck by the church as a whole—popes, bishops, clergy, monks, theologians, families, lay men and women, pastoral ministers, and missionaries.

The debate about Vatican II undoubtedly feels outside pressure from that world to which Vatican II sent its message for the entire duration the council, from the opening speech of Pope John XXIII *Gaudet Mater Ecclesia* of October 11, 1962, to the pastoral constitution *Gaudium et Spes* of December 7, 1965.

The "incident" of January 2009 concerning Benedict XVI's decision to lift the excommunication of the Lefebvrian bishops of the Priestly Fraternity of St. Pius X revealed how profoundly the culture of Vatican II has penetrated the modern world and that the modern world is now begging the church to be faithful to those teachings *ad extra*.[17]

The complexity of the debate also has to do with the fact that the history of the post-conciliar church intertwines with the growth in knowledge and awareness of Catholic theology about Vatican II. It is a remarkable fact that during the first decades of the debate about Vatican II the historical and theological research on the council has acquired information and developed approaches to the "thing"—the Second Vatican Council—that were only imaginable in the 1970s or 1980s. Scholars of very different theological affiliations now know much more about Vatican II, both in its day-by-day unfolding and in its overall and epoch-making dimension, that is, as an event of church history, of the history of theology, of the history of ideas, and of political and social history.

The amount of information about the change that happened at Vatican II is probably more than Catholic theology expected and maybe more than the church as an institution was ready to handle.

But the communion of the church is much better equipped to handle the rediscovery of its past than the intellectuals on the payroll of the Communist Party of the Soviet Union, who, when faced with the permanent, ideological manipulation of recent history, were mocked with this popular Soviet-era joke: "We know exactly what the future will be. Our problem is with the past: that keeps changing."

The past has not been changed by the lively historical and theological debate about Vatican II—a comforting sign of the vitality of the church in a world where the so-called neo-atheism takes pride in seeing faith and debate as opposite terms. The historicization of Vatican II starting in the late 1980s has clearly introduced a hermeneutical shift in the theology of Vatican II. One of the key principles of that hermeneutical shift was the new understanding of modernity and the modern world with the expression of "joy and hope." Undermining that message of joy and hope coming from Vatican II is nothing less than undermining the intention of the council itself.

NOTES

1. See Massimo Faggioli, *Vatican II: The Battle for Meaning* (New York: Paulist Press, 2012); *History of Vatican II*, volumes 1–5, ed. Giuseppe Alberigo, English version ed. Joseph A. Komonchak (Maryknoll, NY: Orbis Books, 1995–2006).

2. See Joseph Ratzinger, "A Review of Post-Conciliar Era," in Joseph Ratzinger, *Principles of Catholic Theology* (San Francisco: Ignatius Press, 1987), 367–93.

3. For a bibliography about Vatican II, see Massimo Faggioli, "Concilio Vaticano II: bollettino bibliografico (2000–2002)," *Cristianesimo nella Storia* 24, no. 2 (2003): 335–60; "Concilio Vaticano II: bollettino bibliografico

(2002–2005)," *Cristianesimo nella Storia* 26, no. 3 (2005): 743–67; "Council Vatican II: Bibliographical Overview 2005–2007," *Cristianesimo nella Storia* 29, no. 2 (2008): 567–610; "Council Vatican II: Bibliographical Overview 2007–2010," *Cristianesimo nella Storia* 32 (2011/12): 755–91.

4. See John W. O'Malley, *What Happened at Vatican II* (Cambridge, MA: The Belknap Press of Harvard University Press, 2008), 53–92.

5. For Cardinal Suenens's formulation of the ecclesiological dimension *ad intra–ad extra*, see Alberto Melloni, "Ecclesiologie al Vaticano II (autunno 1962—estate 1963)," in *Les commissions conciliaires à Vatican II*, ed. Mathijs Lamberigts, Claude Soetens, and Jan Grootaers, 91–179 (Leuven: Bibliotheek van de Faulteit Godgeleerdheid,1996); Komonchak, *History of Vatican II*, 2:281–357.

6. See Massimo Faggioli, *True Reform: Liturgy and Ecclesiology in "Sacrosanctum Concilium"* (Collegeville, MN: Liturgical Press, 2012).

7. See Raymond Loonbeek and Jacques Mortiau, *Un pionnier, Dom Lambert Beauduin (1873–1960): Liturgie et unité des chrétiens*, 2 vols. (Louvain-la-Neuve: Collège Erasme, 2001), esp. 1:907–9. See also Jacques Mortiau and Raymond Loonbeek, *Dom Lambert Beauduin: Visionnaire et précurseur (1873–1960); un moine au coeur libre* (Paris: Cerf, 2005).

8. See Giuseppe Dossetti, *Per una "chiesa eucaristica": Rilettura della portata dottrinale della Costituzione liturgica del Vaticano II; lezioni del 1965*, ed. Giuseppe Alberigo and Giuseppe Ruggieri (Bologna: Il Mulino, 2002), 41.

9. For all this, see Massimo Faggioli, *Il vescovo e il concilio: Modello episcopale e aggiornamento al Vaticano II* (Bologna: Il Mulino, 2005).

10. See Richard Gaillardetz, *Ecclesiology for a Global Church: A People Called and Sent* (Maryknoll, NY: Orbis Books, 2008); Peter Hünermann, "Theologischer Kommentar zur dogmatischen Konstitution über die Kirche," in *Herders Theologischer Kommentar zum Zweiten Vatikanischen Konzil*, vol. 2, ed. Hans Jochen Hilberath and Peter Hünermann (Freiburg im Breisgau: Herder, 2004).

11. See Mauro Velati, *Dialogo e rinnovamento: Verbali e testi del Segretariato per l'unità dei cristiani nella preparazione del concilio Vaticano II (1960–1962)* (Bologna: Il Mulino, 2011).

12. See Peter Hünermann, "Kriterien für die Rezeption des II. Vatikanischen Konzils," *Theologische Quartalschrift* 191, no. 2 (2011): 126–47.

13. See Christoph Theobald, *La réception du concile Vatican II, I. Accéder à la source* (Paris: Cerf, 2009).

14. Giuseppe Alberigo, *La chiesa nella storia* (Brescia: Paideia, 1988), 218–39.

15. Richard John Neuhaus, "The Councils Called Vatican II," in Richard John Neuhaus, *The Catholic Moment: The Paradox of the Church in the Postmodern World* (San Francisco: Harper and Row, 1987), 61.

16. Concerning the almost classical division of the first decades of post–Vatican II into three different periods (1965–75; 1975–85; 1985–), see Hermann Josef Pottmeyer, "A New Phase in the Reception of Vatican II: Twenty Years of Interpretation of Vatican II," in *The Reception of Vatican II*, ed. Giuseppe Alberigo, Jean-Pierre Jossua, and Joseph Komonchak (Washington DC: Catholic University of America Press, 1985), 27–43; Walter Kasper, "Die bleibende Herausforderung durch das II. Vatikanische Konzil. Zur Hermeneutik der Konzilsaussagen," in Walter Kasper, *Die Kirche Jesu Christi. Schriften zur Ekklesiologie, I* (Walter Kasper Gesammelte Schriften, 11) (Herder: Freiburg im Breisgau, 2008), 200–211, esp. 200–201; Karl Lehmann, "Das II. Vatikanum—Ein Wegweiser. Verständnis—Rezeption—Bedeutung," in *Das Zweite Vatikanische Konzil und die Zeichen der Zeit heute*, ed. Peter Hünermann (Freiburg im Breisgau: Herder, 2006), 11–28, esp. 22–24.

17. See Massimo Faggioli, "Die kulturelle und politische Relevanz des II. Vatikanischen Konzils als konstitutiver Faktor der Interpretation," in *Exkommunikation oder Kommunikation? Der Weg der Kirche nach dem II. Vatikanum und die Pius-Brüder*, ed. Peter Hünermann (Freiburg im Breisgau: Herder, 2009), 153–74; and Massimo Faggioli, "Vatican II Comes of Age," *The Tablet*, April 11, 2009.

II.

LITURGY IN THE
TWENTY-FIRST CENTURY

BENJAMIN DURHEIM

Perhaps the most readily recognizable theological developments to spring from the Second Vatican Council are those that have affected the sacraments and the liturgy. Massimo Faggioli has argued as much in his work for this volume; the way in which Christians worship embodies their beliefs about God and themselves—as well as their beliefs about how God and humans relate. Liturgical shifts—even those considered relatively minor—have the power to reshape or reemphasize aspects of the divine-human dynamic precisely by reshaping or reemphasizing the practices, phrases, or prayers that concretize such a dynamic (which is one reason that the critiques of the Vatican II liturgical reforms have been—again as Faggioli has indicated—so vehement; such reforms cast the divine-human relationship in a different light). For example, the shift from liturgy celebrated in Latin to liturgy celebrated in the vernacular, while it could be said to have provided the liturgical space to highlight a number of Christian religious claims, certainly highlighted at least one: God does not speak Latin exclusively, and we humans need not operate as if that were the case.

The shift to celebrating liturgy in the vernacular is only one of the many liturgical moves made in and after the Second Vatican Council, but changes in liturgical practice constitute only a portion of the gifts the legacy of Vatican II offers with regard to the liturgy. Since the council the reforms inspired there have provided fertile ground for pursuing under-examined questions of liturgical theology, as well as for pursuing well-documented issues from new (or newly clarified) angles. The question of Christian sacrifice (especially the sacrifice of the Eucharist) has never been far from Christian discourse, but in the years since the Second Vatican Council this issue has enjoyed a prominent place in liturgical theological study. Similarly, the question of liturgy's connection to ethics—a connection implicit in the whole of the Christian tradition—has surfaced in recent years as another topic of theological interest. To be sure, the Second Vatican Council is not the exclusive (or even necessarily the primary) source of inspiration for these and other late-modern or postmodern takes on liturgical questions, but it is a significant part of the backdrop to the current stage of liturgical/sacramental theology. This being the case, what follows are two liturgical-theological works, done using Vatican II as their springboard and oriented toward a vision of what Vatican II still offers the contemporary church as it looks to the future.

Gina Ingiosi, in her chapter, builds on an aspect of liturgical theology that was emphasized in and since the Second Vatican Council—namely, the church as the mystical body of Christ—by cultivating a conversation between this impulse toward speaking of the church as the body of Christ on the one hand, and a thinker who attempts to rework the very word *body* on the other. As Ingiosi readily admits, Judith Butler would not immediately come to mind as an ideal conversation partner for the church on issues of liturgical theology. However, Ingiosi nevertheless develops a set of parallels and points of possible dialogue between the two conceptions of *body*. For example, Ingiosi acknowledges that the Second Vatican Council's conception of the body of Christ was heavily indebted to Pope Pius XII's *Mystici Corporis Christi*, and at least partially as a result, conceived of body as a "visible, ordered agency" (Ingiosi). On the other hand, Butler has maintained that the body itself—not just concepts such as gender that spring from it—is constructed rather than a given. In this light it is possible to see the church's liturgical body both in terms of being given (as the mystical body of Christ), and in terms of being made, especially in the celebration of the Eucharist.

Drawing further on the theme of the body, Elizabeth Antus's essay emphasizes the issue of inclusivity in the body of Christ. How are Christians to reckon with the fact that Christian liturgy can sometimes fall into excluding some of God's children from participating fully in the celebration, even without fully realizing it? Antus wrestles with this issue by exploring questions of how necessary (or not) intellectual understanding might or ought to be for participating in liturgy, how the "order" of liturgy may or may not accommodate persons for whom such order is difficult or incomprehensible, and how conceiving of the liturgical assembly as the body of Christ may inform the way in which the church approaches liturgical hospitality. Hospitality, in Antus's sense, does not mean the ability as "normal" people to welcome those who may not be seen as "normal"; instead, she interprets the language of the body of Christ as making each person an integral part of the church. With this in mind, it is not only the church as the body of Christ that informs how those with intellectual disabilities ought to be welcomed as participants in the liturgy, but it is also exactly those participants who can better inform the church's understanding of its liturgical self as the body of Christ.

Our Fragile Flesh

Sacramental Hospitality Toward Persons with Intellectual Disabilities and Its Implications for Theology

ELIZABETH L. ANTUS

The Second Vatican Council's constitution on the sacred liturgy, *Sacrosanctum Concilium*, strongly encourages the entire church, particularly the laity, to participate intentionally and actively at the sacraments, especially the Eucharist.[1] In the past several decades since the council we have witnessed the effects of this initiative, as Catholics have celebrated the mass in the vernacular and have acted as readers and extraordinary eucharistic ministers. This liturgical engagement has sparked a particular vibrancy among the faithful that underscores the church's truly corporate identity as the fully engaged, richly complex body of Christ.[2] Furthermore, as we noted throughout the Emerging Theologians conference, this vibrancy and emphasis on participation also highlights the importance of ecclesial activity at the level of the *local*: the church is expressed precisely through the activities of particular parishes worshiping together day in and day out. The concrete actions of the worshipers at the parish level, then, ultimately shape the church's existence in the world.

However, the potential limitations of the council's call for active and conscious participation come to our attention when we examine it from the perspectives of Catholics with disabilities. In the wake of legislation such as the Americans with Disabilities Act of 1990, Christians such as Nancy Eiesland have reflected on Christians with disabilities and how non-disabled, or "temporarily able-bodied," Christians should welcome these persons within the church community.[3] In particular, these authors have called for various accommodations such as increased accessibility to worship as well as a moratorium on hymnal lyrics, images, and preaching that depict physical impairments as telltale signs of sinfulness.[4]

Even more recently, and for the purposes of this chapter, Christians have begun to reflect upon the lives of people with *intellectual* disabilities such as Down syndrome, profound developmental delay, and autism spectrum disorders. In these cases crucial questions come to the fore: How can Christian churches encourage the full inclusion of those who may not possess the use of reason or full consciousness and who may struggle to conform their "out of control" bodies to the liturgical order?[5] What does active participation mean for such people, and how can Christian worship become more inclusive of it? However we contemplate these questions, it is wrong-headed to presume that these people participate less because of their disabilities. Such a presumption is a distortion of the spirit of *Sacrosanctum Concilium*.

Thus, to place intellectually disabled persons at the center of theological reflection on liturgical participation, I delineate the contours of the problem with contemporary sacramental theology. I then employ Thomas Reynolds's 2008 text *Vulnerable Communion: A Theology of Disability and Hospitality*, specifically his argument that we must situate discussions about intellectually disabled persons squarely within an understanding of bodily vulnerability that characterizes *everybody's* existence. This use of Reynolds facilitates a reimagining of *Sacrosanctum Concilium* and post-conciliar sacramental theology (as articulated by Louis-Marie Chauvet and Nathan Mitchell) so that we can move beyond construing liturgical participation in exclusively cognitivist, and therefore ableist, terms.[6] Rather, liturgical participation may come to be understood as an inclusive activity of the entire body of Christ precisely in all the fragility, spontaneity, and limitation that is enfleshed within its members.

My central claims are thus the following: first, to enact the best of *Sacrosanctum Concilium*'s vision, in which the Eucharist is a unique practice of charity engaging *all* the members of Christ's body (SC, 59), Catholic priests, laity, and theologians must in their own respective ways work to incorporate the bodies of intellectually disabled members into the church's worship life. However, second, to enact such hospitality, Catholic sacramental theology must also accommodate a more expansive understanding of embodiment in which the body is considered not only the "rational" medium of one's ordered self-expression within the world, but also as a site of potential disruption and *disorder* that outpaces and sometimes frustrates conscious intentionality, for everybody. These two tasks will mutually reinforce each other: the more we (namely, Catholics who are not intellectually disabled and are somewhat educated in the finer points of sacramental theology) recognize intellectually disabled persons as integral to the church, the more we can expand our appreciation for one another's bodies, and vice versa. These points will ultimately illuminate how this earthly liturgy can more fully be a "foretaste of that heavenly liturgy" (SC, 8).

THE POSITIVE VISION OF *SACROSANCTUM CONCILIUM*

Before all else one must emphasize that *Sacrosanctum Concilium*, and Catholic sacramental theology in its wake, contains a powerful vision of the worshiping body of Christ that has the potential to spur Catholics to welcome intellectually disabled members more fully into the church. The liturgy is necessary for such a task because, as it is described in the constitution, it is "the summit toward which the activity of the church is directed; [and] it is also the source from which all its power flows" (SC, 10). It is through liturgical worship that Catholics are being rebuilt by the Spirit as the body of Christ (SC, 2). Specifically, this means that Catholics are being empowered to love others—friend and enemy—in the way that Christ loved friend and enemy in his life and death (SC, 10). Chauvet emphasizes this expansion of communal relationships, stating, "It is precisely a *new relation of places between subjects*, a relationship of filial and brotherly and sisterly alliance, that the sacramental 'expression' aims at instituting or restoring in faith."[7] Sacramental grace is thus meant to inaugurate—and repeatedly purify—a new mode of communion between Christians that dissolves biases and makes neighbors out of strangers.

In the wake of the council the church has given some reflection to how the liturgy needs to include persons with disabilities. The United States bishops authored a document about this very thing in 1995 in which they provided general principles for pastors to incorporate persons with disabilities into Christ's body through the sacraments.[8] In so doing, the bishops emphasized that inclusion of persons with disabilities is not a mere option; it a necessary task that requires discernment and attitude adjustments on the part of ministers and the laity as a whole. Regarding the mass, the bishops emphasized that ministers should make a concerted effort to assign persons with disabilities to the roles filled by the laity as much as possible.[9]

This desire to draw persons with intellectual disabilities from the margins to the center of the church's worship life receives support in the conciliar and post-conciliar emphasis on the church as the body of Christ.[10] The church's identity as the body of Christ signifies not only that Catholics are a community, but also that this communal conformity to Christ happens precisely *through* our bodily presence, together and with one another, at the Eucharist. Our bodies matter. This idea has resonance with earlier insights from the Christian tradition. Augustine of Hippo preaches to his congregation, "So if our Lord Jesus Christ had only taken on a human soul, only our souls would be his members. But in fact he also took on a body, and thus is a real head for us, who consist of soul and body; and therefore our bodies too are his members."[11] Because God has become fully human, fully *embodied*, in the incarnation, our embodiment is ineradicably important to God, and this incarnational affirmation of the body, of *everyone's body*, becomes clear through the necessarily concrete sacraments.[12] Chauvet declares that Christianity's arch-sacramentality "indicates that *there is no faith unless somewhere inscribed, inscribed in a body*—a body from a specific culture, a body with a concrete history, a body of desire."[13] Because God has become human, we can never forego the particularity of our own bodies or the sacraments that we return to repeatedly.

Sacrosanctum Concilium freshly elucidates this central commitment of Christianity. Liturgical participation thus happens not only through receiving the scripture readings and the homily, but also through the physical presence of the congregants and bodily activities such as singing, speaking the responses, and shaking hands (SC, 33). Indeed, Nathan Mitchell underscores the intentionality behind *Sacrosanctum Concilium's* affirmation of our embodiment, stating, "The council . . . made, as the centerpiece of its reform, the retrieval of worship as an *embodied action by the entire assembly*."[14] Thus, while persons with intellectual disabilities may not possess the kind of high-level rationality or, in certain cases, a rudimentary consciousness that is often presupposed in more cognitivist understandings of liturgical participation, they can be said to participate in and through their bodily presence within the worshiping community. Nobody is excluded from being enfleshed, and our Christian beliefs in the doctrines of creation, incarnation, and resurrection suggest that the flesh is sacred.[15] In sum, then, *Sacrosanctum Concilium* has the potential to encourage robust ecclesial inclusion of persons with intellectual disabilities through richer theological reflection on the church as Christ's body constituted by our bodies.

POTENTIALLY ABLEIST PITFALLS IN ENACTING SACRAMENTAL THEOLOGY

Sacrosanctum Concilium and post-conciliar sacramental reflection, however, may lend themselves all too easily to cognitivist, and therefore ableist, understandings of what it means to participate in the liturgy and what it means to be embodied. Chauvet trenchantly notes that Christians have always struggled to accept our embodied limitations as something good, and that we have also struggled to accept the necessity of the sacraments as mediating God's presence to us. Chauvet laments that Christians are prone to resist the body and the sacraments because we "harbor a nostalgia for an ideal and immediate presence to oneself, to others, and to God," which is characteristic of certain logocentric metaphysical tendencies in the Christian tradition.[16] In other words, we may sometimes fall prey to the desire to transcend our bodily particularity and to achieve an absolute rational comprehension of things unstained by the blood, bone, and guts of fleshly human existence and the water, chrism, and unleavened bread of the sacraments. For Chauvet, this is how we deny our limits as finite, mortal, vulnerable, and always in need of things we can touch, smell, see, and hear.[17]

Sometimes this tendency in Christian theology even undermines explicitly good-faith efforts to value the body. In a document such as *Sacrosanctum Concilium*, in which the affirmation of corporality is certainly present, one sees certain passages nevertheless possibly promoting an exclusively cognitivist or consciousness-based understanding of lay participation in the Eucharist. In addition to the description of lay activity as "conscious," this constitution also speaks of the importance of Catholics cultivating "proper dispositions" in preparation for the liturgy and of "understanding" as easily as possible the texts and rites therein (SC, 11, 21). While we may certainly interpret concepts such disposition and understanding in terms broader than that of cognitive mastery, and therefore may in some sense speak of some intellectually disabled persons as understanding the liturgy at a basic experiential level, we cannot entirely sever the association with truly rational comprehension that such concepts evoke. Indeed, though the 1995 "Guidelines for the Celebration of the Sacraments with Persons with Disabilities" from the U.S. bishops state that receiving the sacraments is a right for Catholics with disabilities and that the mere possession of a disability is not grounds for exclusion from the sacraments, it also states that Catholics with intellectual disabilities must still be able to communicate that they somehow understand the uniqueness of the Eucharist as distinct from regular food.[18] Many intellectually disabled persons may not meet this criterion. Rational understanding thus remains the norm for all Catholics, with the Eucharist as with many of the other sacraments,[19] and in this way it can function as an ableist exclusionary principle according to which many intellectually disabled Catholics do not measure up.

We need not jettison *all* appeals to rational comprehension when it comes to participation in the Eucharist; those who *can* understand in their own ways and even at a depth level the meaning of the texts and rites within the liturgy should strive to do so. However, I suggest that we *broaden* our understanding of eucharistic participation so that rational comprehension need not be applied as the norm in every case, particularly certain cases of intellectually disabled Catholics. We can and should sometimes look beyond the cognitivist standard when it comes to liturgical participation, and it seems that *Sacrosanctum Concilium* itself provides the warrant for so doing; at one point the document enjoins pastors to consider the "age, condition, way of life and standard of religious culture" when making decisions concerning the laity (SC, 19). It seems feasible that pastors may also apply such contextual reasoning to cases involving intellectually disabled Catholics such that they could develop some analogical sense of participation in each instance. This expansion of our understanding of participation will make the liturgy a more inclusive and more effective manifestation of the church as Christ's body.

One might suggest that an appeal to our common embodiment in the body of Christ rescues us from this ableist lurch, but, if left unexamined, post-conciliar sacramental theology still risks restricting the body within ableist parameters. The current emphasis on the body in sacramental theology generally paints the body in terms presupposing a rational agent: the body, which "I" have, is "my" medium for interfacing with others in the world, even if it is acknowledged that "I" am also "it." Karl Rahner, whose particular affirmation of the body as the *Realsymbol* of the soul has deeply influenced sacramental theology, states, "The body is the medium of all communication."[20] Similarly, Chauvet construes the body as the necessary mediation of the layers of meaning within which humans find themselves bound up in the world and among each other: "Each person's own body is structured by the system of values or symbolic network of the group to which each person belongs and which makes up his or her *social and cultural body*. . . . No word escapes the necessity of a laborious inscription in a body, a history, a language, a system of signs."[21] The body's value is thus verified, but typically through intimate proximity to the spiritual agent who controls it. While Rahner and Chauvet do not ascribe to a Cartesian notion of the self as mechanistically instrumentalizing the distanced body as a *res extensa*, they do tend to describe the body as the locus of *ordered self-expression within the world*, which still presupposes intentionality and self-consciousness at some level.[22] While these thinkers do insist that our bodily being conditions our consciousness and reason in ways we cannot even fully acknowledge, this point nevertheless complements the more central point for them that "our" bodies express "our" being in the world.

This particular description of embodiment, standard in much contemporary sacramental theology, always risks excluding persons with intellectual disabilities, many of whom do not possess the conscious and rational mastery of their bodies that is presupposed. When we consider these points in light of the church's celebration of the Eucharist, we see afresh the ways in which "body" is actually encoded as "ordered body" within the liturgy. Voicing this sentiment, Chauvet declares, "The sacraments are thus made of significant materiality: that of a body which cannot experience them without submitting itself to them through a program already specified, a gesture duly prescribed, a word institutionally set."[23] In this paradigm eucharistic celebration centers around Catholics intentionally submitting themselves to ordered ritual activity; for example, as *Sacrosanctum Concilium* emphasizes, there is a time for bodily engagement and a time for silence, and these specifications must be observed for good liturgy to occur.[24] Though in many cases persons with intellectual disabilities can be encouraged to participate in the liturgy through extra-verbal gestures and singing, the common sacramental presupposition of the liturgically ordered body, if left unexamined, leaves us unequipped to think about the unordered bodies of persons with intellectual disabilities during worship.[25] How should we reflect upon those who may not be capable of comporting themselves exactly according to the liturgical order? If we take current sacramental theology to its logical conclusion on this front, then we are left saying that the unpredictable bodies of intellectually disabled Catholics are embarrassing anomalies within the worship life of the church.

Having drawn out the contours of this problem more sharply, we may now turn to one theologian's recent refashioning of embodiment in a mode more hospitable to intellectually disabled people. Thomas Reynolds, who has reflected deeply on disabilities by drawing on his experience of caring for his son Chris, who has struggled with Tourette's syndrome, bipolar disorder, Asperger's syndrome, and obsessive-compulsive disorder, helps contextualize the church's unwitting exclusion of people with intellectual disabilities. Reynolds speaks of "a cult of normalcy" regnant in the United States, wherein we ascribe certain values to the body, such as wealth accumulation, efficiency, capitalistic consumption, and beauty or health, as ways of measuring the worth of bodies. The more one possesses these things, the more one can be said to have a certain amount of "body capital," or "the power to belong," because one literally embodies the values the society associates with the good.[26] Underlying these various measurements of body capital is our fixation on being self-determinative, strong, and independent, and a denial of our own limitations and vulnerabilities.[27] Concomitantly, then, we are socialized to carry on a process of stigmatization of those who lack this kind of capacity: "Instead of facing our own vulnerability directly, we . . . then ignore or pity those ugly, deformed, monstrous, senile, retarded, and otherwise unseemly bodies. In doing so, however, we flee from our own bodies."[28] In other words, what we essentially prize about bodies is our ability to *control* them according to our intentions—to be in control is to be invulnerable. Persons with intellectual disabilities are thus especially subject to stigmatization, then, since they often lack this very ability of self-control and ordered bodily comportment; we are deeply scandalized by such "out of control" bodies.[29]

Reynolds underscores the kinds of questions that these biases raise for people like his son: "Should Chris control his motor and verbal tics in public? Should he avoid hugging others spontaneously in order to preserve the etiquette of keeping space between people who are not family or friends? Should he be required to chew silently with his mouth closed while eating with others?"[30] In mainstream US society, the answers to these questions would push Chris's body to become "docile," conformed to the order of commonly accepted etiquette.[31] It is my contention, however, that the church need not exert this same pressure. Even though post-conciliar sacramental theology has tendencies toward enshrining the ordered body in liturgical celebration and thereby excluding persons with intellectual disabilities from consideration, it need not be this way. The church does not have to promote yet another rigid cult of normalcy.

LOOKING FORWARD: INCLUSION OF INTELLECTUALLY DISABLED PERSONS IN THE FRAGILE BODY OF CHRIST

To realize more fully *Sacrosanctum Concilium*'s vision of the liturgy as a sacrament conforming us to Christ's love, we must recommit to incorporating intellectually disabled persons into the church's worship life, and we can begin to do so through expanding our theology of embodiment and recognizing the bodies of intellectually disabled people as dignified. Rather than restrict the meaning of embodiment to ordered self-expression among others in society and in church, we can also begin to think about the body even more fundamentally as a site of vulnerability, porosity, spontaneity, and sometimes even disruption. To be embodied is to experience the world in one's flesh without ever totally accounting for such experience through rational reflection, to be limited in various ways and at various times throughout one's life, and sometimes to suffer because of these limitations. As Reynolds notes, these conditions apply to *all*, not just to those who have disabilities.[32] I make these points not to deny the rational agency of those who possess it, but rather, to elucidate the fact that we are all at one another's mercy, for good or bad, before we can even hope to become at least somewhat independent (if that can even ever happen at all).

As Reynolds argues, it is from this shared condition of bodily vulnerability that non-disabled Catholics can recognize the place of privilege that intellectually disabled Catholics, as those who are especially vulnerable, should have within the body of Christ. This point is radically crystallized through the actions of Jesus toward those whose bodies were considered undesirable in his own society. Given that Jesus ministered especially to those whose bodies were most stigmatized, the church today, as his body, is called to do the same, not simply by tolerating but by privileging those who are stigmatized in our society. Inclusion in the body of Christ signifies that those whose bodies are despised and deemed out of control find special welcome in the sacraments, especially the Eucharist.[33] As Nathan Mitchell highlights, one consequence of the Pauline metaphor of the body as a description of the church is that commonly accepted social hierarchies are inverted as all are affirmed in Christ.[34] In this case this point means that the church refuses to measure the worth of our bodies according to wealth, beauty, or even the well-intentioned comportment of one's body. In this way the church upsets the ableist standards of the cult of normalcy.[35] One practical implication of such recognition is that Catholics who are not intellectually disabled should enthusiastically go to great lengths to incorporate intellectually disabled members into the various activities of the church at worship whenever possible, especially when intellectually disabled members seem eager to participate.[36]

Furthermore, whenever Catholics with intellectual disabilities "disrupt" the flow of the mass through some kind of spontaneous outburst or generally do not conform to the order of liturgical behaviors asked of the laity, non-disabled Catholics should not presume that such disruptions are merely negative erosions of the authentic worship activity of the church toward which they should then feel embarrassment or pity. Rather, Catholics should convey, through preaching (by priests), various forms of social outreach surrounding the mass (by the laity), and more inclusive theologies of embodiment (by theologians) that such persons are deeply significant to the community. These efforts will require patience, openness, and constant dialogue with intellectually disabled Catholics and their families or guardians.

If we let them, these disruptions can function as opportunities to reveal the calling of the church to be radically inclusive of all, not because anybody has earned this mediation of God's grace through perfect adherence to the liturgical order, but because we are all loved by God in the fragility that underpins our lives and our bodies, and we should love one another in the same way. The more that we can understand the body, and the body of Christ, in terms of shared fragility and interdependence, the more we can practice hospitality toward intellectually disabled Catholics, and this praxis of hospitality will in turn continue to transform our theology of embodiment. The quality of our reflection on the body and of our welcome of persons with intellectual disabilities will rise and fall in tandem with each other. In this way, then, we can begin to think about the "out of order" bodies of intellectually disabled persons as revelatory of God's prevenient love for all of us and our bodies, and we can reinterpret the best of *Sacrosanctum Concilium* for the future of liturgy.[37]

NOTES

1. "It is very much the wish of the church that all the faithful should be led to take that full, conscious, and active part in liturgical celebrations which is demanded by the very nature of the liturgy, and to which the Christian people . . . have a right and to which they are bound by reason of their Baptism" (SC, 14).

2. The document later specifies that the purpose of the sacraments is indeed to fortify the body of Christ, namely, the worshiping people of the church: "The purpose of the sacraments is to sanctify people, to build up the body of Christ, and, finally, to worship God" (SC, 59).

3. The designation "temporarily able-bodied," now common in disability literature, suggests that the line between "disabled" and "non-disabled" is often blurrier than we would think, and that, in general, we will all experience weakness and limitation in our bodies at some point in our lives. See Thomas E. Reynolds, *Vulnerable Communion: A Theology of Disability and Hospitality* (Grand Rapids, MI: Brazos Press, 2008), 1–45.

4. See Nancy L. Eiesland, *The Disabled God: Toward a Liberatory Theology of Disability* (Nashville, TN: Abingdon Press, 1994), 19–30, 69–120. Also see Brett Webb-Michael, *Unexpected Guests at God's Banquet: Welcoming People with Disabilities into the Church* (New York: Crossroad, 1994);

Deborah Beth Creamer, *Disability and Christian Theology: Embodied Limits and Constructive Possibilities* (New York: Oxford, 2009); Mary Jo Iozzio, "Thinking About Disabilities with Justice, Liberation, and Mercy," *Horizons* 36, no. 1 (2009): 32–49.

5. See Amos Yong, *Theology and Down Syndrome: Reimagining Disability in Late Modernity* (Waco, TX: Baylor University Press, 2007); Hans S. Reinders, *Receiving the Gift of Friendship: Profound Disability, Theological Anthropology, and Ethics* (Grand Rapids, MI: Eerdmans, 2009); Molly Haslam, *A Constructive Theology of Intellectual Disability: Human Being as Mutuality and Response* (New York: Fordham University Press, 2012).

6. Louis-Marie Chauvet, *Symbol and Sacrament: A Sacramental Reinterpretation of Christian Existence*, trans. Patrick Madigan, SJ, and Madeleine Beaumont (Collegeville, MN: Liturgical Press, 1995); Nathan D. Mitchell, *Meeting Mystery: Liturgy, Worship, and Sacraments* (Maryknoll, NY: Orbis Books, 2006). Regarding my use of the term *ableist,* I draw upon Thomas Reynolds in defining ableism as attitudes, actions, and words that (i) objectify people with disabilities by entirely defining them according to their disabilities, (ii) render these people as unfortunate, aberrant deviations from certain cultural ideas about "normal" human ability and strength, and (iii) thereby define these people as outside the bounds of what it means to be human, to live a good life, and to form communities with one another. See Reynolds, *Vulnerable Communion,* 27–34, 52–63.

7. Chauvet, *Symbol and Sacrament,* 140.

8. United States Conference of Catholic Bishops (USCCB), "Guidelines for the Celebration of the Sacraments with Persons with Disabilities" (Washington DC: USCCB, 1995).

9. Ibid., 21.

10. Ibid., 59.

11. Augustine of Hippo, "Sermon 161: On the Words of the Apostle, 1 Corinthians 6:15: *Do You Not Know That Your Bodies Are Members of Christ?* Etc.," Selected Sermons *(Sermones ad Populum),* in *The Works of Saint Augustine (Electronic Edition),* vol. 5, ed. John Rotelle, OSA, trans. Edmund Hill (Brooklyn, NY: New City Press, 1992), #1.

12. Mitchell, *Meeting Mystery,* 177.

13. Chauvet, *Symbol and Sacrament,* 154.

14. Mitchell, *Meeting Mystery,* 179.

15. For moving reflections on these doctrines and the role that embodiment plays, see Karl Rahner, "The Resurrection of the Body," *Theological Investigations,* vol. 2 (Limerick, Ireland: The Way, 2000) (online PDF edition), 203–16; "On the Theology of the Incarnation," *Theological Investigations,* vol. 4, 105–20; "The Body in the Order of Salvation," *Theological Investigations,* vol. 17, 71–89.

16. Chauvet, *Symbol and Sacrament*, 154.

17. Ibid., 145.

18. USCCB, "Guidelines for the Celebration of the Sacraments with Persons with Disabilities," nos. 2, 20.

19. The minimal use of reason is necessary in the cases of the Eucharist, confession, holy orders, and matrimony. Regarding baptism and confirmation, the consent of a parent or guardian is sufficient for an intellectually disabled person to receive the sacrament. Regarding anointing of the sick, intellectually disabled people are encouraged to participate through communal celebrations of this sacrament. See ibid., nos. 8–39.

20. Karl Rahner, quoted in Mitchell, *Meeting Mystery*, 160.

21. Chauvet, *Symbol and Sacrament*, 150–51.

22. For an extended treatment of these kinds of distinctions, see Charles Taylor, *Sources of the Self: The Making of the Modern Identity* (New York: Cambridge University Press, 1989).

23. Chauvet, *Symbol and Sacrament*, 152.

24. "To develop active participation, the people should be encouraged to take part by means of acclamations, responses, psalms, antiphons, hymns, as well as by actions, gestures and bodily attitudes. And at the proper time a reverent silence should be observed" (SC, 30).

25. Indeed, there are many ways that persons with certain intellectual disabilities such as Down syndrome and development delay can be encouraged to participate in the mass through singing, handing out bulletins, and managing the collection baskets. For other concrete suggestions and stories of intellectually disabled people being incorporated into (and greatly enhancing) certain preexisting activities of parish life, see Webb-Michael, *Unexpected Guests at God's Banquet*, 170–84.

26. Reynolds, *Vulnerable Communion*, 58–59, 88–98.

27. Ibid., 67, 97.

28. Ibid., 97.

29. Ibid., 73.

30. Ibid., 74.

31. Ibid., 75.

32. Ibid., 105, 222.

33. Ibid., 222.

34. Mitchell, *Meeting Mystery*, 181–83.

35. Reynolds, *Vulnerable Communion*, 235.

36. I should be extremely clear about the fact that not all intellectually disabled persons would like to participate in the liturgy in the same way or to the same degree. This is why it is all the more important for worshiping Christians who are not ntellectually disabled, particularly the laity, to foster relationships with intellectually disabled parishioners and their families.

And even if an intellectually disabled person does not wish to participate in the eucharistic celebration in a special way, fellow parishioners should still attempt to understand the particular needs that such a person might have. Some examples of these other forms of advocacy could include saving an intellectually disabled member's seat before mass or offering to give an intellectually disabled member a ride each week. In any case, dialogue about the particular needs and desires of each individual is indispensable (see Webb-Michael, *Unexpected Guests at God's Banquet*, 1–22).

37. Mitchell, *Meeting Mystery*, 182–83.

Mystical "Body"

An Ecclesiology Informed by Judith Butler

GINA INGIOSI

The church as body has undergone serious reconfigurations since its debut in Paul's letters. The works of de Lubac and of de Certeau evince the (sometimes unintended) malleability of what has come to be known as the mystical body doctrine. Any attempt to speak of it in a stable, non-historicized sense is suspect, but the differences are not so dramatic as to call the various manifestations "doctrines" of the mystical body; they all affirm the basic tenet of unity but accent it differently or apply it to different situations. Changes have been due, in part, to changing understandings of both *mystical* and *body*.[1] Noting the danger and promise of change, but above all its inevitability, this essay seeks to locate the mystical body today, both in the unfurling shadow of Vatican II and in an increasingly postmodern and poststructuralist field. Judith Butler's *Gender Trouble* will act as surrogate mother, contributing new form and flesh to this familiar teaching utilized by the Second Vatican Council; the result will both maintain the traditional insights of the doctrine and incorporate elements of ecclesial life often beyond the scope of the mystical body model.

THE MODERN BODY OF THE MYSTICAL BODY

Discussion of the church as the mystical body of Christ found little popularity in the modern period until the early twentieth century,[2] when it rather suddenly took hold of Catholic imaginations again, particularly in the United States. It became a rallying cry of Catholic social justice movements as well as (harmoniously) a foundation for the hierarchical structure of the church. This renewed emphasis on the mystical body flowed into Vatican II where the mystical body of Christ is taken seriously as an organizational and moral blueprint for the church in the world. The church as the mystical body of Christ appears predominantly in *Sacrosanctum Concilium* (SC) and *Lumen Gentium* (LG) where footnotes attest to the influence of Pope Pius XII's encyclical *Mystici Corporis Christi* (MC).[3] These documents' presentation of the mystical body of Christ relies on Pius XII's understanding of the body as a visible, ordered actor.[4] Vatican II seems to make use of this model of bodiliness as visible, ordered agency to describe the mystical body of Christ as a composite body organized for its own growth. This familiar understanding of *body* will be challenged below by Butler.

In the first half of Pius XII's encyclical he expounds on what bodiliness is; for Pius, bodiliness is recognized by its structure. Promulgated in 1943, a time when the visible unity of the church was in short supply, *Mystici Corporis Christi* addresses the various errors in understanding the church: "false rationalism," "popular naturalism," and "false mysticism" (MC, 9). It is the last on the list that seems to be occupying Pius in this encyclical. This concern perhaps informs Pius XII's decision to describe the body in terms of its composition and capacity.[5] While the documents of Vatican II treated here echo the attributes put forward in Pius XII's encyclical, it is important to note that they do not echo his concerns.

Lumen Gentium expresses the unity of the church in terms of bodiliness; thus, the documents presume that a body must comprise unified parts (LG, 32). It is because the church is the mystical *body* of Christ that the building of the church is incremental and perceivable. That is, the work of the sacraments, principally the celebration of communion (LG, 7), is as organically related to the church as skin is to the body. In this, it simply follows the pattern of any natural body that is delineated and distinct.[6]

The church also exhibits organized interdependence[7] in its members. The exhibition of the organization is no minor point; it is this combination of the ordered and visible qualities of the natural body that allows Pius XII to speak of the centrality of the hierarchy to the ecclesial body. The hierarchical structure of the members figures into *Lumen Gentium*'s presentation of the body of the church as well (LG, 8).[8] In this picture, the diversity of and distinction among roles, offices, and ranks within the church are explained through the model of a body, and a body is constituted by various united, cooperative parts (LG, 30).

In addition to acting as a justification for the importance and distinction of the hierarchy, the mystical body's visibility and organization translates into another quality of body: intelligibility. While Pius XII explicitly reads order and fittingness in the diverse roles of members of the church, Vatican II documents, *Lumen Gentium* in particular, recast this organic relationship between members and their roles as a personal and unique contribution to the church. For *Lumen Gentium* the accent is on the number and diversity of gifts (LG, 7), even while citing Pius XII, who accents the suitability of certain roles to certain members. As noted above, the body is not simply a conglomeration of odds and ends but a unity and a harmony of diverse elements. To refer to this phenomenon as *organization* might be less apt than *interrelation*. It seems then, in either case, "bodiliness" is characterized by members relating to one another in diverse yet predictable ways.

Last, the church can act. In *Sacrosanctum Concilium* the supreme act of the mystical body of Christ is the performance of the liturgy (SC, 7). Designating the liturgy as the "sacred action surpassing all others" (SC, 7) implies that ecclesial action *can* occur outside of the liturgy. Interestingly, the supremacy of the liturgy results from its uniquely holistic character: it is the only act done by the whole church—Christ the head and the church his body—which raises questions about how the church can be church when not united to Christ. This rather limited view of ecclesial action will be discussed below, but it is enough for now to note that agency derives from the united and ordered quality of the body, as *Sacrosanctum Concilium* no. 26 makes clear.[9] Such a united and orderly body can act in the world, but regardless of whether or not it does, it is already and will remain a body. It is the building up of the church body, particularly in the "eucharistic sacrifice" (LG, 7, 26) that is in question and not that Body's very existence, as will be the case in Butler's *Gender Trouble*.

BODY IN *GENDER TROUBLE*

Butler's book *Gender Trouble*, published in 1990, proposed a new feminist criticism of gender. Butler's argument, that the body itself is constructed, including its sex differentiation, is a much more fundamental criticism than prior feminist critiques that sought to invalidate gender as a category or to at least disrupt the presupposed equivalence of gender with sex differentiation. Butler, however, argues that the recognition of the construction and performativity of only *gender* leaves the task half-finished. By challenging gender at its perceived root, the body, she can challenge the soil from which gender grows—heterosexism.[10] Her concern for toppling the operative heterosexism in gender discussions means that her assumptions are at odds with Catholic teachings.

The mystical body does have its own gender troubles, in fact. The historical body of Christ was male, but the ecclesial body of Christ is female in the Catholic tradition. While this clearly denotes a favoring of the nuptial relationship between Christ and his church (perhaps to the neglect of other potential paradigms for the church such as the mystical body), it has often determined the pronouns for the church. That is, even when the church is not spoken of in terms of its being "bride," it is often referred to as *she,* so many discourses on the church implicate gender, even if unintentionally, as an ecclesiological category. Further, the reality of the church as composed of men and women complicates the "gender" of the church. Expressions of the church as female or feminine are very clear instances of nonliteral uses of the terms, allowing common ground between the tradition and Butler.

Despite this common ground, some may find Butler's work to be an inappropriate or unwise choice to illuminate Catholic doctrine. As noted above, however, its application to an ecclesial body and not simply an individual, human body defuses the tension between Butler and the gender essentialism commonly found in Catholic thought. Further, what she has to say about bodiliness is invaluable to and strikingly consistent with the doctrine of the mystical body. With these precautions in mind, this essay proposes that the body in Butler's *Gender Trouble* will ultimately serve the mystical body doctrine well because it (1) exhibits fluidity between meaning and materiality, and (2) depends upon performativity.

First, to speak of the constitutive nature of the interaction between body and meaning entails recognizing that "'the body' is itself a construction."[11] For Butler, the body offers no clean slate with which to work. She rehearses a genealogy of philosophies of gender to argue that discussions of gender have historically relied on or been at the service of heterosexual normativity. Even feminist approaches to gender often have no room for non-heterosexual sexuality. In historicizing gender and proposing the underlying assumption of heterosexuality, Butler can claim that sex-differentiation and the body itself are not objective facts but are constructed and interpreted. Historicizing the constructed nature of the body serves as the first step to seeing bodiliness as an ongoing conversation between meaning and matter.

Next, constructed bodiliness never ossifies. A constructed body is not static; meaning and interpretation do not produce permanent, stable bodies. As Butler sees it, bodies must be reinforced "as a set of boundaries, individual and social, politically signified and maintained." Such maintenance implies that the constitution of bodies is a process. It is ongoing, and its product is mutable: " . . . the body is not a 'being,' but a variable boundary, a surface whose permeability is politically regulated, a signifying practice within a cultural field of gender hierarchy and compulsory heterosexuality."[12] What body is and what a particular body is may be regulated, but this only implies that there is a need to regulate—that the interpretation and the material can renew each other and shift those variable limits. Such fluidity provides the condition for the second key characteristic of bodiliness: performativity.

Performance crystalizes the relationship between matter and interpretation, so without performance there can be no body. Further, performance specifically lies in repetition (made possible by the realization of the degree to which one is constituted):

> The subject is not *determined* by the rules through which it is generated because signification is *not a founding act, but rather a regulated process of repetition* that both conceals itself and enforces its rules precisely through the production of substantializing effects. In a sense, all significations not only restrict, but enable the assertion of alternative domains of cultural intelligibility.[13]

Such a body has no "natural" elements to fall back on, so it must act out its identity, which could mean supporting the meaning ascribed to it or subverting it: "There is no self that is prior to the convergence or who maintains 'integrity' prior to its entrance into this conflicted cultural field. There is only a taking up of the tools where they lie, where the very 'taking up' is enabled by the tool lying there."[14] The acts and the tools are always already in conversation with one another. The body is not obvious or independent, but neither are the meanings given it. Instead, it is that "variable boundary," or point of collision, constantly being pushed and pulled by performance.

Last, to say that the constructed body is always in flux, always repeating itself, is to say that it cannot be pinned down or identified with one moment or explained away by some unseen force: "That the gendered body is performative suggests that it has no ontological status apart from the various acts which constitute its reality. This also suggests that if that reality is fabricated as an interior essence, that very interiority is an effect and function of a decidedly public and social discourse."[15] No place or refuge exists that can claim independence from this schema. To have a body is to be performing that body within whatever limited means are available, because the reality of any body is utterly dependent upon its performance.

THE MYSTICAL "BODY"

Finally, the time has come to propose what the mystical body doctrine might gain—or lose—when founded on the body described in *Gender Trouble*. As outlined above, that body exhibits two chief characteristics. First, the body is not some stable entity with a one-directional relationship to meaning, either flowing to or from it for all time. There is reciprocity between matter and meaning. Describing the body in this way opens up a space to identify a body by its second chief characteristic: performance. The constitutive nature of performance will be the basis of the following ecclesiological reflection. The mystical body of Christ considered thus must, like any other body, *perform* itself in order to *be* itself; this model for the church, then, stresses the need for the church to act as church in order to be recognizable and identifiable.[16]

Of course, that simple statement raises a vital question: How suitable can this performative bodiliness be for the church whose meaning comes from without? To critique the "priority" and "givenness" of a human body already evokes objections from voices within the church, but to imply that there is nothing given or prior in the church itself is a serious ecclesiological problem. Such a view of bodiliness seems to leave no room for Christ's forming the body or his Spirit's subsisting in it. We have seen that Butler, however, makes no naive claims about the limitless possibilities of performance; instead, she insists that the possibilities are given. As quoted above, "There is only a taking up of the tools where they lie, where the very 'taking up' is enabled by the tool lying there."[17] Recognizing performance as limited begins to bridge this apparent gap between *Gender Trouble*'s bodiliness and that of the church.

To bring the two closer, though, Butler's discussion of gender subversion helps. Up until now the discussion has been concerned mainly with the affirming type of performance, and that will continue to be the focus. For a moment, though, remembering that performance can subvert meaning helps to highlight that there was meaning to start with. Butler does not argue that bodies have no meaning; she simply rejects the notion that their meanings are somehow objective, obvious facts found in the composition of the body itself.[18] The great insight of her work is that bodiliness has been given meaning from without that can be affirmed or subverted in performance. The mystical body of Christ, which is united with Christ but not equivalent to him, finds an echo in this relationship between meaning and the body.

Just as the mystical body doctrine as based on modern understandings of bodiliness shows, the question of how to be church goes largely unaddressed. It is not important, then, for this new accent in the doctrine to provide an answer either. As demonstrated above, the role that the body plays in the doctrine is mainly structural—it is always the "of Christ" part that fills in the content of what that body does once it is formed. To say that the bodiliness is constituted by performance does not and need not define the nature and content of that performance, but it makes a further discussion of those details much more urgent. Using *Sacrosanctum Concilium*, *Lumen Gentium*, and also *Gaudium et Spes*, this essay concludes by gesturing toward some of those now constitutive actions of the church.

As noted above, *Sacrosanctum Concilium* selects the liturgy as the greatest action of the church due to its reliance on the whole body; in this new light liturgy is still just as vital to the church, and that vitality is just as rooted in the operative concept of body. The difference, of course, is that instead of implying that the decapitated church-body can act, the liturgy-acts attain importance as moments of expression and reception for the church. Seeing the sacramental life of the church as praxic collisions of input and output further helps to illuminate *Lumen Gentium*'s emphasis on the importance of the celebration of the sacraments—exemplified in its famous touting of the Eucharist as "the fount and apex of the whole Christian life" (LG, 11). The recasting of the mystical body done here dramatically underlines the necessity of liturgical action in the life of the church. When the actions of the church become its identity and existence, it only assists in understanding how liturgy might be so central and how the eucharistic sacrifice might be both the beginning and end of the church.

In *Gaudium et Spes*, and in key passages in *Lumen Gentium*,[19] the concern for the relationship of the Catholic Church to the rest of Christianity is evident, and the mystical body model necessarily drops out. How could a metaphor based on an organic, stable, ordered structure have degrees of communion or fellowship? One of the basic invocations of the mystical body in the past had been as a defense for the obvious boundaries of the church. By redirecting the focus of the mystical body model toward performance, space is provided for those who perform the body but who have not been initiated into the body as part of the contested and fluctuating "set of boundaries, individual and social."[20] Such an interpretation would still maintain the concern for degrees of and distinctions in fellowship that the documents, particularly *Lumen Gentium*, would like to maintain, because performance or actions (liturgical and moral) can be more or less similar in a way that body cannot be more or less whole.

Beyond intensifying traditional elements of the doctrine, an emphasis on ecclesial performativity broadens the scope of the doctrine to include action in the world. First, as mentioned above, the liturgy is the greatest act of the church in *Lumen Gentium*, because it is the only one done by the full church—head and body. Without unseating the supremacy of this act, this proposed mystical body would maintain that place of honor by continuing to recognize its traditional role as the moment of conception for the church: the communal reception of the body of Christ effects the body of Christ, and in a qualified way vice versa.

This recognition would allow for Christ's headship to be part of more than the liturgy, so that actions of the church as church could include a variety of ecclesial activities in addition to consecration. *Gaudium et Spes* needing to refer to the people of God in order to talk about the way that the church could interact with the world implies that this only seemed possible on an individual or personal level;[21] the mystical body as a performative body could make it possible to talk about the church as church in the world—and hold that body accountable to its proclaimed identity in Christ. As paragraph 93 of *Gaudium et Spes* attests in quoting John 13:35, the church must follow Christ in order to be recognizable to the world, and this following often falls outside of the realm of liturgical action.

Of course, all of this focus on the mystical body model should be kept in the context of the collection of other symbols for the church: sacrament, spouse, people of God, pilgrim, and so on. No one model or symbol should try to supplant the rest. The work here has been to show how one particular understanding of the church may be given a new accent to maintain its relevance and overcome some of its previously perceived limitations.[22] Taking Butler's thought seriously as a model for the mystical body doctrine necessitates performance in such a way as to buttress the importance of action in a model like the people of God, not to replace it.

The implications of substituting the body of *Gender Trouble* are clear: whatever it is to be church or Christ must be (1) something doable and (2) must be done. First, the dynamism and potency of Christ and the church must be affirmed, for to conceive of the church and/or Christ as static or abstract could divorce them from the possibility of performance. Second, given dynamic, embodied concepts of Christ and the church, the members *must* perform them. Without performance, the body does not die—it ceases to exist.

NOTES

1. Henri de Lubac, *Corpus Mysticum: The Eucharist and the Church in the Middle Ages*, trans. Gemma Simmonds, CJ, with Richard Price and Christopher Stephens (Notre Dame, IN: University of Notre Dame Press, 2006).

2. Keith F. Pecklers, *The Unread Vision: The Liturgical Movement in the United States of America, 1926–1955* (Collegeville, MN: Liturgical Press, 1998), 49.

3. Ormond Rush, *Still Interpreting Vatican II: Some Hermeneutical Principles* (New York: Paulist Press, 2004), 14.

4. Pius XII, *Mystici Corporis Christi (On the Mystical Body of Christ)*, encyclical letter (June 29, 1943), available on the vatican.va website.

5. In sum, the attributes of a body (which are applicable to the mystical body of Christ) are its visibility (MC, 14), internal diversity and order (15–17), and self-sustaining nature (18–21).

6. Following a comparison to the "natural body" Pius adds, in a pre–Vatican II, Catholic sensibility toward other churches, "Hence they err in a matter of divine truth, who imagine the Church to be invisible, intangible, a something merely 'pneumatological' as they say, by which many Christian communities, though they differ from each other in their profession of faith, are united by an invisible bond" (MC, 14). Vatican II unsurprisingly favors "people of God" as a model for the church when it tries to make sense of ecumenism; yet, it is surprising, given Pius XII's specific application of the "visibility" of the natural body to the mystical body, that Vatican II would borrow from Pius XII at all. This borrowing perhaps speaks to the power and endurance of the mystical body model.

7. "So for this reason above all the Church is called a body, that it is constituted by the coalescence of structurally united parts, and that it has a variety of members reciprocally dependent" (LG, 16).

8. *Lumen Gentium* interestingly uses Pius XII's presentation of the role of the hierarchy, based on the natural ranking of members in a body, several times when expounding the role of the episcopacy without referring to the mystical body doctrine or to the church as mystical body. In this way, mystical body thinking is more pervasive in the document than it seems at first glance.

9. "Liturgical services are not private functions, but are celebrations of the Church, which is the 'sacrament of unity,' namely, the holy people united and ordered under their bishops" (LG, 21).

10. Judith Butler, *Gender Trouble* (New York: Routledge, 2006), xxi; originally published in 1990.

11. Ibid., 15.

12. Ibid., 46, 189.

13. Ibid., 198–99, emphasis in original.

14. Ibid., 199.

15. Ibid., 185.

16. Though what follows will stress the potential for performance to affirm ecclesial identity, it is important to point out that performance in *Gender Trouble* has at least two other dimensions that complicate the picture: (1) limitation, and (2) the possibility for subversion. Both of these are alluded to and taken into consideration, but an explicit analysis of their implications would require papers in their own rights.

17. Butler, *Gender Trouble*, 199.

18. As Butler discusses the potential for subversion that dressing in drag has, she identifies the two associations that she hopes to break down: "I would suggest as well that drag . . . effectively mocks both the expressive model of gender and the notion of a true gender identity" (Butler, *Gender Trouble*, 186). Butler rejects any understanding of gender as real in itself or as expressing something real.

19. *Lumen Gentium* 15 and 16 discuss the connection or potential connection between the Catholic Church and other Christian churches and other faiths.

20. Butler, *Gender Trouble*, 46.

21. Maureen Sullivan, *The Road to Vatican II: Key Changes in Theology* (New York: Paulist Press, 2007), 46. Speaking of *Gaudium et Spes*, Sullivan notes: "Here, unlike previous official church documents, whose starting points would be the truths of the faith, *Gaudium et Spes* suggests a very different starting point: the human person. This document demonstrates a clear shift from a deductive methodology to an inductive methodology, a shift that will open the door to an entirely changed treatment of the church-world relationship" (46). Though she interprets this move differently, she nevertheless notes the conspicuous move from the church in the world to members (Christians) in the world.

22. Cardinal Ratzinger articulates one such limitation of mystical body that is inherited from Pius XII: "Pope Pius XII's encyclical on the mystical body (1943) had made a great step forward . . . but its still too-pointed idea of the Church's visibility made it all but impossible to give any status to Christians separated from Rome. . . . Here the idea of the 'body of Christ' is complemented with that of the "People of God" (Joseph Ratzinger, *Theological Insights of Vatican II* [New York: Paulist Press, 1966], 45).

III.

MINISTRY FOR THE FUTURE

NATHANIEL HIBNER

Ministry is the active hand of the church: the collaboration of clergy, religious, and lay people serving out their faith in the real world. Ministers feed the hungry, clothe the naked, visit the imprisoned, and heal the sick. They spread the good news to foreign lands and celebrate the Eucharist among strangers. To place ministry into a simple definition would only diminish this vast field that encompasses every aspect of Christian life.

The members of the Second Vatican Council understood the importance of the works of the church. For the mission given by Christ to the apostles to be realized, the council extended an open invitation to all the faithful. The church leaders wrote how the gifts of the Spirit "makes them [all people] fit and ready to undertake the various tasks and offices which contribute toward the renewal and building up of the Church" (LG, 12). Fifty years later, Catholics have heeded this call and the world has benefitted by their acts of charity and love.

Georgetown University's Center for Applied Research in the Apostolate tracks ministerial formation in the United States and publishes its results on its website. Its data reveal a 50 percent increase of ministerial education programs in the past thirty years. During this same time the number of participants has tripled. In the 2011–12 year, 17,452 people enrolled in degree and certificate programs in the field of ministry. With the renewal of the permanent diaconate by the council, each year has seen a 3 percent rise in permanent deacons throughout the United States. This totals 16,291 deacons since 1971. These statistics illustrate the dedication of Catholics who wish to become more active members in the church. Catholics have welcomed the invitation to participate in the many good works of the faith.

For the writers in this section and for the fellow emerging leaders in the church, the future of ministry is promising. The church's many ministerial roles remain to act as beacons of hope and administrators of God's love. Our hospitals continue to heal the sick. Our schools continue to develop the minds of tomorrow. Our food banks continue to feed the hungry. But as the population of the world rises, the church must be prepared to minister to the future needs of this ever-expanding humanity. Different structures may be required; new roles for all members of the church may need to be opened. Peter Folan in Chapter 5 uses the categories, outlined by Yves Congar, of *structures* and *Structure* to determine where the two have converged and diverged during the past fifty years. He gives a prescriptive plan to help the church thrive in the future.

First, in order for the church to face these needs, a new invitation must be presented to the faithful. We, as a community, should support the works of one another and open our arms to those who wish to follow in our steps. The simple act of inviting people to help in a soup kitchen can spark a flame that guides their decisions for the rest of their lives. Those teaching theology and ministry in our schools have an obligation to encourage the faithful to discern their role in any form of ministry, whether sacramental, administrative, or academic. The promotion and invitation of ministerial opportunities can help to attract more faithful to the call of our Lord. Opportunities such as the renewal of the permanent diaconate by the council are examined in this part with a critical eye on its effectiveness and possible need for adaptation. For the church to thrive in the coming decades, all members must be invited to share their gifts as ministers of the faith.

Second, the ministers of today and tomorrow need resources and support for their continued works. These include financial, spiritual, and motivational support, but ministers require also a sense of security and empowerment to enter confidently into the chaos of the world. The hierarchy, too, cannot stand in the background criticizing the works of those in the field. For ministers to aid others, the community has the obligation to aid its ministers. The future of ministry needs a strong foundation of the faithful to stand upon as it brings about the kingdom of God.

Finally, younger adults and emerging theologians need to be more aware of the interrelation between their spiritual and secular lives. Adults in the church can act as examples of this communion by living out their faith in service to others. This appreciation among our youth will ensure the continued expansion and evolution of the church to meet the continued needs of the world.

Overall, the structures of ministry have flourished since the Second Vatican Council. Leaders in the field will continue to hear the call of the church to serve one another and to fulfill the mission of our faith. The next fifty years will bring about many new needs, and I trust our ministries will persist in acting as disciples of Christ.

"Pastors" and "the Other Faithful" (LG, 32)

The Sexual-Abuse Scandal and the Emergence of Authority Relationships in the Church

ANSELMA DOLCICH-ASHLEY

INTRODUCTION:
CHURCH AUTHORITY AND SEXUAL ABUSE

My thesis may seem simplistic and even frightfully naive. It is this: The sexual-abuse crisis in the Catholic Church in the United States has enabled the emergence of church authority. This thesis appears simplistic because the Catholic Church, of course, professes the church as one, holy, catholic, and apostolic. The college of bishops in union with the bishop of Rome stands as the *sine qua non* of church authority as willed by Christ, and it is precisely this authority that governs, indeed defines, our denomination as hierarchical (LG, 18–29), in contrast to our separated Christian brethren. Likewise, the thesis appears naive because if the sexual-abuse crisis showed us anything, it is surely that there is, in a sense, *too much* exercise of authority in the Catholic Church. That is, sexual abuse in the church became a crisis precisely because bishops used their authority to respond to allegations however they wished, often in secretive and unjust ways unmoored from constraints of structural accountability or due process within church governance. As a result, known or credibly accused abusers were given new ministry placements where they abused new victims,[1] and there was little the Catholic faithful could do about it.[2]

Indeed, official ecclesial intransigence toward and mishandling of both credible allegations and proven cases have led to the perception that authority in the Catholic Church has exceeded its limits and has nearly destroyed its credibility.[3]

Yet when church governing authority is understood as a *relationship* between the church's official governors (pastors) and the governed (the other faithful), we can begin to see in a new light the sometimes disheartening, sometimes hopeful confrontations between "the other faithful" and "the pastors" in the context of the sexual-abuse crisis. When the hermeneutic of relationship contextualizes the understanding of authority in the Catholic Church, then the depictions of the post–Vatican II church as *either* hierarchical *or* the people of God can now be seen in terms of mutually reliant conjunction rather than hermetic exclusion. My observations here are largely comprised of an ethical analysis of authority and governance in the Catholic Church; while ecclesiology is an essential dialogue partner, the strength of my argument rests on its ethical claims.

CONSERVATIVE AND LIBERAL STEREOTYPES

To begin this analysis I chart an alternative to two stereotypical poles, which here I simply name *conservative* (wherein doctrinal claims of apostolic succession underwrite near-total mastery of a bishop in a diocese) and *liberal* (wherein doctrinal claims of the church as the people of God underwrite the importation of Western-style democracy into the Catholic Church). In so doing I hope to highlight the truth expressed in *Lumen Gentium* that institutional authority in the Catholic Church consists of a viable and dynamic *relationship* between "pastors and the other faithful"—all of whom have been baptized as priests, prophets, and rulers. While the bishop holds the ordinary governing authority in a diocese, this ordinary authority does not displace the baptismal authority of "the other faithful." Thus, by seeking redress and pursuing justice, the survivors of clerical sexual abuse and their advocates were exercising their own baptismal charism of governance. Or, to put it into somewhat traditional language, they overcame, in a pragmatically effective if limited context, the false pre–Vatican II separation between the hierarchy as the actively ruling and teaching church *(ecclesia docens)* and "the other faithful" as the passively receiving and listening church *(ecclesia discens)*. I argue below that in their pursuit of justice, survivors and their advocates effectively replaced this dichotomy with, simply, *authority,* now incarnate in a viable and dynamic relationship between the church's institutional governors (called official because they hold office) and its baptized governors.

First, the conservative stereotype: in this view church governing authority is a capacity given in ordination (even if, in the context of the sexual-abuse crisis, badly abused by actual bishops and pastors). Supporters of this view might point to Pope John Paul II's 2003 post-synodal apostolic exhortation *Pastores Gregis,* which identified the authority of the bishop with that of Christ.[4] However, John Paul was writing within a year of the *Boston Globe* investigations, and in that light his qualification of authority is significant. The grace of ordination is not to be understood mechanically; rather, a bishop is truly authoritative when his ministry aspires to and truly reflects an imitation of Christ, as evidenced by holy pastors such as Pope Saint Gregory the Great, throughout church history. American commentator George Weigel largely echoes this idea, opining that bishops who mishandled sexual-abuse allegations were operating more like spineless corporate functionaries than the great apostles in whose shoes they walk.[5]

A difficulty with such a stance, of course, is that it has a tendency to conflate ordination, personal holiness, and successful ministerial governance. It presumes too easily that bishops of Gregory the Great's ilk are common, or at least ought to be. Comparisons can be drawn here to Plato's philosopher-king, that wise and noble ruler whose authority derives from the correct apprehension of the truth, reflects truth and beauty, and draws all rational persons to follow. It is true that in everyday experience we constantly follow experts possessed of the truth—from the car mechanic to the brain surgeon. It is also true that all Christians are called to follow Christ, the "light of the nations" (LG, 1) and head of the church. But for human persons on pilgrimage in history, the problem at the heart of "theoretical expertise" (to use the philosophical designation) lies in its idealization of leadership. Bishops, like all leaders, are mere mortals, and few of them, observed early twentieth-century German theologian Karl Adam, come close to saintliness. "Eminent popes, bishops of great spiritual force, theologians of genius, priests of extraordinary graces and devout layfolk: these must be, not the rule, but the exception. . . . An immoral laity, bad priests, bishops and popes—these are the open, festering, never-healing wounds of the Body of the mystical Christ."[6]

Ordination cannot be conflated with personal holiness, much less administrative expertise.[7] Indeed, the disjunction between the ideal church and the actual church prompted Pope Paul VI in his 1964 encyclical *Ecclesiam Suam* to call for internal renewal: "The actual image of the Church will never attain to such a degree of perfection, beauty, holiness and splendor that it can be said to correspond perfectly with the original conception in the mind of Him who fashioned it" (11). Pope Paul's words were prescient. During the sexual-abuse crisis it became painfully obvious that an understanding of the bishop as the only one qualified to rule *in persona Christi* rather inevitably opened the door to governance characterized by mastery, understood here as a significant lack of accountability to those whom the bishop governs. This is an ethical problem insofar as governance without accountability, on this side of the Parousia, invariably creates errors and harms preventable by structures designed to protect human dignity. But it is also an ecclesiological problem, given that appeals to rule *in persona Christi* too easily overlook the fact that *all* of the faithful, through baptism, have entered into Christ, from whom their rights and responsibilities within the church arise.

Somewhat analogously, the stereotypical "liberal" pole also seems to conflate ideals of governance—only different ideals. In this view the recognition of the people of God as possessing the baptismal charism of governance can be worked into a kind of social-contract foundation for church authority. Indeed, Vatican II's ecclesiological development seems to echo changes in secular political theory and practice noticeable in the modern period and often associated with the rise of democratic regimes. Instead of relying on (nonexistent) perfection or superiority reserved to the few, justifications for secular governance appealed to a rationale that "people are roughly equal in their abilities to reason and live well."[8] Thus, ideas found in modern social-contract theories—particularly the notion that "the governed" possess the authority and provide the mandate for government leaders to rule—seem to make sense as a way forward.[9] Indeed, it is no wonder that American Catholics made use of their own structures of secular government to exercise simultaneously their rights as citizens and their baptismal authority in pursuit of justice in their church. I suggest that defensiveness on the part of recent popes toward making Catholic Church governance more democratic has shut down a potentially fruitful conversation.[10]

Yet proposals for importing democratic structures into the Catholic Church have arguably failed thus far to take into consideration the famous paradox of authority running through modern stable democracies. In these regimes the governed are not in charge of governing any more than I as a US citizen and resident of Indiana's second congressional district can order my congressional representative or the president of the United States to do my bidding. Yet at the same time I'm not completely powerless to influence government officials. The fact that modern democracies actually work relies upon holding two distinct ideals in a creative and practical tension. As political philosopher Jean Hampton notes, "We who approve of the Lockean idea that . . . an agency relationship exists between ruler and people" find it "remarkably difficult" to explain how and why this works. "If there is such an agency relationship, how does it make sense to consider the people 'ruled'? And if the people who are being 'ruled' are themselves in charge of their rulers, how can their political society last?"[11] So where are we? Is governance "of the people and by the people" in the Catholic Church? Or is governance only of and by the bishops, the successors to the apostles, and empowered by sacramental ordination?

A WAY FORWARD: AUTHORITY AS RELATIONSHIP

I suggest that the difficulty here lies in the perception that church governing authority is some kind of zero-sum game—either the bishops are authorities and order "the other faithful" around, or the people of God are the authorities and set the bishops to do their bidding. I believe that the solution lies in reframing and redefining authority consistent both with philosophical principles that successfully address the paradox of authority and with the ecclesiology of *Lumen Gentium*.

Authority can be seen as *both* the right and power to issue directives that the governed are compelled to obey *and* also "invented" by the people participating in a governing convention.[12] Usually when we think of authority we think of only the former—those who have the right and power to give orders. There is a way in which governing authority is "in" a ruler—whether my congressional representative or my local bishop—but *not* "in" me.

But there is more to authority than that. It is also a relationship. To understand this point fully it behooves us to draw upon philosophical notions of authority and comparisons based upon philosophical distinctions, which I make here in four points. First, authority should be understood within the larger context of a community, within which the right and power of governing office is placed. After all, there would not be much point to governing authority if there were no community to govern.[13]

Ultimately, the purpose of governing authority does not center on the person who holds authority and wields power, but rather on the community for whose sake the authority exercises office. This point is underscored as much in *Lumen Gentium* as it is in the US Constitution. Seen this way, governing authority inherently relies upon the governed people, who respond to governance, and serves the needs of human dignity. Second, however, the response of the people to how they are being governed takes place at a level of removal from the daily exercise of authority (office); thus the people are properly called the governed and those who hold office are properly called authorities. *Lumen Gentium* also calls attention to this dynamic: "If therefore in the Church everyone does not proceed by the same path, nevertheless all are called to sanctity and have received an equal privilege of faith through the justice of God. And if by the will of Christ some are made teachers, pastors and dispensers of mysteries on behalf of others, yet all share a true equality with regard to the dignity and to the activity common to all the faithful for the building up of the Body of Christ" (LG, 32). In a secular venue, Hampton uses "invention of authority" to describe collectively those myriad attitudes and practices by which those who are governed support the ruling regime—even if that support is minimal, that is, characterized merely by the absence of opposition. Every time we obey the law or simply refrain from active disobedience, we implicitly support the kind of governance that oversees our society, as well as the actual individuals who hold government office.

Thus, third, the reality of authority that emerges is much more complex than everyday notions of authority—and certainly more nuanced and mature than the simplistic glorifying or trashing of authorities or candidates for office sadly characteristic of much of American society today. In societies characterized by internal strife and lack of respect for authority, we see the problems accrued when proper authority really does break down. The fundamental problem is not per se disobedience toward official government leaders, but rather the resultant social disruption resulting from the weakening of the regular coordinating and protective tasks of governance. The vulnerable of a society then readily become the victims of those who have managed to wrest power, and against whom authorities are powerless to prevail. We need authority, both in secular society and in the church, to provide vital needs and to protect human dignity and the common good. But, fourth, it would be naive to think that simply leaving official authorities alone to do their jobs is somehow virtuous. Both in secular governance, and certainly in church gover- nance in light of the sexual-abuse crisis, we see that in order for the authorities' rule to be deemed effective, authorities rely upon a level of mutual peace, support, and justice within the social (or ecclesial- communal) fabric. That is, the effect of ruling must support this state of justice and respect, or else governance has gone awry and persons are exposed to potential harm.

How can rulers know whether their rule actually does support this goal? In the American system provision is made for a kind of effective feedback to the ruling regime on the part of the governed. We may alter or tweak the extent and scope of governing authority by regular interventions such as court trials, petitioning for new laws, and casting votes. In these structured ways those ruled influence the scope and direction of governance (and even its foundational ideals, as exemplified by amendments to the Constitution) according to their developing understanding of what justice is, who ought to benefit from it, and in what ways. Although this influence affects and changes the daily exercise of governing office, it takes place at a level of removal from it. So, over the course of American history we have seen continual updates to the governing convention in ways large and small, from defining who can cast votes to due process for prisoners.

Now, although the Catholic Church throughout the modern period developed structures of governance characterized by centralization and mastery, in recent decades church governance has begun to shift away from consolidated forms of authority and toward a governing convention in which the governed participate, even if remotely, in their own governance. *Lumen Gentium* provides the theological foundation for this shift by holding in creative tension the understanding of the Catholic Church as hierarchically structured with the bishops as successors to the apostles, along with the characterizations of the church as the people of God, universally called to holiness yet subject to sin and therefore still in pilgrimage to fulfillment in Christ. Since Vatican II the development of participatory structures of governance—such as lay-majority diocesan finance councils and review boards—has made possible practical exercises of the baptismal charism of governance.

However, the sexual-abuse crisis has revealed that these present structures need to be "reviewed, renewed and revitalized in order to serve better the life and mission of the church."[14] While they do allow for some measure of participation and shared responsibility on the part of the "other faithful," nonetheless the current structures of church governance retain and support many aspects of unilateral, masterful rule on the part of bishops. The sexual-abuse crisis placed into open view the reality that the Catholic Church's relationship of governing authority is a poorly performing one at best. What is missing in the church at present are those meta-level structures of governance, distinct from the immediate "object level" of governance (the ongoing, daily exercise of authority for the sake of the community's needs and goals).[15] Above I described some of the more common meta-levels of American governance, such as court trials, petitions, and voting. These procedures essentially are governing structures by which the governed may influence and provide feedback to their official rulers regarding the functioning of society. As indicated by the prefix *meta*, they are situated behind or beyond the direct job of ruling. They allow for meaningful citizen participation in governance without devolving into anarchism or governance by plebiscite; at the same time, regular citizens not holding public office cannot be identified as proper civic authorities. Analogously, in the Catholic Church, robust meta-level structures would provide "the other faithful" with a healthy means of participating in their own governance while also simultaneously reserving official ruling authority to the bishops.

However, what meta-levels presently exist in the church—such as review boards and finance councils—can be fairly accused of being merely consultative; membership remains under the control of the local bishop. This represents a loss to the entire church, since the effective feedback provided by meta-levels—that is, by persons baptized in Christ and committed to the mission of the Catholic Church—does precisely what Paul VI called for, that is, moves the church as a whole ever closer to a true imitation of Christ. In the case of the sexual-abuse crisis, this means that the church on the basis of structures of accountability, enabling a richer and deeper relationship between pastors and the other faithful, might have better reflected virtues and practices of justice and charity rather than secrecy and privilege.

Yet although the meta-levels of church governance are effectively missing, the sexual-abuse crisis has demonstrated that the other faithful were not helpless in dealing with crimes inflicted upon children by priests and covered up by bishops. I suggest that by utilizing secular American institutions such as law enforcement and the press, the survivors of sexual abuse and their advocates essentially have been inventing on the ground, so to speak, a meta-level of church governance robust enough to ensure that the church's official governors respond to the claims of justice. Admittedly, this intervention has been limited to the extent to which the American legal system can enforce its own laws, yet it is there nonetheless.

HUMAN RIGHTS ADVOCACY IN THE CATHOLIC CHURCH

Thus far, I have been detailing a pragmatic proposal to ensure both the apostolic authority of bishops to rule their own dioceses and the authority of the other faithful as the church's baptized governors. In so doing I have attempted to sketch briefly the nature of authority as a relationship. By this point, however, it may seem as though the church's official governors still retain the upper hand, since it was only by appeal to an extra-ecclesial system of due process and law enforcement that abuse survivors enacted their baptismal authority. Yet there is another reality involved in the "invention" of authority relationships to take into account here, and that is the recognition and claiming of human rights.

The claiming by victim-survivors of the human right to bodily integrity represents one concrete way in which the tables are turned, or as moral theologian Jean Porter argues, "the ruled rule the rulers."[16] By claiming this right through US legal channels, American Catholic survivors of sexual abuse secured limited structural changes prior to broad ecclesial reforms and regardless of competing ecclesiological commitments among the many actors in the crisis. Their advocacy mirrors strategies of contemporary human rights practices in the secular sphere, but also remains consistent with understandings of natural rights in the Catholic tradition. Human rights practice is, of course, a topic too complex to trace within the context of this essay, but nonetheless even its bare outlines offer promise. For example, it is significant to note that despite the differing poles of ecclesiological opinion, probably all Catholics in the United States, pastors and the other faithful alike, were of one mind regarding the basic duty to stop the abuse and to protect the vulnerable.

Drawing upon categories identified by Christian ethicist Sumner Twiss, we can identify this state of affairs in the US Catholic Church as "pragmatic agreement," a significant first step in settling conflicting claims in human rights disputes. In pragmatic agreement, parties in a dispute reach a specific common ground—for example, protecting young persons from sexual harm in ecclesial contexts—that exemplifies "human interests of such fundamental importance that they ought to be socially guaranteed."[17] In response to sexual abuse, Catholics identified a basic human right to bodily protection and integrity grounded in a theological understanding of the human person as constituted in the image and likeness of God. While alongside such a broad and basic agreement there may exist competing and even antagonistic ecclesiological commitments, nonetheless pragmatic agreement on the importance of the protection of the young is a point on which all Catholics can assent.

There are two objections worth highlighting to my proposal that advocacy for the survivors of sexual abuse in the Catholic Church amounts to a kind of intra-ecclesial human rights practice. One is the criticism that advocacy of rights by its own logic impedes the necessary communitarian dimension of the church. In this view, rights-talk elevates individualism at the expense of sociality.[18] I suggest, however, that the claiming of *human* rights (as distinct from certain legal rights) represents a fundamental threshold of justice consistent with the second tablet of the Decalogue and theological anthropology broadly implicit in Catholic social teaching—without which persons cannot fully express either their human dignity or their Christian calling. It is because the idea of human rights cogently expresses to the contemporary world the preciousness and dignity of human persons that all popes since John XXIII in *Pacem in Terris* have supported human rights in contemporary society. The second objection, focusing on early modern philosophical theories that gave rise to many contemporary rights theories, argues that such philosophies are not compatible with Catholic theology and practice and might serve to undermine doctrinal beliefs such as apostolic succession. However, as historian Brian Tierney has persuasively argued, natural-rights theories originated during the medieval period, as Catholic theologians and canon lawyers responded to the requirements of human dignity within the context of faith in a rapidly evolving society.[19]

The development of natural-rights theories within the medieval Christian context lends itself to analogous application today within the Catholic Church. The claims of rights need not move from theory to practice. In the context of internal disputes regarding church governance, the movement might well go in the other direction, as theoretical consensus on natural rights arising from theological claims regarding the human person and pragmatic agreements about protection of the young open doors to dialogue about, and exploration and testing of, new features of interrelationship between pastors and the other faithful. (In the medieval period, Tierney notes, practices preceded theories simply because there weren't any fully articulated rights theories.) As they exchange views, pastors and the other faithful may be able to "identify not only shared human rights norms, but also shared reasons for accepting these norms, for example, similar views of human moral capacity, common vulnerabilities to suffering and oppression, analogous moral principles, rules and virtues and the like."[20] Ideally, this pragmatic arrangement will enable a communal search for rationales and values supportive of it, including incorporating church ethics into an ecclesiology adjusted to account for the failings of the "pilgrim Church" (LG, 48) in history.

Human rights represent fundamental and compelling claims supportive of human persons, understood as created in God's image and likeness. Especially when claimed by the governed, they represent aspects of personhood that ruling authorities—both ecclesial and secular—have duties to respect and protect. How do human rights, then, synchronize with the idea of church authority as I have been developing it here? I suggest that the idea of human rights gives us another resource from within the Catholic tradition to help the Catholic community delineate the broad contours of authority, understood in terms of a relationship. If hierarchy and apostolic succession fundamentally characterize official governing authority, then within the broader church context, "bookending" that doctrine, is the fundamental human dignity of the governed, given practical and ethical articulation as human rights. In terms of normative ethics and concrete practices of applied ethics, the practical exercise of official authority is given limits by the human rights of the other faithful. Between these two poles the relationship of authority exists.

CONCLUSION: RELATION AND RESTORATION

This essay has purposed to analyze an ethics of church authority consistent with Catholic doctrine and theology. I have already gestured toward a theology of baptismal charisms in identifying the other faithful as the Catholic Church's baptismal (not ordained) governors, as well as toward a theological anthropology undergirding the idea of human or natural rights. By manner of conclusion, it is helpful to bring the circle around and identify a working theological understanding of the episcopacy, which gives life to an ethics of authority as relationship.

While we often use the word *official* to describe a bishop's governing authority in the Catholic Church, this very word calls attention only to certain aspects of the episcopacy. The term *office* connotes the task of authority to issue directives compelling obedience on the part of the governed, and the power associated with this task. But this usage of the word *office* can mask the fundamental nature of the episcopacy itself, which is not an office but a *relation,* that is, a subject defined by means of its relationship to others.[21] The episcopal relation has a twofold term: with all other bishops in union with the bishop of Rome, and with the members of each bishop's local see, in which the bishop exercises the triple *munera* of sanctifying, teaching, and governing.

The triple *munera* commonly are understood as a job description of a bishop, accompanied by the power to carry out duties. But the theological meaning is far richer and gives depth to my ethical analysis of church governing authority. As Michael J. Buckley has noted, the *munera* imply not just the bishop's power to exercise duties (the habitual potency), or his actual carrying out of his ministry (actual potency), or merely the laity's "receiving" the bishop's ministry. The triple *munera* signify all the above *together with* the sanctifying, teaching, and governing having real and existential outcomes in building up the life of faith and the vitality of the local diocese. A bishop is fundamentally defined, then, as one who is in a vital relation with the members of his see; these members are absolutely necessary for the church to exist in that place. Their relation with the bishop exists "like the Church itself . . . only in the concrete circumstances of history."[22] Thus, when the power of office is exercised in a way that enables harm or inhibits justice in communal relationships, then not only is ethics compromised, but so is the very actualization of the church in history. In a theological sense, then, structures of governance that enable meaningful participation on the part of the laity also enable the bishop to "be himself." Conversely, without these very structures that hold him to accountability, he is paradoxically lessened as an authority, at least in a de facto sense. That is, a bishop still holds office *de jure*, but his credibility and effectiveness for his see's spiritual vitality suffer when his rule lacks accountability.

In the context of the sexual-abuse crisis in the Catholic Church in the United States, the theological relation of the bishop to his diocese and the ethical relationship of authority between pastors and the other faithful in their respective dioceses have been disrupted, and indeed, violated. Thus the survivors of direct sexual abuse by clerics are themselves the symbol and center of a larger disorder: that a community whose episcopal relation ought to be characterized by Christlike love, humility, and justice became caught up in self-serving secrecy, denial, and equivocation. I suggest that the kind of questions and moral intuitions raised by the sexual-abuse crisis, on the one hand, and the pragmatic consensus on the need to protect the vulnerable, on the other, ought themselves to lead the Catholic Church toward a comprehensive, restorative justice consistent with the church's self-understanding as a community of Christ's disciples.[23] As Dublin Archbishop Diarmuid Martin observed from his experience in handling the sexual-abuse crisis in the Catholic Church in Ireland, "Then the Church becomes a restorative community—a restorative community for all. . . . A precondition for the Church's providing a service of spiritual healing to victims is that the Church learns to be a truly restorative community, a community which welcomes and accepts the wounded into its community on *their* terms."[24]

Although set in motion by the huge and preventable tragedy of sexual abuse, a variety of positive responses have been forthcoming: the claiming of human rights, the search for and enactment of meta-levels of governance on the part of the Catholic Church's "other faithful," and the growing awareness of the episcopacy as a relation. All of these efforts and more will create, I hope, a foundation for such a restorative justice as recently called for by Archbishop Martin. It is in that hope that pastors and the other faithful must continue to press for church reform.

NOTES

1. To cite but one example, a Philadelphia grand jury report noted, "Moreover the evidence established that Cardinal Bevilacqua and his predecessor knowingly transferred priests who had been credibly accused of molesting children to new assignments where they retained access to, and control over, children." Report of the County Investigating Grand Jury, First Judicial District of Pennsylvania, Criminal Trial Division, Sept. 26, 2001, Misc. No. 01–00–8944, 2. Available on the bishop-accountability.org website.

2. Bishop Wilton Gregory of Belleville, Illinois, then president of the United States Conference of Catholic Bishops, admitted in a 2002 address regarding the crisis: "It is we who need to confess; and so we do. We are the ones, whether through ignorance or lack of vigilance or—God forbid—with knowledge, who allowed priest abusers to remain in ministry and reassigned them to communities where they continued to abuse. We are the ones who chose not to report the criminal actions of priests to the authorities because the law did not require this. We are the ones who worried more about the possibility of scandal than in bringing about the kind of openness that helps prevent abuse. And we are the ones who at times responded to victims and their families as adversaries and not as suffering members of the church." Bishop Wilton Gregory, "Presidential Address Opening Dallas Meeting of U.S. Bishops," *Origins* 32, no. 7 (June 27, 2002).

3. See Francis Oakley and Bruce Russett, eds., *Governance, Accountability and the Future of the Catholic Church* (New York: Continuum, 2004).

4. "Each bishop is configured to Christ . . . Through the Bishops and the priests, their co-workers, the Lord Jesus Christ, seated at the right hand of God the Father, remains present in the midst of believers." Pope John Paul II, *Pastores Gregis,* 1, 6. All official church documents are available on the vatican.va website.

5. George Weigel, *The Courage to Be Catholic: Crisis, Reform, and the Future of the Church* (New York: Basic Books, 2002).

6. Karl Adam, *The Spirit of Catholicism,* trans. Dom Justin McCann, OSB (New York: Crossroad, 1997), 216–17.

7. See Jean M. Bartunek, Mary Ann Hinsdale, and James F. Keenan, eds., *Church Ethics and Its Organizational Context: Learning from the Sex Abuse Scandal in the Catholic Church* (Lanham, MD: Rowman and Littlefield, 2006).

8. Jean Hampton, *Political Philosophy* (Boulder, CO: Westview Press, 1997), 28.

9. See Gerard Mannion, "What Do We Mean by Church Authority?" in *Authority in the Roman Catholic Church: Theory and Practice,* ed. Bernard Hoose, 19–36 (Burlington, VT: Ashgate Publishing Company, 2002).

10. Political scientist Bruce Russett's observations are compelling in this regard: "In 2002 Pope John Paul II warned a group of Austrian bishops visiting the Vatican, "The church is not a democracy, and no one from below can decide on the truth." Yes, the church is not a democracy because it lacks institutions of democratic accountability, and that is the problem. Saying the church is not a democracy is not just saying that democracy in the church would be bad, but continues a hierarchical suspicion of democratic government itself. . . . Saying the church is not a democracy becomes the assertion of a point of pride that it is not like those 'others.' The church's lack of democracy is embedded both in its culture and in its lack of adequate institutions to constrain abuses of power. Consequently we have one of several central and pernicious myths: *the myth that democracy is irrelevant to good governance in the church.*" Bruce Russett, "Monarchy, Democracy, or 'Decent Consultation Hierarchy?'" in Oakley and Russett, *Governance, Accountability, and the Future of the Catholic Church.*

11. Hampton, *Political Philosophy,* 63.

12. I understand the term *invention* of authority as Hampton uses it in *Political Philosophy. Invention* in this sense calls to mind the Latin root of the term (*invenire* means "to discover or to come upon"), which calls to mind a mutual search and active cooperation by both rulers and the governed to fashion and perfect the running of a society such that it reflects a society's—in this case, the Catholic Church's—highest ideals.

13. *Lumen Gentium*'s structure famously reflects first Christ, the light of the nations, then proceeds to describe the church as "the People of God" (LG, 9–17), a community where all share in the one priesthood of Christ.

14. Sharon Euart, "Structures for Participation in the Church," *Origins* 35, no. 2 (May 2005).

15. See Hampton, *Political Philosophy,* 70–114.

16. Jean Porter, *Ministers of the Law: A Natural Law Theory of Legal Authority* (Grand Rapids, MI: Eerdmans, 2010), 331.

17. Sumner Twiss, "Moral Grounds and Plural Cultures: Interpreting Human Rights in the International Community," *Journal of Religious Ethics* 26, no. 2 (1998): 271–82.

18. See Mary Ann Glendon, *Rights Talk: The Impoverishment of Political Discourse* (New York: 1st Free Press, 1993).

19. Brian Tierney, *The Idea of Natural Rights: Studies on Natural Rights, Natural Law and Church Law 1150–1625* (Atlanta: Scholars Press 1997).

20. Twiss, "Moral Grounds and Plural Cultures," 297.

21. For these observations I am indebted to Michael J. Buckley's insightful analysis in his *Papal Primacy and the Episcopate: Toward a Relational Understanding* (New York: Crossroad Herder, 1998).

22. Ibid., 44.

23. On the idea of the church as a community of disciples, see the new chapter in the expanded edition of Avery Dulles's classic *Models of the Church* (Garden City, NY: Image Books, 1987).

24. Archbishop Diarmuid Martin, "The Truth Will Make You Free: A Personal Journey," lecture delivered at Marquette University, Milwaukee, Wisconsin, April 4, 2011. See also "Dublin's Archbishop Diarmuid Martin Reflects on the Clergy Sexual Abuse Scandal," Marquette University Law School, Restorative Justice Initiative Conference, April 4–5, 2011. Both are available online.

The Structure and Structures of Ministry

Shaping the Future

PETER FOLAN, SJ

Shortly before Christmas 2011, the Archdiocese of Boston announced its plan "to reorganize the management of its 290 parishes by creating teams to oversee multiple parishes under a single pastor," a story that received considerable coverage in *The Boston Globe* and other local media outlets.[1] Those familiar with the Catholic Church in the United States would be justified in wondering just how new this news really was. For some time now the days of parish rectories housing two, three, or more priests, each assigned to minister to the same manageable community of believers, have been more the stuff of memory than of present experience. Dioceses outside the traditional Catholic strongholds of the Northeast have already spent years, if not decades, implementing the sort of reorganization that Boston just announced. Add to this the fact that "for several decades and in growing numbers, lay men and women have been undertaking a wide variety of roles in Church ministries,"[2] and a clear truth emerges: ministry in the church has changed and is continuing to change.[3]

Given this ferment, considering the future of the church will be futile if *considering* means "predicting." Thus, rather than offer a *descriptive* account of the future, this paper formulates a *prescriptive* plan of how the current state of ministry can be shaped to allow the church of the future to thrive in its "mission of proclaiming and establishing among all peoples the kingdom of Christ and of God" (LG, 5). This forward-looking orientation ultimately wishes to tap into the movement of the Holy Spirit, who urges the church toward its eschatological end. As the church, guided by the Spirit, moves ahead, I argue that the *structures* of the ministry of tomorrow will be shaped both by the *structure* of ministry articulated by the Second Vatican

Council and the strengths and weaknesses of ministerial *structures* in place today.

STRUCTURE AND STRUCTURES

I borrow this distinction of structure and structures from the work of Yves Congar, who contrasts the terms in his *True and False Reform in the Church*. The very first sentence of the book's foreword begins to address the difference Congar has in mind: "Theologians have only studied the *structure* of the church, so to speak, not its actual *life*. Naturally, the church has a structure deriving from its constitutive elements, but with this structure it *lives*, and the faithful within it live in unity."[4] The structure of the church, then, is that which is *necessary* for the church to continue being authentically the church, something "divine and eternal,"[5] something that is not changeable. Put differently, nothing less than God's revelation dictates the structure of the church, thus indicating that the appropriate response to the church's structure is reception into the *life* of the church, or what Congar ultimately calls "ecclesial structures":

> Those who use this rather vague expression, "structures," don't always bother to define what they mean. However, there seems to be a consensus about the following: (i) The question is not about the [essential] structure of the church (dogma, sacraments, hierarchy). No one is calling this essential structure into question. Rather, using my distinction between structure and life, the need for [structural] change has to do with issues about life. (ii) However, within the essential structure of the church, the church's life borrows forms, some of which are adaptable, while others have a certain stability. For example, the eloquence of some preacher is an ephemeral expression of doctrine, but the way the catechism is written, or the style and organizational structure of parishes, or even the manner of celebrating High Mass—these are more stable forms of ecclesial life. Such things do not belong to the essential structure of the church. They are historically introduced as expressions of its life, and so they have only a relative value. They are what we mean when we speak in the plural about "ecclesial structures."[6]

Structures, according to Congar, manifest concretely the church's *structure* at any given point, and as such, are either more or less genuine, effective, and Spirit-inspired means of making present that structure.

This distinction has relevance for shaping the future of ministry in the church. Indeed, it raises a fundamental question: Which dimensions of ministry are part of the church's structure, and which are simply structures? In other words, what can be shaped (because it is, by its very nature, able to be shaped), and what cannot be shaped (because it is, by its very nature, not able to be shaped)? The logic of these questions suggests that one begin with structure, with that which cannot be shaped, and then, within the boundaries it delineates, seek to determine which structures should be added, changed, or eliminated for the future of ministry.

LISTENING TO THE TRADITION: THE STRUCTURE OF MINISTRY

Ministry, to say the very least, is a complex reality, a phenomenon that defies simple definition. True though this is, the task of shaping ministry's future demands at least a basic, albeit necessarily incomplete sketch of it. Thomas F. O'Meara provides this by highlighting ministry's most salient features, work that has acquired quasi-canonical status among theologians of ministry: "Christian ministry is the public activity of a baptized follower of Jesus Christ flowing from the Spirit's charism and an individual personality on behalf of a Christian community to proclaim, serve, and realize the kingdom of God."[7] Ministry, then, is something *active*, as opposed to speculative; *public*, as opposed to private; *collaborative*, as opposed to unilateral; and *ecclesial*, as opposed to individually devotional. With these four features at its heart, ministry becomes a means by which the church lives out its mission "to enlighten the whole world with the message of the Gospel and to gather together in one spirit all women and men of every nation, race and culture" (GS, 92).

Among the documents of the council, no decree will be of greater aid in determining which dimensions of ministry belong to the structure of the church than *Lumen Gentium (The Dogmatic Constitution on the Church)*. Other conciliar documents will buttress *Lumen Gentium*'s vision of the church, but none cuts to the core issues in quite the same way. I shall embed the dimensions in five propositions that the council appears both to affirm and to consider part of the very fabric of the church itself.

1. All ministers are disciples, but not all disciples are ministers.

One of the great innovations of the council came in its affirmation that it is not only the ordained who bear responsibility for realizing the church's mission. On the contrary, as *Lumen Gentium* stresses, the entire people of God is charged with it: "The baptized, by regeneration and the anointing of the holy Spirit, are consecrated as a spiritual house and a holy priesthood, that through all their christian activities they may offer spiritual sacrifices and proclaim the marvels of him who has called them out of darkness into his wonderful light" (LG, 10). *Apostolicam Actuositatem* testifies to this same truth, saying, "On all Christians . . . rests the noble obligation of working to bring all people the whole world over to hear and accept the divine message of salvation" (AA, 3). So many of the documents of the council, in fact, include a clear statement of the mission of the church and an explicit declaration that all the baptized, that is, all disciples, are called to take an active role in this mission (e.g., CD, 15; AD, 1; PO, 2). From this, one can conclude that ministry, in the minds of the council fathers, is something that includes and transcends what all disciples are called to do. Differentiations among the people of God, therefore, all of them disciples, yet some of them ministers in addition to being disciples, can correctly be called part of the church's structure.

2. Ministry itself is part of the structure of the church.

It is important to read this proposition in a minimalist fashion and not to demand that it unpack exactly what it means by *ministry*. Questions about whether, for example, mowing the lawn around the church or arranging flowers in the sanctuary is ministry, remain, at this point, unanswered.

The council argues in numerous places that, among the baptized, there will always be need of people whose work in realizing the mission of the church is active, public, collaborative, and ecclesial. For instance, *Lumen Gentium* says, "Allotting his [the Spirit's] gifts 'at will to each individual,' he also distributes special graces among the faithful of every rank. By these gifts, he makes them fit and ready to undertake the various tasks and offices for the renewal and building up of the church" (LG, 12). Other documents of the council—among them, *Christus Dominus, Presbyterorum Ordinis,* and *Optatam Totius*—are predicated on the assumption that ministry has a place in the structure of the church. The guarantor of this place is no less than the Holy Spirit, who prepares disciples to take up certain "offices" (*officia*) for the sake of the church's mission.

3. Ministries are differentiated.

The preceding excerpt from *Lumen Gentium* (12) reveals that ministry, which is part of the structure of the church, is not monolithic, a "one size fits all" reality that admits of no distinctions. The Spirit prepares people for "various tasks and offices" because ministry has some level of specification. Ministers are not "ministers at large," each ready to plug in to any role at any moment. Again, *Lumen Gentium* speaks to this point, saying, "There is only one Spirit who, out of his own richness and the needs of the ministries, gives his various gifts for the welfare of the church" (LG, 7). The variety of the Spirit's gifts and the corresponding multiplicity of ministries are grounded in Paul's words to the church of Corinth: "To one is given through the Spirit the utterance of wisdom, and to another the utterance of knowledge according to the same Spirit, to another faith by the same Spirit" (1 Cor 12:8–11).

4. Among the differentiations in ministry are the orders of bishop, priest, and deacon.

This proposition lists the ministries that are explicitly named in the documents of the council, ministries that the council includes as part of the structure of the church. At its most general, the council says, "Those among the faithful who have received holy Orders are appointed to nourish the church with the word and grace of God in the name of Christ" (LG, 11). That the ordained are rightly called ministers becomes clear later, when the same document states, "Ministers, invested with a sacred power, are at the service of their brothers and sisters" (18). This broad description of these ministries in *Lumen Gentium* takes on far more detail in the declarations of the council particular to each ministry—*Christus Dominus* for bishops and *Presbyterorum Ordinis* for priests.[8]

5. The laity have a "ministerial" task that is proper to them.

The fifth proposition falls short of asserting that the laity have a *ministry* proper to them. This follows the lead of the council decree that most directly addresses the work of the laity, *Apostolicam Actuositatem* (*The Decree on the* Apostolate *of the Laity,* emphasis added). Numerous parts of the council documentation, however, most notably some passages in *Lumen Gentium*, hint that the council identifies a ministry of the laity and simply withholds the name *ministry*. At one point, the text reads, "Gathered together in the people of God and established in the one body of Christ under one head, the laity, whoever they are, are called as living members to apply to the building up of the church and to its continual sanctification" (LG, 33). While this might look like a restatement of the tasks of discipleship, and thus not be ministry at all, the presence of the word *laity* must be understood as saying something particular about the laity beyond what the council says about all disciples.

At the same time, it would be a misreading of this proposition and the council to interpret either one of them as explicitly instituting what would eventually become lay ecclesial ministry. I take it as obvious—and obviously an indication of the Spirit's movement in the church—that documents like *Lumen Gentium* and *Apostolicam Actuositatem* helped occasion the rise of lay ecclesial ministry, but to draw a direct line from their publication in the mid 1960s to the situation of ministry even twenty years later, much less fifty years later, would be too rash.

RECEIVING THE TRADITION:
THE STRUCTURES OF MINISTRY

If the council presents the most recent iteration of the church's structure with regard to ministry, then the structures that arose, morphed, and disappeared in the wake of the council indicate how the people of God received the council's teachings. The task of reception, which Congar defined as "the process by means of which a church (body) truly takes over as its own a resolution that it did not originate in regard to its self [sic], and acknowledges the measure it promulgates as a rule applicable to its own life," is no easy one.[9] Embracing it as if it implied the right to vote in an ecclesial plebiscite, or rejecting it because the only appropriate response to the words of those in authority ought to be unquestioning obedience, pervert the richness of reception and the important role it has played in the history of the church. Rather than thinking of reception as a juridical act that grants validity to something, I join Congar in framing reception this way: "It attests that these decisions really arise from the Spirit which directs the Church, and that they are of value for the Church as such (and not primarily by virtue of their reception)."[10]

The enormous amount of conversation in the church concerning the fourth and fifth propositions above suggests that the people of God have taken seriously their work of reception, especially as it concerns the ministry of the ordained and the laity. Indeed, the contributions to this conversation by, on the one hand, the hierarchy, and on the other, theologians, have produced a creative tension that has opened up new vistas of reception. I turn now to those two sites of creative tension—the ministry of the ordained, specifically of priests, and the ministry of the laity—with the hope of tracing and ultimately entering the conversation myself. Doing so, of course, entails that I join the conversation in a context, *my* context, namely, the American church in the twenty-first century.

THE MINISTRY OF PRIESTS

The council's decree on the training of priests, *Optatam Totius*, mandated that "a specific 'Program of Priestly Formation' . . . be established by the episcopal conference" (OT, 1), a prescription that the United States Conference of Catholic Bishops (USCCB) fulfilled in its *Program of Priestly Formation* (PPF), currently in its fifth edition, with a sixth set to appear soon. Given the 375 paragraphs of the PPF, it makes good sense to ask about the particular structures that are likely to come about if the PPF is fully implemented. What does the USCCB want the priesthood to look like when it becomes incarnate in individual priests? How does this match or diverge from what theologians envision? If priests are formed with the PPF, the following four structures, again articulated in propositions rather than a checklist of characteristics, will likely obtain. Each of them elicits responses from theologians.

I. The necessity of the priesthood is linked to ministries of the word, sacraments, and governance.

The emphasis here lies on the word *necessity* as the PPF sees the priest as the ordinary minister of the word, the sacraments, and governance. In *extraordinary* situations, the PPF, following the *Code of Canon Law* (CIC), acknowledges the possibility of the non-ordained undertaking some of these functions, but there can never be an instance in which the laity enjoys the fullness of any of them. For instance, no lay person can ever preach a homily (CIC, 767, §1), hear a sacramental confession (CIC, 965), or become the pastor of a parish (CIC, 521, §1). It is the priest's sacramental ordination that calls him to "a specific vocation to holiness," one that empowers him, and him alone, to fulfill these roles.[11]

The structures that enshrine this link face challenges on several fronts, two of which strike me as especially relevant. First, the connection between sanctioned preaching, sacramental presidency, and ordinary governance, on the one hand, and ordination, on the other, could benefit from further clarification. As Anthony Barratt argues:

"An understanding of the sacrament of order in terms of powers" must be exchanged for "one based upon apostolic ministry expressed as the continuing of a number of tasks/offices or *munera*."[12] In ordaining a man to the priesthood, the bishop neither imparts powers that he has nor does he implore God simply to do likewise. Rather, the one who ordains serves as a mouthpiece for Christ, who calls the one being ordained into a new relationship, a relationship that requires the ordinand to stand *in persona Christi* as well as in *persona Ecclesiae*.[13] This requires less the gifting of powers than it does the sharing of responsibility.

Second, too strong an emphasis on the function of the priest loses *who* a priest is in the face of *what* he does. Broad swaths of theologians see the *ontological* question of priestly identity to be at least as important as, if not more important than, the *functional* question of what the priest can do.[14] In the end, of course, the ontological/functional divide is no real divide at all, for one cannot hope to separate what the priest does from who he is, just as one cannot separate the marble of a statue from its shape.

2. Priests are to be "men of communion."

This phrase, which originates in John Paul II's post-synodal Apostolic Exhortation *Pastores Dabo Vobis* (1992), appears six times in the PPF. Seminary formation programs ought to have as a primary goal the formation of such men, men who have "real and deep relational capacities . . . capable of making a gift of [themselves] and of receiving the gift of others" (PPF, 76). This speaks to the heart of what it means for the priest to *be* sacrament, for as Denis Edwards wisely observes, "God's ultimate reality is located not in substance but in personhood, in the freedom and ecstasy of persons in communion."[15]

Undoubtedly, the authors of the PPF are on the right track here. The church needs priests to be men of communion, perhaps never more so than in the devastating wake of the clergy sexual-abuse crisis in this country. Though no one explanation for the cause of such a vast web of abuse and cover-up exists, voices like Eamonn Conway's deserve to be heard when he writes, "Clergy offenders tend to have a higher IQ than most other sexual abusers, with a corresponding strong tendency to rationalize and intellectualize, but a diminished capacity to explore feelings and emotions."[16] The PPF has good instincts here in urging priest candidates to have deep relational tendencies, and it will do even better if, in the sixth edition, they are linked more explicitly to the protection of children. As it stands, the PPF includes several paragraphs related to the horror of the abuse crisis (see nos. 55, 64, and 96), but most of them would benefit from being more steeped in the language of pastoral care for priests and children alike.

3. Priests are to remain celibate for life.

The PPF acknowledges, affirms, and tries to prepare seminarians for the reality of lifelong celibacy. The topic arises scores of times in the PPF, suggesting both that the document takes it seriously and, perhaps, that the document takes it too seriously. In other words, one does well to ask whether all this treatment amounts to a recognition that celibacy is not nearly as straightforward as it was once thought to be. I think it does recognize this, a point for which the church must give thanks. But the church must also ask whether the PPF identifies the layered complexities of celibacy and, if it does so, whether it ultimately helps a man embrace the "evangelical motivations" for living this way: "the undivided love of the Lord, the spousal love for the Church, apostolic availability, and the witness to God's promises and kingdom" (110).

That celibacy has its merits and can enrich the ministry of priests is a proposition that few serious theologians deny. Many make the broader point that celibacy plays a large role in the lives of all people, not just priests and consecrated religious. Ben Kimmerling, for instance, observes, "While the sexual-genital expression of love is an option for some, *the celibate expression of love is an obligation for all*," one that mirrors the choice of Christ himself, who "chose to live a celibate life rather than a married one."[17] Francis George, echoing *Pastores Dabo Vobis*, even calls celibacy "self-gift in generative love to Jesus and a revelation of Jesus' own gift of self in generative love to the Church, which, in turn, reveals the saving love of the Father for the salvation of the world."[18]

Though they grant these merits, many theologians do not believe that they validate the current status of clerical celibacy as mandatory. The body of literature calling for the abrogation of mandatory celibacy is so vast that summarizing just its main points would make for a cumbersome task. Perhaps the words of Sandra Schneiders, who understands celibacy as a charism, a gift of the Holy Spirit given to some but *not all* people, will suffice to encapsulate these views:

> If consecrated celibacy is to be understood and practised as a charism it needs to be realistically re-examined in light of contemporary experience, freely re-appropriated by religious who

choose it in response to a personal vocation, and re-articulated in terms of contemporary theology and spirituality on the one hand and contemporary cultural understandings on the other.[19]

4. All priests are to be men.

This is one point that the PPF never addresses, and I suspect that there are two reasons for this. First, the *Code of Canon Law* is clear and succinct on the matter: "A baptized male alone receives sacred ordination validly" (CIC, 1024). Second, John Paul II's apostolic letter *Ordinatio Sacerdotalis* (1994) effectively aimed to quash all conversation on the topic:

> In order that all doubt may be removed regarding a matter of great importance, a matter which pertains to the Church's divine constitution itself . . . I declare that the Church has no authority whatsoever to confer priestly ordination on women and that this judgment is to be definitively held by all the Church's faithful. (4)

In other words, John Paul declared the non-ordination of women to be part of the unchangeable structure of the church, not simply one of its structures.

Such a strong statement and the centuries of tradition that preceded it have seen Catholic theologians divide into three camps. The first, the unwavering supporters of Canon 1024 and *Ordinatio Sacerdotalis,* say nothing and simply point to these two sources as their ultimate discursive checkmate. The second, which includes many feminist theologians, spend little time contending with this issue because they consider it such an obvious instance of injustice and wrongheadedness. The third position tries to operate within the limited confines set out by the institutional church, but examples of this are exceedingly difficult to find, even more so since 1994. As time passes, the divisions among these camps widen and the amount of communication among them dwindles. Outside of academic circles, the topic, to say the very least, continues to be discussed, at times heatedly so. The church, which includes all of these parties, waits to see how the Spirit will guide it toward genuine unity.

LAY ECCLESIAL MINISTRY

While the phenomenon of lay ecclesial ministry had not arisen in any recognizable form by the close of the council, the decades afterward saw an explosion in the number of, responsibilities of, and institutions designed to train lay ecclesial ministers. The USCCB recognized this in 2005 with its publication of *Co-Workers in the Vineyard of the Lord: A Resource for Guiding the Development of Lay Ecclesial Ministry*. The document sounds a positive tone, one that "expresses our [the bishops'] strong desire for the fruitful collaboration of ordained and lay ministers who, in distinct but complementary ways, continue in the Church the saving mission of Christ for the world, his vineyard" (6). It also puts a great deal of energy into offering suggestions on how best to form lay ecclesial ministers, though the bishops are clear to note that "the Church's experience of lay participation in Christ's ministry is still maturing" (14).

Now, nearly seven years after the publication of *Co-Workers*, the time seems ripe to ask what the church has learned about lay ecclesial ministry and where this ministry is headed. Four propositions can be stated.

1. Lay ecclesial ministers are quickly becoming the primary ministers in the church.

This certainly is the case with respect to numbers, if not responsibilities as well. As of 2011, 240 lay ecclesial ministry formation programs existed across 116 dioceses in this country, and since the start of the twenty-first century, more than 100,000 lay persons have enrolled in these programs.[20] Add to this an ever-decreasing number of priests—in the period spanning from 1965 to 2011, the number of priests in the United States decreased by more than 30 percent—and an ever-increasing number of Catholics—in the same period, the population increased more than 40 percent—and the implications of this proposition become even clearer.[21]

As true as these statistics are, connecting the rise of lay ecclesial ministers with the decline of priests imports a cause and effect or "Plan B" mentality that might be misleading. Why assume that lay ministers began appearing *because* priests started disappearing? Why think this situation is dire rather than exciting, an instance, perhaps, of the Holy Spirit doing something very new in the church?

Bernard Sesboüé opts for such a positive read on this, writing:

> Male and female Christians are putting themselves forward to help the church in its properly pastoral role, and are doing this on the strength of an official mandate from the bishop. They are offering themselves for this task out of Christian conviction, out

of a desire to serve the church and to give it a new ministerial form.[22]

His response to the reality of lay ecclesial ministry is joy and gratitude, not the "okay, but . . . " of those who mourn the disappearance of the "long black line."

2. The laity are called to be ministers.

This call should not be compared to the call of a baseball manager to the bullpen, that is, a call he usually makes because things have gone wrong with the pitcher on the mound. Though *Co-Workers* certainly does not make any such comparison, it also does not broadcast that God and the community are each calling lay men and women to do ministry in the church. Not until the final pages of the document does *Co-Workers* say what probably should have appeared much earlier: "The same God who called Priscilla and Aquila to work with Paul in the first century calls thousands of men and women to minister in our Church in this twenty-first century" (66).

One reason for the reluctance of the bishops to say this is that they appear to be sheepish about putting lay ecclesial ministry and ordained ministry on the same plane. *Co-Workers*, echoing *Lumen Gentium*, reminds its readers that the ministerial priesthood and the priesthood of all believers "differ essentially," and thus the work of priests should not be confused with that of lay ecclesial ministers (24; LG, 10). Their tentativeness is understandable in light of the publication of *Ecclesiae de Mysterio* (1997), a Vatican interdicasterial instruction "regarding collaboration of nonordained faithful in priests' sacred ministry."[23] Much of the document adopts a corrective stance, attempting to eradicate aberrant sacramental praxis and ensure that lay ministers do not encroach into the territory that rightfully belongs to priests. Reading it, one gets the feeling that, were numbers of seminarians to begin swelling again, there would simply be no more need for lay ecclesial ministry, and thus it could just go away.

A more fruitful way forward could include something like Richard Gaillardetz's concept of "ordered church ministry," which he calls "a reality broader than the ministry of the ordained (though inclusive of it) and narrower than Christian discipleship."[24] The "ecclesial re-positioning" that would result in this would likely result in an appreciation of the different ways that priests and lay ecclesial ministers work in the church *without* understanding the latter as anything less than genuine co-workers.[25] To proceed otherwise would simply be to reinscribe clericalism and hierarchy, which would amount to a way backward, not forward.

3. Most lay ecclesial ministers are women.

The third proposition has a different feel to it than virtually any of the other numbered propositions in this essay. It is simply a statement of undeniable fact: "most lay ecclesial ministers are women."[26] The sooner that the entire church realizes that this is both true and graced, the sooner the church will be able to prepare for the future of ministry. Here again, Kimmerling points to a way forward in her work on friendship between women and priests: "On the issue of women, it's not enough for priests to think globally. They must have the courage to love locally."[27]

If priests want to avoid clericalism, they must learn to collaborate more effectively with lay ecclesial ministers, which means learning to work with and befriend women more deeply. That friendship must be a part of every work relationship is simply untrue; that friendship does nothing to help deepen a ministerial collaboration, however, is equally untrue.

4. The church needs new ways of imagining and living the ordained priesthood.

Though it might appear odd to place this fourth and final proposition under the heading of lay ministry, this is where it belongs. The way we talk about and live the priesthood; the way we advertise for "vocations," which still, all too often, means becoming a priest or a religious; and the way that the priest can still be seen as the one with all the power, the one who makes decisions, the *only* one who stands *in persona Christi*, all have a bearing—and usually, a negative bearing—on lay ecclesial ministry.

The church, in its wisdom, does not legislate *one* theology of the priesthood at the expense of all others. Practically speaking, however, this laundry list of elements—power, authority, decision making, and *in persona Christi*—are the basic operative elements in many people's theology of the priesthood. Perhaps the exclusivity of this model ought to be disbanded—preferring, for instance, the model of priest as sacrament—to offer a richer theology of lay ecclesial ministry today and greater hope for ministry as a whole tomorrow.

CONCLUSION

As the fiftieth anniversary of the start of the first session of Vatican II draws near, the proliferation of talks, papers, conferences, and documentaries, all of which have already begun in earnest, will only increase. In other words, the work of receiving the council will continue and, perhaps, gain even more momentum than it has had in these past decades. This can only be a good thing for the church, and maybe most of all, for the church's understanding of ministry. Confident that the Spirit has breathed new life into ancient ministerial offices and inspired the people of God to embrace entirely new forms of ministry, the church joins its voice to the voices of the council fathers, who began each of their sessions by praying to that same Spirit, pleading, "Be the guide of our actions, indicate the path we should take, and show us what we must do so that, with Your help, our work may be in all things pleasing to You."[28]

Where will this path lead? Of course, its contours, sharp turns, gentle curves, and final destination depend on the will of the Spirit. Still, if the past fifty years indicate anything about ministry, they suggest that the Spirit has desired to do something new with ministry, something that the council fathers simply could not have foreseen. The Spirit's work is likely not done, and so Christians do well to pray humbly, *Come, Holy Spirit, and renew the face of the church.*

NOTES

1. Mark Arsenault, "Archdiocese to Group Parishes in Large Clusters," *The Boston Globe* (December 1, 2011).

2. United States Conference of Catholic Bishops (USCCB), *Co-Workers in the Vineyard of the Lord: A Resource for Guiding the Development of Lay Ecclesial Ministry* (Washington, DC: USCCB, 2005), 5.

3. Though I recognize that all ecclesial communities share some common challenges related to ministry in a religiously pluralistic world, I focus here on the Catholic Church (which, in the interest of saving space, I will call "the church") and on some ministerial issues the church faces, many of which are not as prominent in other communities.

4. Yves Congar, *True and False Reform in the Church*, trans. Paul Philibert (Collegeville, MN: Michael Glazier, 2011), 9.

5. Ibid., 11.

6. Ibid., 51n.

7. Thomas F. O'Meara, *Theology of Ministry,* rev. ed. (New York: Paulist Press, 1999), 150.

8. The council itself issued no documents pertaining specifically to the diaconate. Paul VI, however, in his apostolic letter *Sacrum Diaconatus Ordinem: General Norms for Restoring the Permanent Diaconate in the Latin Church* (June 18, 1967), assured that this ordained ministry also received updating.

9. Yves Congar, "Reception as an Ecclesiological Reality," in *Election and Consensus in the Church, Concilium* 77, ed. Giuseppe Alberigo and Antonius Gerardus Weiler, 43–68 (New York: Herder and Herder, 1972), 45.

10. Ibid., 65.

11. USCCB, *Program of Priestly Formation*, 5th ed. (Washington, DC: USCCB, 2006), no. 22.

12. Anthony Barratt, "What Is Ordination? A Roman Catholic Perspective," in *Ecclesiology* 3, no. 1 (2006): 72–73.

13. Susan K. Wood, "Priestly Identity: Sacrament of the Ecclesial Community," in *Worship* 69 (1995): 113.

14. Cf. Wood, "Priestly Identity," 111; Robert Barron, *Bridging the Great Divide: Musings of a Post-Liberal, Post-Conservative Evangelical Catholic* (Lanham, MD: Rowman and Littlefield, 2004), 231; Francis George, *The Difference God Makes: A Catholic Vision of Faith, Communion, and Culture* (New York: Herder and Herder, 2009), 217; and John O'Donohue, "Minding the Threshold: Towards a Theory of Priesthood in Difficult Times," in *The Furrow* 49 (June 1998): 323.

15. Denis Edwards, "Personal Symbol of Communion," in *The Spirituality of the Diocesan Priest*, ed. D. Cozzens (Collegeville, MN: Liturgical Press, 1997), 78.

16. Eamonn Conway, "Operative Theologies of Priesthood: Have They Contributed to Child Sexual Abuse?," in *The Structural Betrayal of Trust, Concilium* 2004/3, ed. Regina Anmicht-Quinn, Hille Haker, and Maureen Junker-Kenny (London: SCM, 2004), 73.

17. Ben Kimmerling, "Friendship Between Women and Priests," in *The Furrow* 41 (1990): 542–43, emphasis in original.

18. George, *The Difference God Makes*, 223.

19. Sandra M. Schneiders, "Celibacy as Charism," in *The Way Supplement* 77 (1993): 13.

20. Mary L. Gautier, "Catholic Ministry Formation Enrollment: Statistical Overview for 2010–2011," published by the Center for Applied Research in the Apostolate (CARA) (Washington, DC: Georgetown University, April 2011), 27.

21. I have taken this information from a CARA study entitled "Frequently Requested Church Statistics," available on the cara.georgetown.edu website.

22. Bernard Sesboüé, "Lay Ecclesial Ministers: A Theological Look into the Future," *The Way* 42 (2003): 69.

23. *Ecclesiae de Mysterio*, in *Origins* 27, no. 24 (November 27, 1997), subtitle.

24. Richard R. Gaillardetz, "The Ecclesiological Foundations of Ministry Within an Ordered Communion," in *Ordering the Baptismal Priesthood: Theologies of Lay and Ordained Ministry*, ed. Susan Wood (Collegeville, MN: Liturgical Press, 2003), 36.

25. Ibid.

26. Sesboüé, "Lay Ecclesial Ministers," 65; Gautier, "Catholic Ministry Formation Enrollment," 32.

27. Kimmerling, "Friendship Between Women and Priests," 546.

28. "Prayer of the Council Fathers," in *The Documents of Vatican II*, ed. Walter M. Abbott, SJ (London: Geoffrey Chapman, 1967), xxii.

Renewing the Permanent Diaconate

SOFIA SEGUEL ÑANCUCHEO

The ecclesiological premise of Vatican II is reflected in the 1983 *Code of Canon Law* (CIC) as affirmed by Pope John Paul II in his apostolic constitution *Sacrae Disciplinae Leges* (1983), which issued the code's promulgation. It states, "in a certain sense, this new Code could be understood as a great effort to translate this same doctrine, that is, the conciliar ecclesiology."[1] One such example of this application through translation is that Vatican II establishes an "equality in dignity" among the members of the Church (LG, 32), an idea now present in the CIC in the category of *christifideles*, which illuminates the ontological equality of all believers in the church under the sacrament of baptism and their subsequent participation in its universal mission (CIC, 204 §1). Likewise, the church is called always to read the "signs of the times" (GS, 4), this mission that has been entrusted by Jesus Christ. It is from this perspective that the issue of the married permanent deacon is presented, which because of its nature poses new questions in the theological, canonical, and pastoral areas as one seeks to understand the relationship among the diaconal vocation of the church, the sacrament of orders, and the sacrament of marriage. In many ways this vocation has become a true sign of the times today.

Theology generally emphasizes the council's Copernican turn on the role of the laity in the church (LG, 30–38), their the "secular" role (see LG, 31), and the vocation of marriage (see GS, 47–52). All this was possible thanks to a new ecclesiological understanding in which the church is recognized as the "people of God," comprised of laity, clergy, and religious (LG, 30). Moreover, the concepts of the common priesthood and the ministerial priesthood, developed by Vatican II, have helped to make this qualitative leap, as both priesthoods are distinct from each other but not far apart: "Each in its own way is a part of the one priesthood of Christ" (LG, 10).

It is very interesting that the conciliar and post-conciliar magisterium have sought to establish the elements of every vocation as well as the mutual complementarity among them. It is from this perspective that one sees the identity of the married permanent deacon. It is the vocation in which the two sacraments converge: holy orders and marriage. It is from this particular theological reality that the following canonical and pastoral questions arise: How should we understand the deacon, as a lay person or as a minister of holy orders? If he is a sacred minister, what happens to the sacrament of marriage? How do we configure marriage with the sacrament of holy orders? Here one can agree with Cardinal Tettamazzi, archbishop of Milan, that the present reality of the married permanent diaconate shows that a "reflection on the relationship between the sacrament of marriage and the sacrament of orders is up till now, frail, poor and almost ephemeral."[2]

The importance of considering the question of the permanent diaconate is seen in a number of other related topics related to ministry. These include: (1) the pastoral care of the family; (2) the ministry of lay people, in light of a decline in vocations to the priesthood and the need for greater lay involvement in pastoral care; (3) the renewal of the sacrament of holy orders following the scandals of clerical sexual abuse; (4) the role of particular churches in determining this renewal; and finally (5) the female diaconate. A reflection on the close connection between the sacrament of orders and the diaconate could help to clarify the doubts about the possibility of a female diaconate. Unfortunately, there have not been many studies on these issues, and in turn, this lacuna indirectly affects the permanent diaconate as it seems difficult to recognize the importance and the need for more research regarding this ministry.

HISTORICAL CONTEXT

There are many studies that present the historic evolution of the ministry of the deacon, and its biblical, patristic, and magisterial antecedents.[3] For now, it is enough to say that this ministry was not created by the Second Vatican Council but was present already in the tradition of the church. Following a period of decline it was "reestablished"[4] finally putting into place the directive of the Council of Trent (1545–63).[5] In fact, *Lumen Gentium* establishes the desire that in the future one remembers, as at one time, the ministry of the permanent deacon "as a proper and permanent rank of the hierarchy" (LG, 29).[6] Because it is not considered an intermediate state that has the priesthood as its end, the permanent deacon's value is recognized in itself.

Prior to Vatican II, the deacon had exercised his ministry in the service of bishops and priests without himself possessing a sense of his own ministry. *Lumen Gentium* provides an identity for this ministry stating that "being in communion with the bishop and priests" (29), deacons serve the people of God.[7]

THEOLOGICAL CONTEXT

To understand the diaconal ministry it is necessary to remember the diaconal vocation of the church comes from Jesus Christ who "came not to be served but to serve" (Mk 10:45). The deacon is perceived as a sign of this ecclesial reality because "the Church has no meaning in itself, but in terms of this world that God loves, and of his kingdom which it celebrates and awaits."[8] This ministry of service alone makes it possible to realize the relationship between the kingdom of God and the church's mission entrusted by Jesus Christ. Once the sacramentality of the episcopate (LG, 21) and priesthood (LG, 28) is established, a great theological debate arises around the ministry of the diaconate centered on the question of the nature of the sacramental diaconate.[9] Here, it is necessary to remember that the sacraments are the gestures that offer grace and have their origin in Christ through the church.[10]

One may argue that holy orders is a sacrament, but one that possesses three basic degrees: episcopate, presbyterate, and diaconate. Such a gradation puts the sacramental diaconate into perspective and helps one understand the consequences of this ministry. One, therefore, is able to see the inseparability of the diaconate by the hierarchical constitution of the church and, in turn, its ontological participation of Christ's ministry.

Several council documents discuss the reestablishment of the permanent diaconate. Among them we find the decree on the mission of the church (AG, 16) and the decree on the Eastern Catholic Churches (OE, 17) both of which refer to the permanent diaconate and its reestablishment. As Petrolino, however, states, "*Gaudium et Spes* makes no reference to the diaconate, except perhaps to show that this ministry is understood, especially if not exclusively, as a task within the Church."[11] Without a doubt, the main text from Vatican II concerning this ministry is *Lumen Gentium* (29). The text consists of three parts: a doctrinal statement, examples of ministries of the deacon, and a decree to restore the permanent diaconate.[12] The detailed implementation is found in two documents by Pope Paul VI: the *motu proprio, Sacrum Diaconatus Ordinem* (1967), and the apostolic letter *Ad Pascendum* (1972).

The theological reflection of Vatican II on the divine institution of the diaconate considers the elements present in scripture, the tradition, and the magisterium of the church, and explicitly recognizes that it is not a human institution. Thus, the diaconate has emerged as one of the three degrees of the sacrament of orders within which it is located at the lowest level, a "distinction that must be understood is in terms of functionality and value"[13] so that "the deacon in his function depends on the bishop and the priests."[14] Petrolino qualifies this location stating that, "this 'Inferiority' is part of the tradition in relation to the Bishop, to which the Deacon is subject, but not with regard to the priest."[15] He continues by citing the Vatican norms:

> In the exercise of their power, deacons, since they share in a lower grade of ecclesiastical ministry, necessarily depend on the Bishops, who have the fullness of the sacrament of orders. In addition, they are placed in a special relationship with the priests, in communion with whom they are called to serve the People of God.[16]

This special relationship between the priest and the deacon shows that both depend on the bishop and both are called to serve the church, each with his particular vocation. There seems to be no subordination of deacon to the priest. However, deacons receive the laying on of hands in order "to perform a service, and not to exercise the priesthood" (LG, 29). This qualification means that deacons cannot preside at the Eucharist or absolve in the sacrament of reconciliation. In this way the order of the diaconate is the entrance into the clerical state (CIC, 266 § 1). This does not mean, however, that the deacon becomes a priest; neither does it imply that he will continue to be part of the lay state. Rather, he is a married member of the clergy.

Normally we think that the functions of a deacon can be done by a lay person, but against this claim it must be said that "the deacons carry out the functions within their ordination that enables them for the role of guarantor of apostolicity of the faith lived."[17] Thus, "this theological foundation of the deacon's function is in the participation of the three *munera* of Christ—the three ministries of Jesus that are of themselves for the entire people of God, but the ministry is to be realized with proper effectiveness."[18] As for the specific tasks to be performed in terms of service, the deacon turns to the people of God in terms of the threefold ministry of liturgy, word, and charity (LG, 29), but, he is called also to be with his family under a model of virtue (1 Tm 3:8–13). Because this ministry involves not only the deacon but also his wife and children, the grace received in this ministry must shine in his marriage and family.

The ministry of the married permanent deacon, in the liturgy of ordination, is established as having relevance to the conjugal state of life of the future deacon, a decisive factor in the preliminary order showing that there is a profound relationship between the stability of the state of life and the sacrament of orders.[19] Moreover, the church receives this state of life and "in some way stabilizes the deacon in marriage."[20] Thus, the candidate for the diaconate *(viri probati)* must discern whether or not his marriage and his family life are compatible with the order to receive the sacrament because "God does not want to jeopardize a sacrament that he has given, by means of another sacrament."[21] The diaconate should be taken then in a state of maturity and stability both in his person and his marriage (CIC, 1031 § 2).

In the order of the sacraments we remember that the deacon is a husband and father as well as a minister of the church. How do we then understand the relationship between the sacrament of holy orders and the sacrament of marriage?

> The Sacrament of Orders is not added to or inserted into the Sacrament of Marriage. . . . Marriage as a Sacrament is ranked, for the baptized, in close continuity with baptism. At the same time, the Sacrament of Orders is not the manifestation of baptismal grace that emerges from divine communion, as the mystery of alliance; we are enrolled in the filial relationship . . . and in a brotherly relationship.[22]

To this we add that "the sacrament of the diaconate is certainly ordered toward the baptismal vocation of the diaconate. . . . Between the sacrament of the diaconate and the baptismal vocation to the diaconate is a difference in nature, and not only in degree. The diaconate is an investment to work in the service of the apostolic faith. It is of the order of grace and a means of grace."[23]

The question is whether or not something has changed in the sacrament of marriage. The answer is yes, at various levels. For example, after receiving the sacrament of orders, the spouse cannot remarry once widowed. The deacon's wife, on the other hand, if she becomes a widow, can remarry. Another example, in liturgy the deacon does not sit with his family at the liturgy but in the choir with appropriate liturgical clothing.[24] The reason for these changes is that only the husband receives the diaconate, not the couple, though there are practical and spiritual consequences for marriage and family. Therefore, "the ordination of the husband does not change the personal status of the wife in the realm of God's people."[25] The marriage conformed by two baptized persons now becomes a marriage conformed by an ordained man and a baptized woman, each one with a particular charism.[26]

Meanwhile, the sacrament of marriage "sanctifies conjugal love and constitutes it a sign of the love with which Christ gives himself to the church (cf. Eph. 5:25). It is a gift from God and should be a source of nourishment for the spiritual life of those deacons who are married." At the same time, "In marriage, love becomes an interpersonal giving of self, a mutual fidelity, a source of new life, a support in times of joy and sorrow: in short, love becomes service. When lived in faith, this *family service* is for the rest of the faithful an example of the love of Christ. The married deacon must use it as a stimulus of his diaconia in the Church."[27]

Without a doubt, the wife participates in the spiritual ministry of her husband. The family of the deacon is also called in some way to change the status of its life, a change that makes even more explicit the ecclesial *diakonia*. Thus, the bishop should provide pastoral care not only to the deacon, but also to the deacon's wife and his family.[28]

CANONICAL CONTEXT

The CIC states that by divine institution the people of God are divided into two categories that complement each other: the group of clerics, who through the sacrament of the orders are part of the hierarchy, and the laity, the faithful who are not part of the hierarchy (CIC, 207 § 1). While all clerics are obliged to observe celibacy (CIC, 1037), there is an exception for permanent deacons who already have received the sacrament of marriage (CIC, 1042 § 1). If, however, they become widowed they cannot remarry because having received the sacrament of orders, they have a matrimonial impediment to its validity (CIC, 1087). The possibility exists that they may, in turn, be admitted to the order of priesthood.

Lumen Gentium (29) illustrates that the deacon receives a special gift at the time of consecration that directs him specifically to the vocation of service to the church. It is a grace that consecrates the faithful leaving an indelible character so that "the deacon is no longer a layman, and cannot be defrocked in the strict sense."[29] Likewise, this grace enables him to perform the functions of teaching, sanctifying, and governing (CIC, 1008). For this reason it is argued that "the diaconate ordination enables ministry."[30] Ordination, which is never "declaratory, but establishing,"[31] is a new status in church life. The permanent deacon "has a sacramental ministry, legally qualified, but conditionally exercised in the world of laymen."[32] In this way he continues to participate fully in the secular life of the laity, both at home and at work. Nevertheless, it is clear that the married deacon must be understood as an ordained minister and a member of the hierarchy of the church (CIC, 1009).

In terms of the formation of the permanent deacon, it is established that formation must follow the requirements of the episcopal conference (CIC, 236) and those norms established by the directory to the permanent diaconate in 1998.[33] With regard to their economic livelihood, "married deacons, who are completely dedicated to the ecclesiastical ministry, deserve remuneration with which they can support themselves and their families, but those who exercise or have exercised a secular profession, and are paid, must supply their own needs and those of his family with what they receive for this title" (CIC, 281 § 3). Their salary will come from the diocese or the parish where he exercises his ministry. The availability of salary "does not however exclude the possibility that a cleric might wish to renounce this right, as the Apostle himself did (1 Cor 9:12), and otherwise make provision for himself."[34] In the case of death, the CIC states that it is necessary "to define the extent of diocesan liability with regard to the widows and orphans of deceased deacons" so that their families "are never neglected and . . . their needs are provided for."[35]

The permanent deacon, to be a member of the clergy, "is incardinated in a particular church or in a personal prelature, for whose service he was promoted" (CIC, 265–66). That is, "diaconal ordination confers a power, enabling it to exercise a ministry. But this is determined and specified in its exercise by an administrative act by which the competent ecclesiastical authority, in this case, the diocesan bishop, gives a role or position and limits its exercise."[36] *Lumen Gentium* (29) establishes a list of these functions, among which it emphasizes "the administration of baptism (CIC 861 § 1), the reservation and distribution of the Eucharist (CIC, 910 § 1), and the blessings of marriages and name of the church" (CIC, 1108).

Finally, it is interesting to note that to receive the diaconate, the man, as is the case for a groom, is required to have the wife's consent[37] (*consensus uxoris,* CIC, 1031 § 2, 1050, 3), who must accept that God has chosen and called her husband for this ministry. The wife "that at one time 'chose' marriage, now must 'accept' the diaconate, and consider that her husband is ordained."[38] The acceptance of this ministry is a gift for the family as well as for the marriage, and the wife now begins a new stage with her husband, one following a personal call of God, who wants to serve his brothers and sisters in Christ. A wife helps with the consent of her husband to say to God: "Here I am, Lord, send me!" (Is 6:8).

CONCLUSION

This brief presentation wished to show an everyday example of something little known but very much present in the church: the reality of the married, permanent diaconate. It is a reality into which the church is called to undertake further research from theological, pastoral, and canonical perspectives in order to show to the world the essential character of *diakonia*, which results in a pro-pastoral care of souls and testifies to the church of *caritas*, which in turn reveals the essence of God, because "God is love" (1 Jn 4:16).

Meanwhile, experience shows that the positive response to this ministry of bishops has resulted in a constant increase in the ordinations of permanent deacons. In 2004, the number of deacons was 32,324. In the latest statistic from 2009, the number rose to 38,155. Between these five years the concentration of ordinations has remained constant. The Americas are the continents with the most permanent deacons (24,582); North America has the highest number (17,192). After the Americas the continent with the most permanent deacons is Europe (12,655), followed by Africa (406), Oceania (346), and finally, Asia (166).[39]

The ministry of the diaconate is a "polymorphic ministry" because the deacon participates in the sacrament of marriage and the sacrament of holy orders and because of the diversity of pastoral realities inherent to this ministry. At the same time this vocation "promot[es] the diversity of ministries." It makes possible a more participatory and organic pastoral work in the church. Married permanent deacons can be called "ministers of proximity, in the sense that they are perceived as the face near to the Church."[40] They participate actively with their testimony of marriage and family life giving "reason for our hope for the world" (1 Pt 3:15). This is possible because the deacon has the ability to proclaim the gospel "through the framework of secular life" (LG, 35) and because the marriage of the deacon is a sign of the love of Christ for his church. Finally, this reflection on the married permanent diaconate may help to deepen knowledge and ecclesial practices, considering this ministry as a sign of the times, especially in light of the challenges facing the church today.

NOTES

1. John Paul II, *Sacrae Disciplinae Leges* (Libreria Editrice Vaticana, 1983). All official church documents are available on the vatican.va website.

2. L. Garbinetto, *Il diaconato permanente in America Latina alla luce del documento della commissione teologica internazionale,* doctoral dissertation (Rome 2006). (The translation is mine.)

3. "Up to the fifth century the Diaconate flourished in the western Church, but after this period, it experienced, for various reasons, a slow decline which ended in its surviving only as an intermediate stage for candidates preparing for priestly ordination. The Council of Trent disposed that the permanent Diaconate, as it existed in ancient times, should be restored, in accord with its proper nature, to its original function in the Church. This prescription, however, was not carried into effect." Pontifical Congregation for Catholic Education Pontifical Congregation for the Clergy, *Basic Norms for the Formation of Permanent Deacons: Directory for the Ministry and Life of Permanent Deacons* (Rome: Libreria Editrice Vaticana, 1998). For a discussion on post-conciliar and conciliar documents on the diaconate, see E. Petrolino, *Diaconato, servizio-missione: dal Concilio Vaticano II a Giovanni Paolo II* (Vatican City: 2006); and E. Petrolino, ed. *Enchiridion sul diaconato: le fonti e i documenti ufficiali della Chiesa* (Vatican City, 2009). For a systematic exposition of the preparatory stages to the Vatican II diaconate, see J. M. Guzman, *El diaconado en "Lumen gentium" 29,* doctoral dissertation (Rome: Pontificium Athenaeum Sanctae Crucis, 1996); L. Bertelli, *Il diaconato permanente nel Concilio Vaticano II,* doctoral dissertation (Venice: Pontificia Università Gregoriana, 1974); and P. Beltrando, *Diaconi per la Chiesa: itinerario ecclesiologico del ripristino del ministero diaconale* (Milan: 1977). Regarding the history and sources of the diaconate, see E. Chizzoniti, *Il diaconato permanente,* doctoral dissertation (Rome: Pontificia Università Lateranense, 2006); S. Zardoni, *I diaconi nella chiesa* (Bologna: 1983). For an updated bibliography on the ministry of the diaconate, see E. Petrolino, *I diaconi: annunziatori della Parola, ministri dell'altare e della carità* (Milan: 1998), 161–70; and M. Bennardo, L. Bortolin, and B. Cutellè, *Il diacono: chi è, cosa fa, come diventarlo* (Cantalupa, Turin: 2008), 143–50.

4. In 1964, following *Lumen Gentium,* "Paul VI approved the will of the Council Fathers of Vatican II and restored (in Latin *restitui*) in the future "the diaconate" as a proper and permanent rank of the hierarchy. . . . A year later, December 7, 1965, the Decree on the Missionary Activity was expressed in these terms: 'Where Episcopal Conferences see fit, the permanent diaconate order is restored, a provision of the Constitution on the Church' (AG 16 f). This time the Fathers used '*restaurare*' as the Latin verb, and spoke of a

'permanent state of life'" (Alphonse Borras, *Il diaconato, vittima della sua novità?* [Bologna: EDB, 2008], 21).

5. Namely, that "the hierarchy established by God's provision is made for bishops, priests and ministers" (see ibid., 22).

6. In this regard, the International Theological Commission said that "the text speaks of the deacons at the end of Chapter III, as the lowest level of the hierarchy, before moving on to Chapter IV of the matter of the laity" (see ibid., 25).

7. See T. Cetrini, *Teologia del diaconato*, in *Il diaconato: percorsi teologici*, ed. G. Bellia (Reggio Emilia: 2001), 23.

8. Borras, *Il diaconato*, 33n2.

9. See T. Cetrini, *Teologia del diaconato*, 13–20. In this regard see the post-conciliar teaching on sacramentality: "The sacramentality of the diaconate is affirmed by the *motu proprio Sacrum diaconatus ordinem* of June 18, 1967, in a continuous way, the *motu propio Ad pascendum* of 1972 to the *Directory* of 1998, through the *Code of Canon Law* of 1983, the *Catechism* of 1992 and its final edition in 1997. In this regard an eminent theological example of the International Theological Commission supports the line of the doctrinal teachings of the Roman Magisterium for the past four decades" (Borras, *Il diaconato*, see 78).

10. Borras, *Il diaconato,* see 87.

11. Enzo Petrolina, *Diaconato, servizio-missione: dal Concilio Vaticano II a Giovanni Paolo II* (Vatican City, 2006), 30. Translations mine.

12. M. Cancouet and B. Violle, *I diaconi, vocazione e missione* (Bologna: 1992), 63.

13. A. M. Pinedo, *Los diaconos permanentes hispanos en los Estados Unidos,* doctoral thesis (Salamanca: Universidad Pontificia de Salamanca, 1991), 56.

14. S. Dianich, *Per un' identita teológica del diacono: documenti del magisterio, problema e propesttive*, in Bellia, *Il diaconato, 69.*

15. Petrolino, *Diaconato, servizio-missione,* see 31.

16. Pontifical Congregation for Catholic Education Pontifical Congregation for the Clergy, *Basic Norms for the Formation of Permanent Deacons,* 8.

17. Borras, *Il diaconato*, 152.

18. The three *munera* of Christ: the office of governing (*munus regendi*), the office of teaching (*munus docendi,*) and the office of sanctification (*munus santificandi*) (LG, 21). See Dianich, *Per un' identita teológica, 69.* Regarding *Tria Munera*, "The ministry of the deacon is characterized by the exercise of the three *munera* held by the ordained ministry, according to the specific perspective of *diakonia*" (proclamation and instruction, prayer, and sacraments, charity). See Pontifical Congregation for Catholic Education Pontifical

Congregation for the Clergy, *Basic Norms for the Formation of Permanent Deacons*, 9.

19. Cancouet and Violle, *I diaconi,* 91.

20. Borras, *Il diaconato*, 171.

21. Cancouet and Violle, *I diaconi,* 92.

22. Borras, *Il diaconato*, 177.

23. Ibid., 177.

24. See Cancouet and Violle, *I diaconi*, 99.

25. Ibid., 105.

26. Ibid., 106.

27. Pontifical Congregation for Catholic Education Pontifical Congregation for the Clergy, *Directory for the Ministry and Life of Permanent Deacons*, 61.

28. Ibid.

29. Petrolino, *Diaconato, servizio-missione*, see 40.

30. Borras, *Il diaconato*, 35.

31. H. Legrand, quoted in Borras, *Il diaconato*, 149.

32. Dianich, *Per un' identita teológica,* 75.

33. Pontifical Congregation for Catholic Education Pontifical Congregation for the Clergy, *Directory for the Ministry and Life of Permanent Deacons*.

34. Ibid., 15.

35. Ibid., 20, 62.

36. Borras, *Il diaconato*, 199.

37. See G. Baracane, *Il diacono, segno-sacramento di Cristo sposo: un contributo alla ricerca teologica* (Assisi: 2010).

38. Borras, *Il diaconato*, 178.

39. See Secretaria Status Rationarium Generale Ecclesiae, *Annuarium Statisticum Ecclesiae 2009* (Vatican City: 2011), 77:86–87.

40. Borras, *Il diaconato*, 30, 55, 37.

IV.

THE FUTURE OF DIALOGUE

CHRISTOPHER CONWAY

If one were to attempt to capture the ethos of the Second Vatican Council in a single word, one would be hard-pressed to do better than *dialogue*. Vatican II was a council convened with an invigorating openness to dialogue and closed with a promise to be a church that not only speaks to the world, but also a church that converses with it. From the ecumenically inclusive invitation to Protestant and Orthodox observers, through the increased participatory presence of the laity, and to the call for a critically reflective engagement with secular society and the world's religions, the council and its resultant constitutions, decrees, and declarations have set a standard for the Catholic Church to a be a people and a faith in dialogue. It is a standard that the church has at times met enthusiastically and at other times retreated from reactively, a history in which Assisi stands next to Regensburg.

The creation of the Secretariat for Non-Christians, now named the Pontifical Council for Interreligious Dialogue, as well as the Pontifical Council for Promoting Christian Unity, have created new opportunities for institutional and individual dialogue. Joint doctrinal declarations have been made, fields like comparative theology have emerged, and formal and informal interreligious engagements continue to sprout. For all these positive developments, we nevertheless remain at a critical crossroads today. Religious and sectarian violence, culture wars, hostility, and apathy have made the need for dialogue all the more pressing, but they have also filled us with trepidation. The security found in turning inward, in "circling the wagons," while seemingly comforting betrays the hope we have and the mission to which we are called. Dialogue will not be our panacea, but it can be a balm for a wounded church and a broken world.

The essays presented here demonstrate the promise as well as the breadth and depth of dialogue. Heather Miller Rubens, positioned at the Institute for Christian and Jewish Studies, assesses the present, and often unexplored, relationship between proclamation and dialogue through a skillful exegesis of conciliar and post-conciliar documents including the recent ecumenically drafted statement "Christian Witness in a Multi-Religious World." Sandra Arenas thoughtfully explores the intersection between ecumenics and ecclesiology by posing the possibility of achieving a *consensus ecclesiarum* in matters of doctrine. Reflecting upon his own experiences in interreligious, intercultural, and intergenerational dialogue, Charles Ochero Cornelio provides a firsthand account of the ways in which dialogue can help foster peaceful conflict resolution in places where Christians are the minority, as in his home country, the Sudan, or where they are the majority, as in Canada where Christian-Muslim dialogues have eased the tensions between these communities. All these contributions make clear the significant impact dialogue has made since the Second Vatican Council.

The Emerging Theologians conference at which these three essays were first presented provided an opportunity for a collective reflection that looked back at the council and the fifty years since its commencement as well as looked ahead to the future of the church. Nearly a decade ago, reflecting then on the fortieth anniversary of Vatican II, Cardinal Avery Dulles, SJ, wrote, "History does not stop. . . . Progress must be made, but progress always depends upon an acceptance of prior achievements so that it is not necessary to begin each time from the beginning."[1] It is in such a spirit that our conference convened. The final statement drafted by the conference participants, which concludes this volume, builds upon the council's contributions and moves in hope toward the future.

The progress we envision for the place and role of dialogue in the church is rooted firmly in the spirit of Vatican II. It is our hope that dialogue becomes a constitutive posture of the church—that we remain a church that can speak confidently to the world and listen humbly to it. To achieve this end we seek to develop a more robust conception of dialogue that further delineates its relationship to proclamation, that is buttressed by scripture and tradition, and that recognizes dialogue's true breadth and depth theologically and culturally. Humility, hospitality, responsibility, and mutuality will be our watchwords going forward.

NOTE

1. Cardinal Avery Dulles, SJ, "Vatican II: They Myth and Reality," *America* (February 24, 2003): 11.

Interreligious Dialogue
in a Post–*Nostra Aetate* Church

The Tension Between Mutuality and Evangelization

HEATHER MILLER RUBENS

Meeting three times over a five year period (2006–11), the Pontifical Council for Interreligious Dialogue of the Holy See (PCID), the World Council of Churches (WCC), and the World Evangelical Alliance (WEA) engaged in a collaborative, ecumenical project to craft "shared recommendations for conduct on Christian witness." On June 28, 2011, this historic gathering of Christian religious leaders produced the document "Christian Witness in a Multi-Religious World: Recommendations for Conduct."[1]

What should Roman Catholics make of this ecumenically crafted document on missionary witness to non-Christians? If this document is a contemporary snapshot of both ecumenism and interreligious relations, what does it indicate about the status of dialogue with religious others, both Christian and non-Christian? With regards to ecumenism, should Catholics highlight this moment as an unparalleled achievement in Christian cooperation, a sort of ecumenical triumph? Or should Catholics puzzle over how this document relates to a continued Roman Catholic witness to non-Catholic Christians? With regards to interreligious dialogue, how should this text on Christian witness

I wish to thank the organizers of the Boston College Conference entitled Visions of Hope for including me in its engaging proceedings in March 2012. I had the privilege of sharing an earlier draft of this paper with the participants assembled in Newton, Massachusetts, each of whom offered valuable insights. In addition, I received constructive feedback from my colleagues Rosann Catalano and Christopher Leighton at the Institute for Christian and Jewish Studies.

inform a Catholic understanding of dialogue with non-Christians? Should Catholics welcome a document that reaffirms the centrality of Christian witness in interreligious relations? Or should Catholics be troubled by the unilateral (non-dialogical) nature of this Christian statement offering "recommendations for [missionary] conduct" in our pluralistic world?

The following is not an exhaustive attempt to answer the assorted questions raised for Roman Catholics by such an ecumenical Christian statement on witness. Rather, I examine brief excerpts from this latest PCID co-authored document in order to probe one specific question as it relates to my work in interreligious dialogue: how is the relationship between missionary witness and dialogue understood in this particular text?

In brief, I argue below that "Christian Witness in a Multi-Religious World" collapses the distinctive spheres of dialogue and missionary witness. I suggest that this collapse occurs because the definition of dialogue offered in the document relies heavily upon a single scriptural citation (Acts 17:22–28). I question whether such a narrowly circumscribed scripturally based sense of *dialogue* is truly representative of a Roman Catholic understanding of the term since *Nostra Aetate*. I conclude with an open question: can adequate scriptural citation(s) be found to support a definition of interreligious dialogue that honors the legacy of *Nostra Aetate*?

MISSION AND DIALOGUE

John Pawlikowski recently observed that "mission and dialogue remain in considerable tension in contemporary Catholicism," and in his estimation this tension has deepened noticeably in recent years.[2] However, this tension is a relatively recent development in the history of the Roman Catholic Church. Prior to the Second Vatican Council there was no uncertainty about the final aim of Roman Catholic interactions with other Christian and non-Christian peoples. The church believed that mission entailed evangelization aimed at the proselytization of all persons. Successful mission, in a classical Roman Catholic sense, concluded with baptism and new membership in the Roman Catholic Church. At the Second Vatican Council, the church suggested that Roman Catholics seek additional aims when pursuing relationships with religious others—namely, to dialogue and collaborate. In *Nostra Aetate* the church "exhorts her sons, that through dialogue and collaboration with the followers of other religions, carried out with prudence and love and in witness to the Christian faith and life, they recognize, preserve and promote the good things, spiritual and moral, as well as the socio-cultural values found among these men" (NA, 2). Questions quickly arose: Should Catholics understand dialogue as an end unto itself, or is it to be understood as part of a broader notion of mission? What is the relationship between *Nostra Aetate* and *Ad Gentes*?

The unresolved nature of the post–Vatican II tension between mission and dialogue has created a fecund space for Roman Catholic thought and action.[3] Whereas previously conversion was the goal of contact with non-Christians, *Nostra Aetate* suggested other possibilities could result from encounters with Christians and non-Christians alike. There was a fruitful ambiguity surrounding the dialogical option, and the concept of mission was more expansive. Relationships with religious others provided an opportunity for mutuality in learning and growth. While witness to one's own faith commitments was an essential part of dialogue, thus placing dialogue firmly within the context of mission broadly defined, the seemingly one-way work of evangelization and proselytization no longer monopolized the church's understanding of mission. Yet while a broader architecture of the relationship between mission and dialogue was suggested, fleshing out the intellectual and practical territory of the two categories required further theological reflection.

In his 1990 encyclical *Redemptoris Missio: On the Permanent Validity of the Church's Missionary Mandate* (RM), Pope John Paul II directly addressed the tension between missionary activity and dialogue created by Vatican II, emphasizing that the church's mission to evangelize remains central to its self-understanding:

> Nevertheless, also as a result of the changes which have taken place in modern times and the spread of new theological ideas, some people wonder: Is missionary work among non-Christians still relevant? Has it not been replaced by inter-religious dialogue? Is not human development an adequate goal of the church's mission? Does not respect for conscience and for freedom exclude all efforts at conversion? Is it not possible to attain salvation in any religion? Why then should there be missionary activity?
>
> . . .
>
> In the light of the economy of salvation, the church sees no conflict between proclaiming Christ and engaging in interreligious dialogue. Instead, she feels the need to link the two in the context of her mission *ad gentes*. These two elements must

maintain both their intimate connection and their distinctiveness; therefore they should not be confused, manipulated or regarded as identical, as though they were interchangeable. (RM, 4, 55).

While emphasizing the continued centrality of missionary activity, John Paul II strongly affirmed the distinction between evangelization and dialogue in the service of mission. In the pope's view evangelization and dialogue are intimately linked yet not interchangeable spheres. Closely following the publication of the encyclical, the PCID and the Congregation for the Evangelization of Peoples (CEP) published *Dialogue and Proclamation: Reflection and Orientations on Interreligious Dialogue and the Proclamation of The Gospel of Jesus Christ*. In this document the basic architecture for understanding the relationship among mission, dialogue, and proclamation is once again made clear. The church's evangelizing mission is central to its identity and is a complex reality. Both proclamation and dialogue are part of mission and are in mutual relationship, yet they should not be understood as interchangeable (DP, 2).

As the church continues to wrestle with the relationship between evangelization and dialogue in the service of mission, it is important to examine critically statements that might indicate the current state of the deliberation. Hence below I pursue a Roman Catholic exegesis of "Christian Witness in a Multi-Religious World" in search of the dialogic implications that might be found in a document focused on the role of witness and evangelization. I agree with Pawlikowski's assessment that the tension between mission and dialogue is very real, and that examining the contemporary work of the Vatican on this issue is vital to understanding the future of dialogue fifty years after the Second Vatican Council. So I ask: how does this text, on the subject of Christian witness, understand the place of dialogue in the interreligious encounter?

THE ROMAN CATHOLIC AUTHORS: THE PONTIFICAL COUNCIL FOR INTERRELIGIOUS DIALOGUE

The Roman Catholic participants in the drafting of "Christian Witness in a Multi-Religious World" were from the PCID, which is the special department of the Roman Curia for Roman Catholic relations with people of non-Christian religions. The work of the PCID is grounded in *Nostra Aetate*, and the PCID has self-defined its methodology as dialogical. Thus, my current exploration into the definition and usage of the term *dialogue* in "Christian Witness in a Multi-Religious

World" by the PCID seeks comparative grounding in the PCID's own foundational definition of the term. The following is an excerpt from the PCID's profile on the Vatican website:

A) Nature and Goals of PCID

The central office for the promotion of interreligious dialogue in accordance with the spirit of the Second Vatican Council, in particular the declaration 'Nostra Aetate.' It has the following responsibilities:

1) to promote mutual understanding, respect and collaboration between Catholics and the followers of other religious traditions;

2) to encourage the study of religion;

3) to promote the formation of persons dedicated to dialogue.

B) Methodology of PCID:

1) Dialogue is a two-way communication. It implies speaking and listening, giving and receiving, for mutual growth and enrichment. It includes witness to one's own faith as well as an openness to that of the other. It is not a betrayal of the mission of the Church, nor is it a new method of Conversion to Christianity. This has been clearly stated in the encyclical letter of Pope John Paul II: 'Redemptoris missio.' This view is also developed in the two documents produced by the PCID: 'The Attitude of the Catholic Church towards the Followers of Other Religious Traditions: Reflections on Dialogue and Mission' (1984), and 'Dialogue and Proclamation' (1991).

In brief, *dialogue* is defined in the PCID profile as (1) a two-way communication that is mutually beneficial, and (2) specifically *not* a new method of conversion to Christianity. Understanding that according to the PCID's own mission statement the principal work of the PCID is to engage non-Christians in dialogue, it seems peculiar that this particular group represented the Roman Catholic Church at this ecumenical gathering of Christians to reflect on missionary practices that favor evangelization. The choice of whom the church sent to these proceedings is significant, as at least two other pontifical delegations appear, at first blush, better suited to attend. The Pontifical Council for Promoting Christian Unity (PCPCU) is the permanent dicastery of the Holy See that promotes ecumenism and works on intra-Christian collaborations. If the Vatican prioritized the substantive ecumenical work involved in crafting this document, the

PCPCU might have had more experience expressing a Catholic voice in an intra-Christian conversation. Alternatively, the Vatican could have sent representatives from the Congregation for the Evangelization of Peoples (CEP), which is responsible for the dissemination of the faith throughout the whole world and is the coordinating body for all the church's missionary initiatives. Sending representatives from the CEP would have demonstrated that the Vatican prioritized sharing the theological and practical expertise of Roman Catholics focused on missionary work.

Thus, the Vatican's choice to send the PCID to represent the Roman Catholic Church at this ecumenical event focused on missionary efforts is somewhat surprising. As mentioned above, the collaborative crafting of "Christian Witness in a Multi-Religious World" is remarkable on two fronts: (1) it is an ecumenical meeting of Christians that (2) formulated a shared understanding on the methodology of mission to non-Christians. In choosing the PCID as the Roman Catholic voice at these proceedings, the church chose not to send Vatican representatives who specialize in ecumenical collaboration or those who specialize in missionary activity.[4] Rather, the Vatican sent the PCID, the Roman Catholic steward of dialogue and interreligious relations, which grounds its mission in *Nostra Aetate*. With the Catholic stewards of dialogue at the table, it seems even more crucial to determine how dialogue is understood in the context of this ecumenically crafted, missionary-focused document.

DIALOGUE AS DEFINED IN "CHRISTIAN WITNESS IN A MULTI-RELIGIOUS WORLD"

"Christian Witness in a Multi-Religious World," while a brief five pages long, is broken into four sections, with an appendix. The excerpt below comes from the second section, which bears the heading "A Basis for Christian Witness." This section lays the biblical foundation for Christian witness, coupling descriptive statements about the nature of witness with scriptural citation. To a large extent this section defines the terms of the document through its propositional nature and its appeal to revelation in support of its claims. Item number four in this section directly addresses the topic of dialogue: "Christian Witness in a pluralistic world includes engaging in dialogue with people of different religions and cultures" (cf. Acts 17:22–28). Looking first at the declarative statement on the most literal level, the authors of "Christian Witness in a Multi-Religious World" assert that dialogue is a legitimate part of contemporary witness. They also imply that the dialogical mode should be understood as a response to the contemporary context of religious pluralism. In examining the sentence alone, the reader could be led to believe that dialogue is a tool of witness rather than an object in its own end. It would seem that dialogue is therefore secondary to witness, which is in keeping with church teachings if witness is understood broadly. There is also a hint of the temporal fleetingness of dialogue: while it is the preferred mode of interaction in a pluralistic world, the centrality of witness to Christian life is eternal. While dialogue seemingly fairs poorly, there is some ambiguity in the statement regarding the relationship between witness and dialogue.

The scriptural text cited to augment the claim, Paul at the Areopagus (Acts 17:22–28), seems to support the conclusion that the document's authors consider dialogue to be a tool of evangelization. This biblical citation is meant to illuminate the relationship between witness and dialogue offered in the document's propositional statement. Rather than perform a full exegesis of the scriptural text, I put this biblical passage in conversation with the understanding of dialogue offered in the PCID's own profile. In brief, the following is a study in stark contrasts, as the biblical citation used to illuminate the mysterious tension between witness and dialogue collapses the work of dialogue into the work of evangelization.

In agreeing to use this biblical text to define the relationship between witness and dialogue in "Christian Witness," the PCID moves away from understanding dialogue as a two-way communication that need not have conversion as its aim. This biblical text is not dialogical in the sense of *Nostra Aetate* as enacted by the Pontifical Council for Interreligious Dialogue's own directive. In Athens, Paul is not engaged in an act of two-way communication. Paul is speaking and not listening. He is giving and not receiving. Paul is witnessing his own faith, not being open to that of the Athenians. Instead, Paul mines the sacred spaces of Athens in search of a place to insert Jesus. There, sacred text does not evoke a sense of mutuality or reciprocity. Paul is not looking for what is "true and holy in these religions," in the spirit of *Nostra Aetate*, but for a place to insert the truth of Christ. Paul is not in dialogue but is engaged in evangelization and proselytization. If this is what dialogue looks like in the context of witness, it would seem that the PCID should reconsider its mandate. This reversion reflects a sense of dialogue that sees the practice within the context of a pre–Vatican II notion of mission that privileges evangelization and proselytization. This most recent articulation of dialogue is a meaningful departure from the definition offered in *Nostra Aetate*, the PCID's own profile,

Redemptoris Missio and *Dialogue and Proclamation,* and such a shift in definition deserves serious reflection on the part of Roman Catholics. I question whether it can be taken as a true expression of the current status of dialogue in the Catholic Church.

A SCRIPTURAL BASIS FOR INTERRELIGIOUS DIALOGUE

The dialogue proffered in "Christian Witness," which I call a dialogue of evangelization, stands in sharp contrast to the dialogue developed in the tradition of *Nostra Aetate,* which I call a dialogue of mutuality.

There is an undeniable ambiguity about the place of dialogue in the context of mission, an ambiguity that has been with Roman Catholics since the Second Vatican Council. Yet that uncertain space has been a site for tremendous growth in Catholic thought and action. While the importance of witness and evangelization have been reaffirmed in recent years, so too has the dialogue of mutuality been defended as a distinct sphere of action. The legacy of *Nostra Aetate* and the work of the PCID up until recently has promoted a dialogue of mutuality that emphasized reciprocity and that affirmed that dialogue was not solely an act of evangelization. Such a dialogue, as *Nostra Aetate* maintains, was not a betrayal of Christian mission. Now it seems that the PCID favors a dialogue of evangelization, which lacks the component of mutual enrichment. I am unwilling to accept this most recent articulation of dialogue by the PCID uncritically.

However, in an attempt to contextualize this shift, I suggest the following: the movement from a dialogue of mutuality to a dialogue of evangelization in this document could be the result of the fact that dialogue was defined in a section requiring biblical prooftext. A dialogue of mutuality, as it has been understood and practiced since *Nostra Aetate,* does not engage scripture in such a manner. Rather, the ground-breaking development of a dialogue of mutuality has been done by philosophers and theologians who have not required direct biblical warrant. In that way a dialogue of mutuality has been baptized by Roman Catholic tradition and not by the Bible. This makes the discussion of dialogue, particularly a dialogue of mutuality, in an ecumenical context, especially challenging. While all Christians find grounding in scripture, Roman Catholics differ from their Protestant and evangelical co-authors on the availability of other grounds for Christian belief and practice. The PCID is the Roman Catholic representative best positioned to champion the validity and import of a dialogue of mutuality. Using Acts 17:22–28 to define dialogue's relationship to Christian witness in this ecumenical text does not appropriately reflect the full Catholic teaching on the issue of dialogue. Rather, it privileges a dialogue of evangelization over and against a dialogue of mutuality. I contend that the fact that the PCID agreed to utilize this scripture reflects an ecumenical compromise. However, it is a compromise of great import to the future of dialogue that is mindful of both evangelization and mutuality.

Thus, I close with a final question: is there a biblical passage that could serve as a warrant for a dialogue of mutuality in the spirit of *Nostra Aetate*? As practitioner of Jewish-Christian dialogue, Acts 17:22–28 will not suffice. I do not see that scriptural passage as a mandate that brings me to the table with my Jewish colleagues, nor would I reference that particular scripture when explaining my theological commitment to interreligious dialogue. It should not be the "go to" biblical text for understanding a Christian view of dialogue that is defined by mutuality and reciprocity. But what would be a good scriptural text? In *Nostra Aetate* itself, Acts 17:26 is cited alone, and might be a possibility. The Gospel of John also offers a promising starting point for developing a biblically based dialogue of mutuality: "In my Father's house there are many dwelling places. If it were not so, would I have told you that I go to prepare a place for you?" (Jn 14:2). And the Gospel stories of Jesus and the Syrophoenician/ Cannanite Woman also might prove to be fruitful scriptural ground from which to develop a dialogue of mutuality (Mk 7:24–30; Mt 15:21–28). Yet each of these suggested texts poses serious challenges to such exegetical work. I am not ready to concede that the dialogue of mutuality, as developed since *Nostra Aetate*, is ascriptural. However, it will take a scripturally minded theologian far more skilled than myself to identify a biblical passage that animates the dialogue identified in *Nostra Aetate*.

NOTES

1. The Pontifical Council for Interreligious Dialogue (PCID) is the principal office of the Roman Catholic Church responsible for the promotion of Roman Catholic relations with persons of other religions, mainly through interreligious dialogue. The World Council of Churches (WCC) is a fellowship of 349 Christian Churches that promotes ecumenical cooperation among its member churches in response to social and religious issues. It represents most of the world's Orthodox Churches, many Anglican, Baptist, Lutheran, Methodist and Reformed Churches, as well as several United and Independent Churches. The World Evangelical Alliance (WEA) is a global network of evangelical Christian churches that represents 600 million evangelical Christians

in 129 countries. According to the WEA press release about the publication of "Christian Witness in a Multi-Religious World," the ecumenical group crafting this document represented "over 90% of the world's Christians" and that this co-authored document was the "first document of its kind" (see the worldea.org website). These two claims also appeared in several news stories about the document's release.

2. John T. Pawlikowski, "Mission and Dialogue in Contemporary Catholicism," *Modern Believing* 51, no. 3 (2010): 47–55.

3. For some examples, see the works of Francis X. Clooney, Catherine Cornille, Jacques Dupuis, Paul F. Knitter, John T. Pawlikowski, and Peter C. Phan.

4. An attendant question that deserves further reflection is whether this collaboration implies that the Roman Catholic Church no longer sees non-Catholic Christians as objects of witness and evangelization.

Consensus Ecclesiarum
Viewed in the Light of
Elementa Ecclesiae and Sensus Fidelium

SANDRA ARENAS

In the Roman Catholic tradition we refer to *sensus fidelium* as the "sense of the faithful." Present theological literature has focused primarily on its function as a criterion for the reception of church teaching by the faithful. However, its weight and meaning in actual deliberations and decisions on Catholic doctrine are minimal, if not absent.

Foundational to *sensus fidelium* is indeed establishing whom among Christians constitutes the *fidelium*. Does this term refer to all who have been baptized, or are there qualifiers among the baptized that denote some as the faithful and others as not? The question of membership then becomes crucial and must be taken as a starting point to explore possible ways to reach a *consensus* among the Christian churches. To examine this ecumenical issue this essay explores the background and content of Vatican II's doctrine of *elementa ecclesiae*—a doctrine directly connected to membership.

By receiving the ecclesiological developments born from the fruitful theological discussions on membership immediately prior to Vatican II, the council recognizes in an innovative way in *Lumen Gentium* and *Unitatis Redintegratio* (UR) the *bona* or *elementa* of sanctification and the truth it claims to be present in other churches and ecclesial communities (LG, 8; UR, 3). This reception could be understood as an explicit recognition of the basic right to believe that the church of Christ legitimately expresses itself within these Christian communities. This chapter brings the categories of *sensus fidelium* and *elementa ecclesiae* together through an ecclesiological viewpoint in order to underline possibilities in the search for consensus.

In this context *consensus* implies a process of understanding that passes through stages of common discernment. This *consensus* would develop within the historical framework of the church's perception of God's self-communication in history. The members of the church join together in the finding of the truth, and when the entire body of the Christian faithful recognizes the truth through a process of communal discernment, *sensus fidelium* becomes the prophetic witness spoken of in *Lumen Gentium*. We refer to this as *consensus ecclesiarum*. Here the object of such a *consensus* would be the whole *depositum fidei*, and its subject would be indeed the whole body of the Christian believers.

The first part of this chapter briefly examines the doctrine of *sensus fidelium* focusing particularly on its historical background and its content as exposed in *Lumen Gentium* no. 12. By exploring the history and content of the doctrine of *elementa ecclesiae* (LG, 8; UR, 3), the second part revisits the traditional ecclesiological subject of membership. Finally, attention is paid to the natural ecclesiological link as it exists between the categories of *elementa ecclesiae* and *sensus fidelium* as foundational doctrines in the search for a *consensus ecclesiarum*. By focusing on the recognition of the ecclesial elements outside the Catholic Church in relation to the doctrine of *sensus fidelium*, we come to the core point where the council worked toward a non-exclusive notion of church membership.

THE CONCILIAR DOCTRINE OF *SENSUS FIDELIUM* REVISITED

The doctrine of the *sensus fidelium* was an important topic of debate in the process of drafting *Lumen Gentium,* with important interventions made by bishops Paulus Beope, Mauritis De Keyzer, and Emile Joseph de Smedt, and Cardinal Leon Suenens.[1] This majority considered the *sensus fidelium* as a divine gift and certainly a God-given instinct of faith; it is hereby understood from a supernatural viewpoint as a charism that draws from the Spirit. Because this gift resides in the people of God as a whole, when it comes to matters of faith and morals, this instinct has a principal function in aiding the faithful to avoid doctrinal error while also penetrating deeply into the truth of faith.[2] This is reflected in *Lumen Gentium*:

> The whole body of the faithful who have an anointing that comes from the holy one (cf. 1 Jn. 2:20 and 27) cannot err in matters of belief. The characteristic is shown in the supernatural appreciation of faith *(sensus fidei)* of the whole people, when,

"from the bishops to the last of the faithful," they manifest a universal consent in matters of faith and morals. By this appreciation of the faith, aroused and sustained by the Spirit of truth, the People of God, guided by the sacred teaching authority *(magisterium)*, and obeying it, receives not the mere word of people, but truly the word of God (cf. 1 Th. 2:13), the faith once for all delivered to the saints (cf. Jude 3). (LG, 12)[3]

It is important to pay attention to the clarification given in the *Relatio* with regard to the section on the *sensus fidelium*. It specifies that the expression "indefectibility in believing" that appeared in the former draft had been replaced by "cannot err" (or cannot be mistaken in belief).[4] That is to say, "indefectibility" would mean to signify to perpetuity while "infallibility" is intended to refer to truth. Moreover, the charism of infallibility is rooted in the presence of Christ along with the assistance of the Spirit.[5]

After examining the meaning of the doctrine of *sensus fidelium* in Vatican II, what can we say about the *fidelium*? What does "universal body of the faithful" mean? To answer this question we must pay attention to other crucial aspects of the ecclesiology of Vatican II; among them, the ecclesiology of *elementa ecclesiae* proves particularly significant. The recovery of the concept of people of God, the affirmation of the common priesthood of the faithful as well as the positive description of the charismatic gifts among the faithful, was an important innovation in ecclesiological doctrine.[6] Nevertheless, in this study we focus only on the recognition of the ecclesial elements outside the Catholic Church in relation to the doctrine of *sensus fidelium* because it is precisely through this doctrine on the *elementa* that the council worked toward a nonexclusive notion of the church and, consequently, of membership.

RETHINKING MEMBERSHIP THROUGH THE CONCILIAR DOCTRINE OF *ELEMENTA ECCLESIAE*

The identification of the true "Church of Christ" has for centuries been taken into consideration from the relatively narrow perspective of one's own confessional background. Either one was a member in the full sense of the word, or one was outside the church and deprived of all hope of salvation.[7] In the twentieth century a key group of Catholic theologians actively called for a reconsideration of the membership of the church. In circles devoted to theological and historical research, important works appeared to be presenting the issue of the Christian unity in a new way that still remained sympathetically rooted in the tradition. All these contributions prepared the way for the council to revisit the ancient issue of membership.

Theological Preparations for the Conciliar Reception of the Doctrine of Elementa Ecclesiae

Especially within francophone circles, crucial contributions were made on this subject, most notably from the French Dominican Yves Congar, who was the first Catholic to reflect on the issue of *vestigia/ elementa*.[8] The Belgian theologian Gustave Thils also developed important ecclesiological-ecumenical reflections before, during, and after the council regarding this subject, and having been one of the main drafters of the *De Oecumenismo*, his views must also be considered.[9] These two contributors have a foundational place in the twentieth-century reception of the doctrine, including the council. Along with Congar's and Thils's contributions, there have been other significant works in this field, including those of Bea,[10] Gribomont,[11] Hamer,[12] Dumont, and Lialine from the francophone side,[13] and Witte and Willebrands from the Dutch side. Willebrands's efforts have particularly informed this present reflection—a point that we shall come back to later.[14] The majority of these figures were connected with one another through important official and unofficial meetings that addressed our subject prior to the council.[15]

Beginning with Congar, these elements have been characterized by him as *principles* of the "One Church."[16] He enumerates a series of principles that have as their source the sacramental realities, namely, baptism, Eucharist, and the sacrament of orders. These principles also refer to the communion in the true faith as well as in true *caritas*. Whether or not dissident Christians conserve the *principles* of communion with God through Christ into the church and although they remain in error, they would still possess something of the church. Even if they will not find in their own confession the totality of these principles or elements, they encounter them in an imperfect form.[17] They are of the church to the extent that they belong to Christ, for that which unites them to Christ is a constitutive element of the church. If such an element exists in whatever manner outside the church, it belongs to the church and therefore to Christ. Consequently, outside the Catholic Church, these principles are able to keep their effectiveness by reason of the good faith of the believer and therefore are able to bring a real incorporation into the communion of Christ and his church. All baptized Christians are to be considered then members of the church in a way that their Christian life tends toward a full and real *(in re)* incorporation in the Catholic ecclesiastical body, not only in a spiritual sense, or *in voto*.[18]

From a non-Catholic perspective, the World Council of Churches (WCC) discussed in its 1950 Toronto Assembly the classical theme of *vestigia* and *elementa ecclesiae*.[19] On this occasion it presented the thesis that elements of the true church—that is, elements of truth—are to be found among all members of the WCC. Having left the concept of *vestigia*, it approached the *elementa* as follows: the preaching of the word, the teaching of the scripture, and the administration of the sacraments. The WCC bases its ecumenism on these elements or traces and understands them to be not remnants of the past, but powerful means of God's action in the present.

The Elementa Ecclesiae at the Council and the Sensus Fidelium

The council, taking up these contributions, explicitly recognizes the *bona* or *elementa* of sanctification and truth to be present in other churches and ecclesial communities (LG, 8; UR, 3). The recognition of the presence of ecclesiality in their structures determined the core of its ecclesiological affirmations. It is not our intention to explicate thoroughly the history of the reception of the ancient doctrine of *vestigia/elementa ecclesiae*.[20] Here, we only emphasize its principal historical-theological aspects as they relate to the doctrine of sensus fidelium.

The notion of *elementa ecclesiae* was not a new idea developed in the course of the conciliar debate. During the ante-conciliar period one can find easily a collection of recurrences that brought up the issue of the *vestigia* or *elementa* into the ecclesiological discussion. The context usually concerned membership.[21] Thereafter, the sub-commissions involved developed their ideas on this subject by discussing the draft schemas among the theologians. A great number of the participants were active members of the CCQOe. The *Relatio* of the Secretariat, Ordination of the Dissident Christians to the Church, dated March 29, 1961, was discussed by several theologians on April 7. Among those present were Cardinal Augustine Bea, Jérôme Hamer, Charles Boyer, Johannes Willebrands, Frans Thijssen, and Gustave Thils, all of whom were previously involved in discussions and meetings concerning the subject of *vestigia/elementa*.

Having noted this, we can now affirm that magisterially speaking the doctrine of the *elementa ecclesiae* was indeed developed within the ecclesiology of Vatican II. In fact, *Lumen Gentium* no. 8 takes up the delicate point of the relationship between the Roman Catholic Church and the notion of the church of Christ as a whole. According to the constitution, the "Church of Christ" survives in the world of today in its institutional fullness in the Roman Catholic Church, although elements of the church are acknowledged in other churches and ecclesial communities.

This notion of *elementa ecclesiae* was developed also in the council's decree *Unitatis Redintegratio*. The elements in other churches and ecclesial communities are presented as dynamic realities that increase the sense of unity among those who believe in Christ and who have received the sacrament of baptism. Hence, through the new doctrine of the *elementa ecclesiae*, the ancient issue of identifying the members of the true "Church of Christ" was approached in a new way. Examples of these elements/gifts present in the separated churches are said to be the scriptures as the word of God; the life of grace; faith, hope and charity; the interior gifts of the Spirit; and finally, the visible elements, namely, the sacramental and hierarchical gifts. These *elementa* must not only be considered in their being Roman Catholic but also in their ecclesial character.

The Theological Commission tried to clarify the salvific mediation of the church through the doctrine of *subsistit in* and the relationship between the Catholic Church and the non-Catholic churches or confessions precisely through the doctrine of *elementa ecclesiae*. The *Relatio* explaining the use of the theological category *subsistit in* makes it clear that the council gave primary importance to the doctrine of *elementa ecclesiae* by subordinating the former to the latter as follows: "*subsistit in* is used instead of *est* as an expression more in harmony with what is said elsewhere about ecclesial elements."[22]

By way of taking further ecclesiological inferences of these facts, Cardinal Johannes Willebrands had noticed the close link that exists between *Lumen Gentium* no. 12, and *Unitatis Redintegratio* no. 3, stating:

> in the immediate context of the council this change from *est* to *subsistit in* was conditioned not only by the ecclesiastical study of the elements of the Church or traces of the Church. There was a parallel reflection on the place in the body of Christ of Christians living in communion with the Roman See. This aimed at opening up somewhat the position of *Mystici Corporis* on membership of the Church, keeping its essential insight but interpreting it by a theological reading in an ecumenical context.[23]

These ecclesiological implications, however, have been overlooked in official post-conciliar documents as well as in the work of theologians. The doctrine of *elementa ecclesiae* as it contains the recognition of ecclesiality outside of the Roman Catholic Church calls for a reexamination of the way the *sensus fidelium* commonly has been understood especially in past occurrences of doctrinal elaboration. To be sure, it would be ecclesiologically incongruous to confine the notion of *sensus fidelium* within the boundaries of the Roman Catholic Church. As a supernatural gift of faith, it must be recognized as residing and operating in all the faithful by virtue of their baptism. In giving expression to a doctrine, therefore, the Roman Catholic Church should no longer avoid taking into consideration the faith of other Christians and the communities to which they belong.[24]

IN SEARCH OF A *CONSENSUS ECCLESIARUM*

Given the inclusive image of the church provided by the doctrine of *elementa ecclesiae,* in order to arrive at a consensus not only must the Roman Catholic faithful be considered in the whole process of discernment but so must other Christian believers: a *consensus ecclesiarum.*[25]

In this new context, what can be said about a *consensus ecclesiarum?* First of all, if it would be theologically unsuitable to confine the notion of *sensus fidelium* within the borders of the Roman Catholic Church, we then also must acknowledge that in general terms *consensus* would infer a process of understanding that passes through stages of common discernment.[26] This consensus develops in the historical background of the church's perception of God's self-communication in history. Therefore, the members of the church are a body joined together in the finding of the truth. When the entire body of the Christian faithful recognizes truth through a communal discernment, *sensus fidelium* turns out to be the prophetic witness enunciated in *Lumen Gentium.* This is the meaning of *consensus ecclesiarum.* The object of such a consensus is the whole *depositum fidei,* and the subject is indeed the whole body of the Christian believers. When the category of *sensus fidelium* is considered in the context of the entire conciliar ecclesiology, a necessary conclusion is that such a charism applies to all Christians regardless of their denominational identities. As the category of *sensus fidelium* enters progressively into ecumenical dialogue, its influence is being reflected in several questions that concern the unity among the churches. These questions, which include the membership, the nature, and the mission of the church, always form the ecclesiological background.

Ecumenical debate on the *sensus fidelium* arises within the wider context of the action of the Spirit in the community of believers and, consequently, within the promise of the church being preserved in the truth. The 1998 WCC paper titled "The Nature and Purpose of the Church" is a good example of receiving this category within the frame of the ecumenical affairs.[27] This document, dedicated to explore doctrinally the nature and mission of the church, explores the idea of the *sensus fidelium* in connection with the ministry of discernment.[28] The argument that the gift of the *sensus fidei* is present in every member of the community infers that the whole community takes dynamic part in the discernment of the truth of the faith in order to build up the communion and fulfillment of the mission of the church.[29] The basic condition to be able to participate in such a task is receiving the sacrament of baptism. In fact, baptism is taken as the basis through which the whole body of the faithful is prepared to contribute in the process of common discernment. Thus, not only does the ecumenical understanding of the concept run from the conviction of the Spirit's action in the church, but it also admits that the Spirit's truth is noticeable in the heart of the community of believers.[30]

This discernment, however, might be problematic because of two interconnected issues: first, the lack of proper criteria for discerning the authenticity of the Spirit's action in the community of the faithful; and second, the diverse ways Christian communities use to designate the reality of the body of the faithful being preserved from doctrinal errors.[31] In terms of the criteria for discerning the genuineness of the Spirit's action in the body of the faithful, it is important to note that *Lumen Gentium* no. 12 possesses a lacuna. Even if we take into account that the criteria for the *sensus fidelium* must be found within the whole ecclesiology of the council as well as from tradition,[32] we still have to offer some possible criteria precisely because we claim that the *sensus fidelium* should lead to a *consensus ecclesiarum*.

Post-conciliar debate has made important contributions concerning the way in which the *sensus fidelium* leads to a consensus of the faithful in moral and doctrinal matters. Roman Catholic theology emphasizes, first, that a *consensus fidelium* is realized in a thriving relationship between the faithful and the pastors as being part of the same body.[33] As Tillard rightly points out, one of the major problems is that while ecumenical dialogue has been chiefly built on the normative doctrinal formulations of the various churches, the challenge is still on how popular expressions of the faith from the faithful can contribute to the development of consensus among the churches,[34] not to mention the correspondingly relevant question of plurality.

In considering that the true "Church of Christ" is not identified with any particular Christian community, we must consequently admit that the present realization of the church calls for plurality. In this context the task of the church is to strive for the palpable realization of the consensus of the faithful. Such consensus has to scrutinize from the plurality of views. Therefore, a genuine *consensus fidelium* leading to a *consensus ecclesiarum* rises from an honest dialogue marked with wide consultation.[35]

If the *sensus fidei* is to be considered as a consciousness illuminated by faith[36] that resides in not only Roman Catholic but in every Christian believer, then as a consequence, *consensus ecclesiarum* must also be considered as the agreement among churches that results from the sense of faith of their members. Because of this, consensus must never be taken as a completed agenda but rather as a process. The churches gradually become more likely to assume the doctrinal insights that arise from the agreed doctrine of the faith in the body of the faithful as a whole, the *sensus fidelium*. As a consequence of this, each and every church disposes itself to consult the others when it comes to common matters. It is a dynamic process that necessarily takes history seriously, because it is in history where the sense of the faithful comes into praxis. It is precisely because the *sensus fidelium* is concretized in Christian lives that a consensus among the churches draws from the very core of their praxis.

CONCLUSION

In view of the ecumenical consequences implied in the two conciliar doctrines, we call for interpreting *Lumen Gentium* no. 12 in light of *Lumen Gentium* no. 8 and *Unitatis Redintegratio* no. 3. Yet, the conciliar doctrine of the *sensus fidelium* must be interpreted in the context of the entire ecclesiology of the Second Vatican Council. Such ecclesiology is to be taken as an inclusive one. As a matter of fact, the doctrine of *elementa ecclesiae* (LG, 8; UR, 3) officially recognizes the saving grace of Christ outside the Roman Catholic Church. Because there is a parallel reflection on the place in the body of Christ of Christians living in communion with Roman See, the inevitable conclusion is that this charism—the *sensus fidei* of the faithful—applies to all Christians, regardless of their denominational identities.

As a supernatural gift of faith, the *sensus fidei* should be considered as residing and operating in all the faithful by virtue of their baptism and by other ecclesial elements. In our view, the council sanctions the consensus of the "universal body of the faithful" as an authority or a criterion for doctrinal discernment. The concrete way by which the *sensus fidelium* operates in the process of doctrinal discernment or development, however, has been overlooked. Thus, it remains the duty of theology to consider both the dynamics that strengthen the process of doctrinal development and the means through which to accomplish it.

For this consideration, the first step would be to take seriously the history of the conciliar texts and to interpret them appropriately. The second step would be to recognize the definite indispensability of the experiences of believers if the church is to determine with precision the manner in which the lived life of faith informs doctrine. Doing so would grant different contexts their rightful voice and value in ecclesial discernments. Moreover, by definition, a common discernment implies a common consultation. But does this imply also a democratization of the structures? Should the church/churches take a civil-political model to guarantee a good discernment process? While this is a topic worth pursuing in another essay altogether, I would venture a negative response. The church should not embrace a civil-political model, as it still is confronted by problems with the monarchical structures it has transposed previously. An a-critical transposition of democracy as the means to arrive at a *consensus ecclesiarum* might lead to the dissolution of the religious mission of the churches, which first and foremost maintains their social relevance.

NOTES

1. See Robert W. Schmucker, *Sensus Fidei: Der Glaubenssinn in seiner vorkonziliaren Entwicklungsgeschichte und in den Documenten des Zweiten Vatikanischen Konzils*, in *Theorie und Forschung: Theologie* (Regensburg: Roderer Verlag, 1998), 172.

2. See Bishop Petrus Cantero Cuadrado's contribution on the *sensus fidei* in *AS*, II/3, 284.

3. *AS*, III/1, 185.

4. The Latin reads "Loco in credendo indefectibilis est ponitur falli nequit" (*AS*, III/1, 198), and is normally translated into English as "cannot err," though it is also translated as "cannot be mistaken in belief." Translation provided by Norman Tanner, ed., *Decrees of the Ecumenical Councils*, vol. 2, *Trent to Vatican II* (London: Sheed and Ward, 1990), 858. See also Christoph Ohly, *Sensus fidei fidelium: Zur Einordnung des Glaubenssinnes aller Gläubigen in den Communio-Struktur der Kirche im geschichtlichen Spiegel*

dogmatisch-kanonistischer Erkenntnisse und der Aussagen des II. Vaticanum, vol. 3/57, in *Münchener Theologische Studien,* ed. Winfried Aymans, Manfred Weitlauff, and Gerhard L. Müller (Munich: Verlag, 1999).

5. *AS,* III/1, 198.

6. For the relation between the ecclesiology of people of God and *sensus fidelium,* see Alois Grillmeier, "The People of God," in *Commentary of the Documents of Vatican II,* ed. Herbert Vorgrimler (Freiburg: Herder and Herder, 1967), 1:153–85, esp. 156. See also John J. Burkhard, "*Sensus fidei*: Meaning, Role, and Future of a Teaching of Vatican II," in *Louvain Studies* 17, no. 1 (1992): 25–31.

7. See Karl Rahner, "Membership in the Church According to the Teaching of Pius XII's Encyclical 'Mystici Corporis Christi,'" in *Theological Investigations,* vol. 2, *Man, in the Church* (London: Darton, Longman and Todd, 1963), 139–55.

8. See Yves Congar, *Chrétiens désunis: Principes d'un "oecuménisme" catholique* (Paris: Cerf, 1937).

9. Gustave Thils presents his understanding regarding "*les éléments d'Église*" or "*vestigia Ecclesiae*," as he called them, in *Histoire Doctrinaire du Mouvement Oecuménique* (Leuven: BETL 8, 1955, rev. 1963).

10. Talking about the obstacles to union with Protestants, Bea points to the fact that they still conserve "non poco del prezioso patrimonio di verità e di pieta della Chiesa-Madre" (Augustine Bea, *L'unione dei Cristiani, Problemi e principi, ostacoli e mezzi, realizzazioni e prospettive* (Rome: La Civiltà Cattolica, 1962), 30. As president of the Secretariat for Christian Unity he also referred to an ecclesiastical patrimony present in Christian non-Roman communions (see *Documentation Catholique, November 9 of 1960* [January 15, 1961]: 79–94). He defines this patrimony as "elements" that include sincere piety, veneration for the word of God which is in the scripture, and a sincere effort to uphold God's commandments.

11. The benediction recognizes ecclesial values as Catholic elements within the non-Catholic Christian communities. See Jean Gribomont, "Du sacrement de l'Église et de ses réalisations imperfaites," in *Irénikon* 22 (1949): 345–67.

12. In 1952 the Dominican theologian wrote a study on the subject of *vestigia ecclesiae,* thereby concentrating on the reality of the sacrament of baptism. See Jérôme Hamer, "Le Baptême et l'Église: A propos des 'Vestigia Ecclesiae,'" in *Irénikon* 25 (1952): 142–64.

13. The topic of *vestigia ecclesiae* was taken up in November 1951 again at Bosey. This encounter was prepared in Paris between Tompkins and Dumont in April of the same year. See *Istina* Archive, *Correspondance Dom Clément Lialine (1948–1952),* Travée 3, droite, Christophe Dumont (April 14, 1951).

14. By means of concluding the foundational meeting of the Conférence Catholique pour les Questions Oecuméniques (CCQOe), Johannes Willebrands

stated that Catholic theologians with a clear ecumenical sensitivity recognize "la grande utilité d'un approfondissement d'une théologie des 'vestigia ecclesiae' subsistant dans les communions dissidents" because of its great potential with respects to the unity of the church. See Johannes Willebrands, *CCQOe: Réunie à Fribourg du 11 au 13 aout 1952. Conclusions sur les rapports et discussions.*

15. In September 1949 some Protestant and Roman Catholic theologians met at the Istina Centre in Paris, in which encounter a common language focused upon the concept of *vestigia ecclesiae*. See Willem Visser 't Hooft, *Memoirs* (Geneva: WCC Publications, 1987), 32. The Central Committee of the WCC gathered in Toronto in 1950 and this subject was explicitly treated. See WCC, *Minutes and Report of the Third Meeting of the Central Committee* (Toronto: July 9–15, 1950), IV: 5. The topic of *vestigia ecclesiae* was taken up again in November 1951. See *Report Rencontre de Présinge*, a report in French and Dutch, twenty-four typed pages plus two introductory pages. Chèvetogne, Willebrands' Archive, No. 32–54. In the Evanston 1954 WCC Assembly the concept of *elementa* was approached in line with Toronto. See Willem Visser 't Hooft, ed., *The Evanston Report. The Second Assembly of the World Council of Churches, 1954* (London: SCM Press, 1955).

16. Congar, *Chrétiens désunis*, 302.

17. Ibid., 289.

18. This is an ecclesiological conviction further developed in "Note sur les mots 'Confession,' 'Église' et 'Communion,'" in *Irénikon* (1950): 3–36; "Chrétiens en dialogue," *Unam Sanctam* 50 (Paris, 1964); 211–42; and "Les ruptures de l'unité," in *Istina* (1964): 133–78. Gustave Thils describes the *elementa* as "authentic Christian values" as they reply to the duty to recognize the church in the Christian churches. He takes the issue up again after the council by stressing that Vatican II was a source of new orientations for regarding the bonds among Christian churches, largely from the aforementioned doctrine of the "elements of the Church." See Gustave Thils, *L'Eglise et les églises: Perspectives nouvelles en oecuménisme* (Paris: Desclée de Brouwer, 1967), 21, 23.

19. See WCC, *Minutes and Report of the Third Meeting of the Central Committee*, IV: 5.

20. For the history of the doctrine of *vestigia ecclesiae* and its reception in the doctrine of *elementa*, see Sandra Arenas, "Merely Quantifable Realities? The 'Vestigia Ecclesiae' in the Thought of Calvin and Its Twentieth-Century Reception," in *John Calvin's Ecclesiology: Ecumenical Perspectives*, ed. Gerard Mannion and Eduardus Van der Borght, *Continuum* (2011): 69–89.

21. The *vota* of the Dutch bishops (Nierman, Jansen, Moors, and Alfrink) deserve special consideration here. See *Acta et Documenta Concilio Oecumenico Vaticano II Apparando*, first series, (antepreparatoria) *Typis Polyglottis*

Vaticanis (1960–61), *AD*, II/2, 486n5, 20/11/1959; *AD* II/2, 499n2; *AD* II/2, 493n2; and *AD* II/2, 513.

22. See *AS,* III/I, 177. Regarding this *Relatio,* Johannes Willebrands has pointed to the two tendencies that were reflected in the council with regard to the interpretation of the *subsistit in.* The same tendencies still can be found among theologians and theological schools. For an example, see the 2009 document promulgated by the Congregation of the Doctrine of Faith and the discussion that followed thereafter. For the debate see Francis Sullivan, "*Questio Disputata*: The Meaning of *Subsistit In* as Explained by the Congregation for the Doctrine of Faith," in *Theological Studies* 69, no. 1 (2008): 116–24; see also the lucid response given by Karim Schelkens, "*Lumen Gentium 'Subsistit In'* Revisited: The Catholic Church and Christian Unity After Vatican II," in *Theological Studies* 69, no. 4 (2008): 875–93.

23. Johannes Willebrands, "Vatican II's Ecclesiology of Communion," in *One in Christ* 23, no. 3 (1987): 180.

24. This is seen as one of the ecumenical potentials inherent in *Lumen Gentium* no. 8. See Patrick Hartin, "*Sensus Fidelium*: A Roman Catholic Reflection on Its Significance for Ecumenical Thought," in *Journal of Ecumenical Studies* 28, no. 1 (1991): 74–87.

25. There are several other theological issues involved in this discussion that we cannot address here. See Nicholas Rescher, *Pluralism: Against the Demand for Consensus* (Oxford: Oxford University Press, 1993), 3; and Jósef Fuisz, *Konsens, Kompromiss, Konvergenz in der ökumenischen Diskussion* (Münster: LIT Verlag, 2000), 22.

26. See Zoltán Alszeghy, "The *Sensus Fidei* and the Development of Dogma," in *Vatican II: Assessment and Perspectives: Twenty-Five Years After (1962–1987),* ed. René Latourelle (New York: Paulist Press, 1988), 1:138–56.

27. WCC/Faith and Order, "The Nature and Purpose of the Church: A Stage on the Way to a Common Statement," Faith and Order paper no. 181 (Bialystok: Orthdruk Orthodox Printing House, 1998). See Harding Meyer and Lukas Vischer, eds., *Growth in Agreement: Reports and Agreed Statements of Ecumenical Conversations on a World Level* (New York: Paulist Press, 1984).

28. WCC, *The Nature,* 99.

29. Ibid., 82.

30. Ibid., 99.

31. There exists a kind of consensus among the churches that in every Christian baptized there is a *sensus fidei* or God-given sense that flows from the Holy Spirit's action.

32. In line with Luigi Sartori, "What is the Criterion for the *Sensus Fidelium*?," in *Concilium* 148, no. 8 (1981): 57.

33. See Leo Scheffczyk, "*Sensus Fidelium*—Witness on the Part of the Community," in *Communio* 15, no. 2 (1988): 182–98.

34. See Jean-Marie Tillard, "Reception-Communion," in *One in Christ* 28, no. 4 (1992): 307–22, esp. 322.

35. We are not talking about a democratization of the structures of the church/churches; for this discussion see Leonard Swidler, "*Demo-kratía*, The Rule of the People of God, or *Consensus Fidelium*," in *Journal of Ecumenical Studies* 19, no. 2 (1982): 226–43; John Coleman, "Not Democracy but Democratization," in *A Democratic Catholic Church: The Reconstruction of Roman Catholicism*, ed. E. Bianchi and R. Ruether (New York: Crossroad, 1992).

36. As defined by Herbert Vorgrimler, "From *Sensus Fidei* to *Consensus Fidelium*," in *Concilium* 180, no. 4 (1985): 3–11.

Dialogue for Peacebuilding
in the Light of Human Rights

CHARLES OCHERO CORNELIO

The Catholic Church rejects nothing of what is true and holy in these religions. She has a high regard for the manner of life and conduct, the precepts and doctrines which although differing in many ways from her own teaching nevertheless often reflect a ray of truth which enlightens all people.

— *Nostra Aetate*

One of the lasting impacts of the Second Vatican Council is the church's commitment to dialogue with culture and other religions. This commitment is present in many of the documents of Vatican II and Pope Paul's encyclical on the church, *Ecclesiam Suam* (1964). With the creation of the Pontifical Council for Interreligious Dialogue in 1964 and its 1991 document *Dialogue and Proclamation*, the Catholic Church has played an important role in the promotion of dialogue among believers, religious leaders, theologians, and religious activists committed to justice and peace. Inspired by the council, Catholic movements, such as the International Movement of Catholic Student (IMCS–Pax Romana), have worked to train youth around the world to value tolerance and to join with others in the "dialogue of action" in common efforts to reduce poverty and promote sustainable development.[1]

A PERSONAL EXPERIENCE OF DIALOGUE

Fifty years after Vatican II, there remains an urgent need for practices of dialogue in our world. Cultural and religious differences play great roles in most of the conflicts in the world today. In my own experience as a Catholic in Sudan, I have been inspired by the church's commitment to dialogue.

I cannot begin my refection on dialogue without echoing the famous words of Ralph Waldo Emerson, "A religion that is afraid of science dishonors God and commits suicide." In other words, religion must engage culture. This idea, for me, has been a motivating force and a reason to embrace others and engage in different forms of dialogue (such as interreligious, intercultural, and intergenerational) with the ultimate goal of peacebuilding. I strongly agree with Emerson (and the council) that science and culture should be integrated with faith. When culture and faith are separated, a disastrous outcome is generally assured.

In 2002, my first year of college, I became involved in Pax Romana Sudan. Through this experience I learned about the church's teachings and came to appreciate the role of dialogue as a peaceful solution to different problems. Coming from South Sudan, I fell in love with this process. Twenty-two years of civil war (I was born one year before it began) was enough to learn and appreciate the values of dialogue in achieving peaceful solutions. Spending one's whole childhood and adolescence in a warring country is the worst thing I can ever think of for any child.

When I began college, the colleges in Sudan were primarily in the north; the civil war forced the ones in the south to move to the north. As a southern (Christian) Sudanese in the mostly Muslim and Arabic-speaking north, I could not escape the "dialogue of life" with Muslim students. This was a difficult time. The "war on terror" and the Iraqi war were seen by many Muslims to be a war on Islam. This made it almost impossible to convince my peers and other students that Christians and Muslims can live together regardless of their races, faiths, traditions, and cultures.

As students in the midst of the conflicts, we were forced to respond to the question: If the governments are fighting, must we necessarily join them in the conflict? This was a challenging question for us, since most students were grouped according to religious, regional, and worst of all racial affiliations. This made it necessary, especially in the years leading up to the breakaway of South Sudan, for us to engage in practices of interreligious and intercultural dialogue. At the same time, we were also experiencing intertribal conflicts in the south. As Catholic students we tried to mobilize students to talk to their tribal elders. However, this was difficult due to the cultural belief that the young should always listen to the elders.

In response to this complex situation the Catholic students worked with others to organize dialogue forums, trainings, and workshops aimed at peacebuilding and embracing of one another as creatures with equal rights to live. We organized these programs with the slogan "All different; all equal." We drew inspiration from many sources, not only the council. We took to heart what Martin Luther King, Jr., said, "We must learn to live together as brothers or we will perish together as fools."

It was very difficult to get this message across. The image of seeing a black human being as a slave and an infidel is deeply rooted in the northern Islamic community. At the same time, the image of the northerners as the enemy and oppressors (colonizer) was also very strong among the black southerners. Despite these very present hurdles, our programs and workshops were successful in bringing together Muslim and Christian students to share about life, faith, and the promotion of peace and sustainable development. In the end, the efforts in Sudan had several concrete successes:

- Christian students were welcomed into mosques and entered into discussions about faith with imams. We shared and learned from each other's scriptures.
- As students, we learned that race does not determine belonging to a religion and vice versa.
- Muslim Arab students joined with Christian African students to speak about the coexistence and beauties of having a multicultural country.
- Intermarriages occurred between some of the participants with different faiths and cultures.
- We all left with the satisfaction of having done something great for our community.

DIALOGUE FOR PEACE: A LASTING CHALLENGE OF VATICAN II

The efforts made by the Catholic students in Sudan are not isolated incidents. IMCS–Pax Romana has responded to the challenges of Vatican II by organizing dialogue efforts among students in different parts of the world. This, we believe, is critical for establishing peace. IMCS–Pax Romana has partnered with the United Nations Alliance for Civilizations in organizing dialogue programs for Muslim and Christian students under the theme: Speaking and Listening with Respect: Students, Faith, and Dialogue. The outcomes of this program were highlighted by the United Nations as a "best practice" in 2009.

In Canada, where Christians are the majority, we have seen how the Christian concerns for dialogue is very different than in Sudan. In Canada, Muslims are often unjustly linked to terrorism, which can be psychologically devastating to young Muslims. This has made dialogue challenging, with some Muslims afraid to voice their beliefs and others operating from a more defensive posture. We believe that it is important for the church (and Christian students) to work for dialogue not only in places where Christians are in the minority, like Sudan, but also in places where Christians are in the majority, and then to share these experiences across borders. We must find ways to support religious freedom, destroy all the stereotypes revolving around Islam, and encourage Muslim students.

At many universities cultural, tribal, and religious divisions, which had existed for many years, were deepened by the occasionally violent conflicts among students, teachers, and administrators over tuition, salaries, and services. In response to these divisions, IMCS launched the Peace Unit Program in 1999. Since then, it has spread to several campuses. The students have been mobilized and trained in the practices of peacebuilding, conflict resolution, and dialogue with the aim of being "an effective and all inclusive movement of students promoting peace, human rights, harmonious existence and resolution of conflict in a non-violent manner within tertiary institutions and the society."

Among the many activities of the Peace Unit Program are the organization of "roundtable forums" where students, professors, and university officials meet to discuss the root causes of conflicts before they become violent. While these dialogue sessions are not directly interreligious, they draw from the church's recent efforts and practices at dialogue. The program has developed "peacemaking with nature" projects, where dialogue develops as students and professors plant trees and clean up the environment together.

One of the most successful efforts of IMCS–Pax Romana in facilitating dialogue has been in Kenya, where the post-election violence in 2007 illustrated many bitter divisions—even among students at the same university.

PEACE = ACTIVE NONVIOLENCE + DIALOGUE

The teaching of the Second Vatican Council on dialogue and peace has a great potential to shape the lived experience of young people around the world. I have a strong hope that youth can take the council's spirit of dialogue and work to address the conflicts facing our world, including ones that are not directly religious conflicts. In *Apostolicam Actuositatem* (AA), the council speaks of the great potential of young people to help transform our society. "The young," we read, "should become the first apostles to the young, in direct contact with them, exercising the apostolate by themselves among themselves, taking account of their social environment" (AA, 12).

University youth, in particular, occupy an important space in our society. They are at the exit of the young world and at the same time at the entrance of the "stake-holding world." Who else should be targeted, then, if we need an effective and positive change for the society? Again, I believe that dialogue is the key to peaceful solutions. Many die due to conflicts that easily could be prevented, and it is up to us to act. As Edmund Burke is often credited with saying, "All that is necessary for the triumph of evil is for good people to do nothing."

NOTE

1. The "dialogue of action," in which Christians and others collaborate for the integral development and liberation of people," is one of the four forms of dialogue promoted in *Dialogue and Proclamation.*

V.

THE ENDURING ETHICAL VISION OF *GAUDIUM ET SPES:* CATHOLIC MORAL ENGAGEMENT IN THE TWENTY-FIRST CENTURY

MICHAEL P. JAYCOX

In a historically unprecedented move, the assembled bishops of the Second Vatican Council affirmed in the pastoral constitution (an entirely new genre for a council document) *Gaudium et Spes* (GS) that the Catholic Church embraces all genuinely human values as its own and seeks to involve itself in the global struggle to realize the deepest aspirations of human freedom in this world (GS, 1, 3, 4, 42). The work of Catholic theological ethicists during the almost fifty years since this affirmation was uttered can be summarized as a dual process of reflection upon the radical implications of this conciliar statement and social engagement to enact the ethical vision it suggests. Therefore, in view of the broad influence of *Gaudium et Spes,* it would be foolish for me to attempt a grand tour of fifty years of Catholic ethical thought and practice within the confines of this introductory essay. Rather, in a spirit of realism and modesty, this essay seeks to understand the extent to which the vision of *Gaudium et Spes* remains the key point of departure for the newest generation of Catholic theological ethicists beginning their work in the twenty-first-century world. Stated differently, we might ask whether the moral vision of the council will be able to survive in a recognizable form and to remain culturally relevant.

A potentially fruitful approach to this question would begin by recognizing that the church's perceptions of the world it inhabits—whether the world of 1965 or that of 2012—largely depend upon how the church's members are situated in the world. The contemporary Catholic Church is a global and inescapably multicultural church, and most of its members inhabit non-Western cultures. Moreover, this church is part of a world characterized not only by other major religious traditions but also by rapidly globalizing economic structures, inequitable access to basic necessities, and grassroots movements oriented toward democratic ideals, social justice, and institutional reform. Therefore, if the ethical vision of the council succeeds in being a vital source of hope for the church and for humanity as a whole, it will do so because it proves to be flexible enough to accommodate and integrate an irreducible pluralism of moral perspectives, as well as credible enough to equip a new generation of theologians and church leaders to proclaim the gospel through active solidarity with those who suffer injustice.

The ethics essays included in this volume represent three constructive proposals inspired by the council's vision. The first, authored by Ellen Van Stichel of Belgium, upholds and develops the methodological foundation of *Gaudium et Spes,* theological anthropology. It was a true watershed moment in the development of Catholic social thought when the council turned away from a sterile, neo-Scholastic conception of natural law in favor of a dynamic, scripturally informed account of the dignity of the human person in order to ground an ethics of the common good and human rights (GS, 12–18, 22, 24–32, 41). Even as Van Stichel notes certain limitations of this renewed approach, her conviction that a theological anthropology adequate for the contemporary world must remain the sine qua non of Catholic moral methodology lies at the heart of her argument concerning the profoundly relational and trinitarian aspects of human personhood. She contends that a relational account of the human person vis-à-vis the Trinity can function as a theological-ethical resource for articulating an incisive social critique of any human relationship that fails to meet the standards of equality, reciprocity, and solidarity.[1]

The second essay, authored by Gonzalo Villagrán, SJ, of Spain, expands and updates the council's fundamental attitude of openness and dialogue toward its worldly interlocutors for a contemporary context simultaneously marked by a more confident post-Christian secularism and a more complex situation of religious pluralism. *Gaudium et Spes* proclaimed an end to the church's long-standing antagonism toward modernity, giving theologians and other Catholic professionals a mandate to engage as fully as possible in the institutions and cultural life of the world around them, even going so far as to affirm that the church can learn something from the world (GS, 40–44). This sea change created the conditions for a Catholic public theology to emerge and thrive, a public theology that necessarily reinvents and reinterprets itself as it adapts to particular contexts of church-world dialogue. Villagrán draws upon the work of David Tracy and others in order to propose a narrative- and symbol-based version of public theology intended to enhance the quality of dialogue between the church and its secular partners. Through his sensitivity to the role of communally formed subjectivity in dialogical encounters, Villagrán offers a viable model for elaborating the kind of contextually appropriate public theologies so badly needed by the contemporary church as it seeks to become a vital participant in global and local conversations about urgent moral challenges.

The third essay, authored by Krista Stevens of the United States, addresses what is among the most serious moral challenges confronting the church and the world at large: systemic racism. *Gaudium et Spes* condemned racism and other oppressive ideologies as social evils and recognized that persons tend to participate in them as a result of negative socialization (GS, 4, 25, 29). Given this general orientation, the council delegated the work of developing sophisticated methods of social analysis, conceptual frameworks (for example, structural sin, preferential option for the poor), and practical strategies to bishops' conferences, theologians, and lay specialists reading the signs of the times in specific contexts of oppression around the globe.[2] Writing from the United States context, where systemic racism has been and continues to be an integral component of the unjust social hierarchy and cultural ethos, Stevens draws upon the work of Bryan Massingale as she deplores the American Catholic clergy's insufficient response to this critical moral issue. Her specific diagnosis of the causes of their failure and her retrieval of critical resources from *Gaudium et Spes* indicate that, in large part, both the content and the core spirit of the council's moral vision are quite far from being fully received by the clergy and the laity of the American church.

It lies outside the scope of this introduction to determine whether these three authors are representative of their demographic in the theological academy, but their work stands as evidence that young Catholic ethicists still take *Gaudium et Spes* as a crucial point of departure for approaching the urgent moral challenges of the twenty-first century.

The fact that this document still brings relevant insight to bear upon these challenges indicates that its moral vision is not a mere historical relic, not an exercise in exhortative rhetoric, and not an overly optimistic appraisal of the possibilities for positive social change. To be sure, *Gaudium et Spes* was written to speak to the world of 1965, but the creative and successful appropriation of this document by Van Stichel, Villagrán, and Stevens in response to current issues indicates that it remains flexible and credible enough to be a bearer of hope in the face of the moral realities of the contemporary world.

NOTES

1. These insights are integral to feminist theologies of the Trinity; see, for example, Margaret A. Farley, "New Patterns of Relationship: Beginnings of a Moral Revolution," *Theological Studies* 36, no. 4 (1975): 642–44; and Elizabeth A. Johnson, *She Who Is: The Mystery of God in Feminist Theological Discourse* (New York: Crossroad, 1992), 205–23.

2. For example, see CELAM (Consejo Episcopal Latinoamericano), *The Church in the Present-Day Transformation of Latin America in the Light of the Council: Part II: Conclusions* (Bogotá and Medellín, Colombia: General Secretariat of CELAM, 1968 and 1970); and Gustavo Gutiérrez, *A Theology of Liberation: History, Politics, and Salvation,* rev. ed. (Maryknoll, NY: Orbis Books, 1988).

The Ethical Potential of Communal Movements for Catholic Social Thought

The Trinitarian Anthropology of the Focolare Movement

ELLEN VAN STICHEL

For an "emerging social ethicist," adequately commemorating the fiftieth anniversary of the Second Vatican Council necessitates engagement with the *Pastoral Constitution on the Church in the Modern World (Gaudium et Spes)*. In fact, one is even eager to immerse oneself in this document because—from a moral theological point of view, at least—it seems that the council fathers have kept the best until the end. Indeed, five decades later it is still a highly relevant source for theological ethicists, as I hope to show in this chapter. The document title itself reflects an important shift in how the church perceives its relation to the world: the church is *in* the world rather than opposed to it. This small prepositional change might seem of minor importance, but it reflects a major transition within Catholic social thought from one worldview to another; with it, a corresponding change in anthropology—how one understands the human being—also applies, resulting in a more personalist approach to ethics.

Ground-breaking as this shift was for the future of Catholic social thought, I believe recent developments in theology challenge it, particularly at this point. Half a century later this personalist anthropology appears outdated, requiring theological renewal. I do not intend to claim that this anthropology has gotten it all wrong, but rather that other dimensions have come into focus in the continuing process of developing an appropriate theological anthropology for Catholic social thought. In particular, I argue that, within today's interdependent world, a stronger emphasis on the relationality of the human person might be helpful in meeting current social challenges that have become manifest as a result of increasing global interdependency. While some

133

kind of relational anthropology was inchoately present in *Gaudium et Spes*, I believe it can be taken a step further with trinitarian theological anthropology, which so far has not yet been developed within Catholic social thought.

In the broader Catholic tradition, such a trinitarian anthropology is gaining influence, both inside and outside academic theology. The most widely known in this regard are systematic theologians Catherine Mowry LaCugna and Leonardo Boff, who have each reflected on the implications of the Trinity for theological anthropology. In this chapter, however, I want to address this trinitarian anthropology from the perspective of the spirituality of a new religious movement, namely, the Focolare movement. Founded during the Second World War by Chiara Lubich in Trent, the Focolare movement is characterized by a spirituality of unity. By trying to live up to the gospel, the word of life in daily practice, this movement of priests, religious people, and lay persons, together with their families, seeks to embody Jesus' testament "that they all may be one" (Jn 17:11–21). Currently, its spirituality is a source of inspiration across denominational boundaries and even interreligious boundaries. My reason for starting from this movement's spirituality is the conviction that academic theology is not the only well-suited conversation partner to develop Catholic social thought. Indeed, reflections on such spiritualities can also enrich a theo-social anthropology both materially and methodologically: materially, as a source of relevant theological data; methodologically, because lived theological movements have the ability to link spirituality and concrete daily life as incarnated by the movements' members. As this movement seems to have achieved a critical following, it is time to take stock of its theology and to discern to what extent Catholic social thought should gain insights from its specific understanding of the human person as being-in-relation.

VATICAN II:
SHIFTING WORLDVIEW, SHIFTING ANTHROPOLOGY

Although written under the pontificate of Paul VI, *Gaudium et Spes* actually recalls the legacy of John XXIII's view of the church and its relationship with the world. During his pontificate the church was confronted with a rapidly changing world characterized by internationalization and economic integration. The increasing economic interdependence contrasted with a lack of political and cultural unity; the world seemed more divided than ever between West and East (as the Cold War clearly showed) and between North and South (as the former colonies' struggles for independence illustrated). Yet these threats did not undermine John XXIII's hope; he gave witness to a remarkable optimism and openness to worldly development, resulting in a new perspective on the relationship between the church and the world.

It had only been one century earlier that Pius IX had promulgated *Syllabus Errorum* (1864), which condemned the "mistakes" of modernity and liberalism. This suspicion with regard to modernity resulted in a general opposition to the world and its development, one that characterized later pontificates until John XXIII. For example, Leo XIII's retrieval of neo-Scholastic Thomism was a strategy to avoid the threat he saw modernity posing to the faith. Politically, the papacy was often more concerned with local politics as the battlefield for the church's power struggle, as the focus on the relationship between church and state within official teachings illustrates.[1] Unlike his predecessors, John XXIII recognized the crucial importance of social problems for revealing to us the "signs of the times" that must be discerned—even at the global level.[2] Instead of using politics to achieve his own goals, he aimed to build a new world together with others—even if they were socialist or communist. This concern for, but also openness to, the possibilities the world offers stimulated him to announce a new Vatican council that should reflect and inspire *aggiornamento*. As such, John XXIII was shown to be a true cosmopolitan, who attempted to end the church's "fortress mentality."[3] When we read in *Gaudium et Spes* that "the joys and the hopes, the griefs and the anxieties of the men of this age, especially those who are poor or in any way afflicted, these are the joys and hopes, the griefs and anxieties of the followers of Christ" (GS, 1) and that "the church has always had the duty of scrutinizing the signs of the times and of interpreting them in the light of the Gospel" (GS, 4), the two most important aspects of John XXIII's inspiration can be seen to determine the outlook of the pastoral constitution; namely, his cosmopolitan perspective and the methodological focus on the world. Indeed, these are the legacy of this visionary pope.

With John XXIII as the mediating figure between two periods, the council's approach and documents thus reflect what Charles Curran has called the shift from a "classicist" to a "historical" worldview.[4] The classicist worldview considers reality to be "an eternal and unchanging order" determined by God, the "rational Creator," an order that is objectively perceivable by humanity through its rationality. Characteristic terms for this worldview are *essence* and *substance*, while *time* and *space* are merely considered *accidental* in that they do not as such influence this eternal, fixed world—let alone influence it in a determining, sustainable manner. Truth, then, has to be discovered through the isolation of the fixed, eternal structures from their historical context. With regard to morality, the classicist worldview coincides with the revival of neo-Scholastic Thomism.[5] This approach methodologically retains a deductive approach that searches for universalistic norms as one looks for the essence of reality. Eternal, absolute, and objective norms are formulated in its consequent natural law, based on this fixed order of things, their so-called nature.

In contrast, characterizing terms for the historical approach are *change, experience,* and *historicity,* for the world is involved in a dynamic process of development within history. Time and space determine the world so that reading and rereading the "signs of the times" becomes crucial for an appropriate analysis and understanding of the world. As such, *Gaudium et Spes* seems exemplary of this approach. This inductive method is also applied at the moral level: human beings not so much discover but rather develop moral norms. Moral judgments do not merely depend on the description of the objective act to which they are often reduced within the neo-Scholastic framework, but elements such as intention and circumstances complicate moral analysis. It is important to notice that the neo-Scholastic interpretation is a specific, particular interpretation of natural law, for various interpretations exist within Catholic theology. According to John Kelly, this static interpretation goes against Thomas Aquinas's own view, stating that we cannot directly deduce "detailed specific conclusions with certitude" from natural law.[6] In contrast to this static and essentialist interpretation, a more "dynamic" notion of essences and "revisionist" or "teleological" interpretations of natural law in general might have more similarities with the historical approach.[7] Since the neo-Scholastic interpretation sustained the official social teachings at least until *Gaudium et Spes,* however, I believe the sharp distinction made between the classicist and the historical approach is appropriate.

More interesting for the purpose of this chapter are the implications of this shift in worldviews for theological anthropology in general and its conception of the social nature of human beings in particular. A *neoclassical natural law* approach conceives of persons as essences, fixed substances characterized by natural processes operating rationally. It looks for what is universally common in being human while ignoring particularity and historicity in individual cases. The *historical approach,* in contrast, coincides with a personalist anthropology as developed by such European thinkers as Emmanuel Mounier, Jacques Maritain, and—from my own context—Louis Janssens; the human person is considered as an embodied, historical subject for which equality as well as uniqueness and particularity ("fundamentally equal but uniquely original," as Janssens stated) are central.[8] Moreover, as norms are not merely objectively deducible once and for all, both personal conscience and intentionality become increasingly important. Interpreting the natural law not as biological but rather as personalist, some authors thus refer to what I call the personalist ethic within *Gaudium et Spes* as the personalist interpretation of natural law.[9] Whether there is then a difference between a personalist natural law and the personalist ethic I refer to remains to be seen. In order to avoid confusion, I hold the distinction between natural law as interpreted by Scholasticism and personalism.

With regard to human beings' relationality, the first approach considers human beings as separate entities with each person having his or her own functioning, so that relationality is a characteristic of what human beings have based on their nature (as the notion of a social animal indicates). Personalists, on the other hand, argue that human beings *cannot* in reality survive or live without others. Neither *should* they, because persons realize their perfection in communion with others. Unlike the natural law approach, where relationships are something persons *have,* personalists state that they (and we) *are* relationships; that is, relations are constitutive of and essential to existence and vocation. As such, this European personalism reflects its origin, namely, the polarization between the two extremes of communism and individualism, which it not only questions but also brings to a higher synthesis by emphasizing that individuality and community are not mutually exclusive.

In line with its methodological stance reflecting the historical approach, the anthropology of *Gaudium et Spes* is decidedly personalistic.[10] Indeed, the section titled "The Dignity of the Human Person" describes not only the unity of the human person as embodied subject (GS, 14) with its rationality and wisdom (15), but also—and more fundamentally from the perspective of personalism—the role of conscience (16), freedom (17), sinfulness, and salvation (13). First and foremost, however, a person's social dimension is addressed, immediately grounded in a theological framework.

But what is man? . . . For Sacred Scripture teaches that man was created "to the image of God," is capable of knowing and loving his Creator, and was appointed by Him as master of all earthly creatures that he might subdue them and use them to God's glory. "What is man that you should care for him? You have made him little less than the angels, and crowned him with glory and honor. You have given him rule over the works of your hands, putting all things under his feet" (Ps. 8:5–7).

But God did not create man as a solitary, for from the beginning "male and female he created them" (Gen. 1:27). Their companionship produces the primary form of interpersonal communion. For by his innermost nature man is a social being, and unless he relates himself to others he can neither live nor develop his potential.

Therefore, as we read elsewhere in Holy Scripture God saw "all that he had made, and it was very good" (Gen. 1:31). (GS, 12)

Here we find two theological foundations of this anthropology. First, human persons are created as *imago Dei*, and the *Dei* of which we are the *imago* is interpreted as God, the Creator whom human persons can know and love. Second, the intrinsic sociality of persons is grounded in the creation of Adam and Eve, who from the beginning were created together, created for community. This sequencing of human generation implies that relationality is a necessary condition for the full development of self. In short, the sociability of personhood is situated in their being created together as two distinct though related persons, on the initiative of God. It is God's acting, in particular God's creative act, that clarifies our relationality.

Considering the context and the neo-Scholastic tradition in official church teachings prior to the Second Vatican Council, it is rather remarkable that the council fathers decided not to define the nature of human persons primarily on the basis of natural law; rather, they went back to one of the most original sources of the faith, namely, scripture.[11] Within recent Catholic social thought, these personalist arguments—though not exclusively belonging to a personalist anthropology, personalism is indeed based on these theological arguments—are still the main theological underpinnings of its anthropology.

(RE)DISCOVERY OF THE TRINITY
AS THE *DEI* OF THE *IMAGO DEI*

The anthropology underlying official social teachings since the Second Vatican Council is thus the idea of human beings as the *imago Dei* of the creational God. Gradually, however, a new theological anthropology appeared on the radar of Catholic social teaching, an anthropology reflecting the implications of the Trinity for the common life of human beings. Certainly in more recent documents, such as the latest social encyclical *Caritas in Veritate,* links to what might helpfully be called a trinitarian anthropology are increasingly present.[12] Moreover, within *Gaudium et Spes* itself there is a passage that hints at the link between the Trinity and humanity's unity:

> Indeed, the Lord Jesus, when He prayed to the Father, "that all may be one . . . as we are one" (John 17:21–22) opened up vistas closed to human reason, for He implied a certain *likeness between the union of the divine Persons, and the unity of God's sons in truth and charity.* This likeness reveals that man, who is the only creature on earth which God willed for itself, cannot fully find himself except through a sincere gift of himself. (GS, 24, emphasis added)

The implications of this statement lack elaboration, resulting in a tendency to overlook this passage, as has often happened in the continuous tradition of developing Catholic social thought since Vatican II. Moreover, since the statement touches upon the theme without further explanation of its practical ramifications, it can hardly be considered a full trinitarian anthropology. As the rest of the document shows, the theological foundations for a theological anthropology lie elsewhere, namely, in the *imago Dei,* as described above. When the council answered the question "What is the human being?" it did not refer to the Trinity as the basis of its answer. This reestablishment of this traditional creational account for the subsequent tradition of Catholic thought overshadows the potential of a truly trinitarian anthropology.

Beyond Catholic social teaching, the implication for God's identity as Trinity—and not just God's acts—for human personal and social life has been the object of discussion within systematic theology since the 1990s. One can see the seeds of this development even earlier (1970s) in the work of Karl Rahner, with his plea for the interaction between the "immanent" and "economic" Trinity. While Catholic theology up to that point made a sharp distinction between the immanent (God's eternal identity and inner structure) and economic (God's salvific activity as Father, Son and Holy Spirit) Trinity with a preeminent focus on the former, Rahner holds that one cannot discuss the nature or identity of the Trinity apart from the revelation of its members in history; there is close "connection" between "God-for-us" and "God-in-eternity."[13] Although Rahner himself did not go so far as to claim that this connection results in an analogy between the human person and God in terms of relationality, he has set the stage for this theological anthropology to arise. Consequently, theologians such as Leonardo Boff and Catherine LaCugna have explored the theological-anthropological implications of the focus on the economic Trinity. And this should not be seen as a coincidence, as these thinkers represent currents of theology that rediscover the importance of the economic Trinity for their theological purposes, in particular, as a source for reflections on how our communal life should appear. A rediscovery of trinitarian anthropology indeed seems very popular with theologies that envision a new humanity, a new global society, in their reaction against different kinds of oppression (for example, liberation theology against the dividing lines of poverty and wealth, feminist theology against sexism, womanist/Hispanic/black theology against racism).

A few decades before the rediscovery of the doctrine of the Trinity for theological anthropology within academic theology, the Focolare movement started to reflect—although in the beginning implicitly—on an anthropology that takes the Trinity seriously as the *Dei* of which we are the *imago*. Faced with the bombing of Trent during the Second World War and other atrocities, Chiara Lubich and her companions discovered the love of God as the eternal ideal that can never be destroyed. But how to put this ideal into practice? Scripture gave them the answer they needed: by loving their neighbors. So they started to feed the hungry around them, help the injured, dress the unclothed, and so on. Inspired by Jesus' sayings, "Ask and you shall be given" and "Give and it shall be given," they discovered God's love and Christ's living presence through their encounters with others, in their mutual support and help. The main phrase that caught their attention—rather coincidentally they started to read this passage in scripture—was Jesus' prayer in John 17:21, "That they may all be one." This passage recounts Christ's dream for humanity to live in unity as he is one with the Father. For God is Love; God as *the Trinity* is love.

From this discovery onward, to live the trinitarian unity became the core of the spirituality of the Focolare. The so-called spirituality of unity is indeed the watermark of the Focolare movement: "Unity is our specific vocation. . . . Unity is the word that sums up the life of our movement," Chiara Lubich has written. Because God is triune and longs for human unity (with God and among one another), spirituality necessarily has a communal character. Unlike other movements, which have "focused primarily on the advance of the individual toward God," Focolare spirituality discourages individual union with God if it happens at the expense of the community. For them, one always goes to God together with others. Even more so, "one advances toward

God by going through one's neighbor."[14] In addition, this divine love humans are called to imitate includes humanity as a whole, bringing a universal perspective to the spirituality. The unity of the whole human family is its goal; the recognition of our primordial interdependence its starting point.

This experience of God's love must be embodied in daily life, must be reflected in all our undertakings and relations: "This Trinitarian love is the pattern and dynamic thrust of human existence. This new element is lived out in all of humanity's expressions—ecclesial, social, cultural—at all levels of human life—personal, communal, social—with all the necessary consequences. It is a love that makes the presence and action of the risen Christ in history something we can experience."[15] It is interesting to note how this living and embodying the spirituality has itself a "communitarian dimension." In fact, "it is lived by people not only individually, but also as groups small and large."[16] Spread across the world, one can find the so-called *Mariapolis*, where people who are dedicated to this spirituality—as married couples, lay persons, or religious—live together in an intentional community. Living the spirituality is in itself embodying the trinitarian anthropology behind it. The link between this spirituality of unity and a trinitarian anthropology is thus not at all far-fetched; if the aim is to live in such a way as to realize a more united world, a trinitarian anthropology is well-suited and appropriate to help sustain this goal. How this trinitarian anthropology, grounded in the spirituality of unity, can become incarnate has been elaborated upon by the *focolarino* Enrique Cambón.[17]

TRINITARIAN ANTHROPOLOGY OF THE FOCOLARE MOVEMENT: ENRIQUE CAMBÓN'S APPROACH

In line with the general spirituality of the Focolare to seek a close connection between faith and daily life, Cambón states that the Trinity must be "repatriated" and its relevance and necessary link with daily life recovered.[18] Indeed, a trinitarian anthropology can never be limited to mere claims for some characteristics of the human person without reference to all the aspects of the person's life. For if one states that human beings are the image of the Trinity, of God-in-relation, questions on the kind of relationships one has to have follow automatically. While a creative account of the human person's sociality can merely state that humans are social because of their creation as Adam and Eve, a trinitarian perspective cannot escape the consequent question of what the practical implications of this anthropology are with regard to views on communal life, society, and global relationships.

According to the perception of the nature of the trinitarian relations and their implications for human relations, different approaches within theological anthropology emerge. To investigate the ways in which God's love manifests itself in the three divine persons is one approach. The three persons are then considered as prime examples to follow because each of them has characteristics a person can apply and live by individually. Yet another, say communal, trinitarian perspective goes further; it focuses on the "trinitarian *relations* which, if they are lived by, participate in the life of God within the human community."[19] The question for theological ethics thus becomes not so much how does a *human person* reflect the image of the trinitarian God; rather, the question is what does a trinitarian *relationship* consist of and how should our (global) society be structured to mirror adequately that series of relations. This is exactly the approach that Cambón holds in his book. A detailed analysis is not possible within the limits of this essay, but I briefly summarize the main characteristics of his trinitarian worldview.

Cambón distinguishes a few paradoxical dichotomies of the trinitarian-based relationships and the persons living the relations.[20] The first one is "person-relation";[21] considering the interrelations of the Trinity, "to be" and "to give" conflate so that personal identity and the community *(communio)* have the same origin. One becomes more oneself by giving oneself; one realizes one's most complete potential in a free relationship with others, and it is one's vocation to enable this *kenosis* to become reciprocal. The intradivine relations become the paradigm of each relation in the universe, and every worldly relation resembles and reflects this divine way of relating. That human beings are social animals is widely accepted, not only within theology, and can thus be considered as a form of trinitarian anthropology. Only an extreme focus on autonomy would deny that relationships are constitutive of human life. Consequently, the specificity of such an anthropology will not so much be the statement that relationships are fundamental, but rather the qualification of these relationships as *agapic,* this giving love to which the idea of *kenosis* points.

The second dichotomy is "unity in diversity." After having stated that the Trinity makes us aware of the unity of God, Cambón clarifies that this unity itself is trinitarian: God is united in diversity, one in three persons. Traditionally, *perichoresis* refers to the idea that the "divine persons exist one in the other, without conflating because each one keeps its identity."[22] Hence, the *kenosis,* the emptying of oneself, is not the same as to become nothing: "A trinitarian relationship between two or more persons means that each one is himself or herself while bringing the other to be." Note that Cambón assumes a trinitarian relationship is possible between two persons, because *trinitarian,* for him, refers to the kind of relationship among the divine persons rather than to the fact they are three persons. In short, in enabling the other to realize oneself, one realizes oneself as well.

A final dichotomy is "altruism-reciprocity," summarized descriptively as "persons act[ing] in a trinitarian way when they live *with* others, *for* others, *in* others, and *thanks to* others."[23] If one leaves one element out, the relationship is not truly trinitarian. For example, to live *with* others is not sufficient, for this might imply merely living in close proximity to one another, as in modern suburbia. Nor is to live *for* others truly trinitarian because the reciprocal element would be missing, in addition to the fact that one only becomes oneself through the other. True *perichoresis* requires the "interplay" of all four factors. In short, by aiding in bringing the other into existence, one also realizes oneself more completely. Structuring human relations as trinitarian relations thus means: (1) to need each other to become oneself; (2) to accept diversity and particularity without resulting in separation but rather in strengthening the unity; (3) to live in reciprocal relations; and (4) to empty oneself (which is not the same as to reduce oneself to nothing) in order to give freedom to others to live. Humanity will and should always try to live up to these trinitarian relationships, realizing, however, that it can never become the Trinity. For while God *is* relationship, we only *have* relationships. Our attempts will never realize the divine unity, but this should not keep us from trying.

All this seems very abstract, and one might start to wonder how this in any way relates to daily life, the starting point of our reflection. Or, one might spontaneously think that this similarity between the divine trinitarian relations and the human variants is far too idealistic to be applicable in "real life." As a social ethicist working on the idea of global justice, for example, I felt at first a hesitance in speaking all too easily of love as the starting point for my reflections. Does not the idea of love, and a kenotic interpretation of it in particular, risk neglecting the demands of justice, as has often happened when one prioritizes charity over justice? Put boldly, ethicists striving for justice, including me, seem in the first instance almost allergic to the idea of a self-giving love as a solution for injustices and inequalities. Cambón's analysis of trinitarian relationships shows, however, that this is not what he argues for. For those who do not think these abstract descriptions of trinitarian relations are convincing, he elaborates in his book both on principles and applied fields. As an example, I focus on the practical applications of a trinitarian anthropology for the theme of global justice. For one might wonder whether kenotic love does not eliminate or reject the idea of global justice. Cambón shows it does not. The central principles that these trinitarian relationships exemplify are solidarity, freedom, participation, subsidiarity, openness, and equality. The fact that Cambón explicitly refers to participation is remarkable, considering the ambiguous stance of official Catholic social thought on this principle. For example, the only explicit reference to this principle was by the Bishops' Synod in 1971. In its concluding document, *Justice in the World*, the bishops emphasize the need for participation as part of development; mere economic growth is insufficient. This participation should enable countries to "develop their own personalization" (17). Moreover, the bishops add an important nuance by linking participation and the global common good: the distant poor not only should participate in building up their own culture and prosperity but also have a specific contribution to make to the enrichment of the global common good, which makes their participation both valuable and necessary (71). Never has this concept of justice as participation been repeated, at least not in official—papal—Catholic social teachings. Quite the opposite, as there has been a recent tendency within these teachings to separate love and justice, with a consequent prioritization of the former over the latter.[24] Considering these recent developments, it is even more striking that Cambón links a trinitarian anthropology grounded in the notion of kenotic, self-giving love to justice as participation. A similar tendency is present within Catholic social thought springing from more local levels, although it is almost completely absent within official Catholic social teachings; for example, the documents of the Latin American and North American bishops refer to the Trinity to ground their reflections on social life and their analysis of worldwide developments.[25] My hypothesis is that a trinitarian perspective prevents social thought from separating *charity* and justice and enables it to reflect on the relationship between *love* and justice, whereby the former is the motivation to strive for the latter.

When Cambón discusses later the domain in which trinitarian relationships should apply, he first discusses the financial economy and refers again to the challenges of global inequalities and injustices. Particularly as Christians, believing in a Triune God, we should be challenged by these injustices. Cambón is very critical, however, that this challenge does not seem to be taken up by the church. In an earlier passage he wonders which image of God is present in the so-called Christian countries if they allow these inequalities to remain present:

> When one looks at the inequality between the rich and the poor countries and the lack of interest, marginalization and exploitation which characterize their relations, and one furthermore is aware that . . . a majority of the rich countries are countries with a "christian" tradition, it is only logical that one starts to wonder what image of God dominates over there. Every injustice and every form of exploitation are fundamentally caused by a lack of real encounter with the (uni-trinitarian) love of God and by a lack of awareness of its consequences for our daily life. The opinion one holds of God . . . is determining for the type of relationships and, more generally, for the type of society one envisions.[26]

In a later passage he sharply criticizes the hypocrisy of those confessing a trinitarian God but not changing today's economic reality:

> If the statistics of some Latin-American countries show that 2% of the population owns 65% of the land, or that 5% of the population monopolizes the majority of the available resources while 80% lives in poverty and misery, this reveals an existential contrast with trinitarian faith, although it is—in general with sincere intentions—professed publicly and illustrated with religious deeds by policy makers and rich layers of the population. Historical experience shows abundantly that a theoretical orthodoxy can coincide in reality with a practical heresy, which undermines this orthodoxy completely.[27]

Our present economic structures are all but "trinitarianly" organized. In fact, these global realities should not only be considered as "inhuman" but also—for a Christian at least—as "anti-trinitarian" and "completely opposite to God's will for this world."[28] On the other hand, small-scale initiatives, projects, and reflections are important steps in the direction of an incarnated economic trinitarianism, such as the increasing awareness of the need for sustainable development based on participation, respect for diversity, equality, and so on. One should thus not get desperate, because "of one's loving relationship with God-Trinity that supports oneself and history and of one's trinitarian experience in relationship with others which, although on a small scale, proves that another world is not only possible but also credible."[29] So *that they may all be one . . .*

WHY IS A TRINITARIAN ANTHROPOLOGY PARTICULARLY INTERESTING FOR TODAY?

Fifty years after Vatican II, I want to formulate some hypotheses as to why this trinitarian anthropology should be important for Catholic social thought of the next five decades.

(1) Our globalized world calls for a relational anthropology. At the Second Vatican Council the bishops proved to have an awareness of the growing interdependence in the world. Though recognizing the increasing mutual interconnectedness and the global character of the common good, it was at that time, however, impossible to foresee the shape this nascent globalization would take. Today, for example, we are aware not only of the living conditions at the opposite side of the world but also of the extent to which these conditions are the outcome of the living standards of others. Globalization shows us that we *are* related; trinitarian anthropology shows us the appropriate nature of that relation. Since our world is (for better or for worse) interconnected, the only adequate anthropology for twenty-first-century social ethics is a relational anthropology. Due to this interdependence, our world also appears ready for this anthropology. For it is probably not deliberate that heretofore Western theology has not seen the value and importance of a trinitarian anthropology; the context made theologians unaware. The sensitivities of this particular momentum today—with globalization as a primary factor—enables us now to see this in the dynamic of a continuing process. As Cambón argues: "If we see more clearly today that the Trinity stimulates us to achieve more equality, democracy, dialogue, solidarity, participation, etc., this is not only due to the fact that we reflect on the Trinity, but also thanks to the sensitivities and the achievements of our time which stimulate these reflections."[30]

(2) A trinitarian anthropology safeguards us from dualistic thinking. The Trinity not only is interesting as a framework to ground a theological anthropology but also requires us to think differently at all levels. Because of our Greek philosophic heritage, Western minds have been accustomed to thinking a binary, dualistic logic—being or not-being, subject or object, divine or human—but also me or you, where relationality is only a side effect. Even personalism did not avoid this trap in its distinction between persons and non-persons. A trinitarian rationality changes not only how we look to relationships

but also how we look as such; it changes our perspective by bringing relationality to the center of our worldview.

(3) Movements and their spiritualities might become increasingly important in the worldwide church. Although some of them were already founded at the moment of the council, movements within the church after the council clearly boomed. Because of their strong link between spirituality and social practice, they not only embody orthodoxy but also enrich it through their specific account of and emphasis on what is important in our tradition; they give new interpretations to theological frameworks that can illuminate the way to new theological thinking. Moreover, since the official church is undergoing a severe crisis at its institutional level—in terms of its credibility and likelihood to survive, at least in the West—these movements might play an increasing role in the church as it renews and interprets the church's teachings. To what extent this linkage might be desirable and possible for the various movements remains to be seen. I have aimed to show that the church's social teachings might be at least enriched by one such particular movement, namely, the Focolare movement. For "by sharing the new 'spirituality of unity,' Chiara Lubich and her 'people' around the globe have sought to promote and spread a culture of interdependence and universal brotherhood and so offer their contribution to the human family."[31]

In conclusion, what I find intriguing is that, at a time when the church started to rediscover its sources and refer to them by using biblical language and christological arguments (as it did in the council), it not only turned to be more open toward the world but also was heard by that world. This is in contrast to the marked resistance it faced when relying on natural law, which was supposed to be a framework for a secular audience as well (since all human beings were thought able to discern the eternal and natural law on the basis of their rationality). Hence, I am very hopeful for what this specifically Christian trinitarian perspective might add to the world and to the church.

NOTES

1. For a description of the "pre-leonine" and "leonine" period of the papacy, see, for example, Michael Schuck, *That They Be One: The Social Teaching of the Papal Encyclicals, 1740–1989* (Washington, DC: Georgetown University Press, 1991).

2. John XXIII introduces this phrase in *Humanae Salutis* (1961). See Peter Hebblethwaite, "The Popes and Politics: Shifting Patterns of Catholic Social Doctrine," in *Official Catholic Social Teaching, Readings in Moral Theology*

no. 5, ed. Charles E. Curran and Richard A. McCormick (New York: Paulist Press, 1986), 269.

3. Allan Figueroa Deck, "Commentary on *Populorum progressio*," in *Modern Catholic Social Teaching: Commentaries and Interpretations*, ed. Kenneth R. Himes et al. (Washington, DC: Georgetown University Press, 2004), 295.

4. Charles E. Curran, *Catholic Social Teaching, 1891–Present: A Historical, Theological and Ethical Analysis* (Washington, DC: Georgetown University Press, 2002), 54.

5. See also Joe Holland, *Modern Catholic Social Teaching: The Popes Confront the Industrial Age, 1740–1958* (New York: Paulist Press, 2003), 120–23.

6. John E. Kelly, "The Influence of Aquinas' Natural Law Theory on the Principle of 'Corporatism' in the Thought of Leo XIII and Pius XI," in *Things Old and New: Catholic Social Teaching Revisited*, ed. Francis P. McHugh and Samuel M. Natale, 104–43 (Lanham, MD: Catholic University Press, 1993), 106.

7. For a "dynamic" notion of essences, see Bernard Hoose, "Natural Law, Acts and Persons," in *Method and Catholic Moral Theology: The Ongoing Reconstruction,* ed. Todd A. Salzman (Omaha, NE: Creighton University Press, 1999), 46. For a "revisionist" interpretation of natural law, see Stephen J. Pope, "Natural Law and Christian Ethics," in *The Cambridge Companion to Christian Ethics*, ed. Robin Gill, 77–95 (Cambridge: Cambridge University Press, 2001), 89–90. For a "teleological" interpretation, see Curran, *Catholic Social Teaching, 1891–Present*, 82.

8. Louis Janssens, "Personalist Morals," in *Louvain Studies* 3 (1970): 5–16.

9. See, for example, Todd A. Salzman and Michael G. Lawler, *The Sexual Person: Toward a Renewed Sexual Anthropology* (Washington, DC: Georgetown University Press, 2003), 103.

10. See ibid., for example.

11. Schuck clarifies how the popes before the council "acknowledged the elevated status of human beings as the *imago Dei*, [but] this is not a claim around which their social teaching revolves" (*That They Be One*, 179). By starting its anthropology and the description of the dignity of the human person with this explicit link, the council fathers can be said to use the *imago Dei* in a paradigmatic and programmatic manner.

12. Benedict XVI, *Caritas in Veritate*, no. 54. Considering the encyclical's reflections on the economy of communion, an initiative of the Focolare movement, I wonder whether this paragraph might also be inspired by this spirituality.

13. Karl Rahner, *The Trinity* (New York: Crossroad, 2003. See also Stanley J. Grenz, *Rediscovering the Truine God: The Trinity in Contemporary Theology* (Minneapolis, MN: Augsburg Fortress Press, 2004), 64.

14. Chiara Lubich, *Essential Writings: Spirituality, Dialogue, Culture* (Hyde Park: New City Press, 2007), 16, 27, 28.

15. Piero Coda, "Introduction," in Lubich, *Essential Writings*, xx.

16. Lubich, *Essential Writings*, 3.

17. See Enrique Cambón, *Trinità: Modello sociale*, Contributti di theologia 25 (Rome: Città Nuova, 1995). English translation forthcoming: Enrique Cambón, *Trinity: Model and Society* (Hyde Park, NY: New City Press, 2013).

18. Ibid., 22.

19. Ibid., 29.

20. Canbón describes five dichotomies (person-relation; unity in diversity; total-total; altruism-reciprocity; self-emptying–fullness), but I believe that they tend to overlap and thus can be reduced to three.

21. See Cambón, *Trinità*, 44–46.

22. Ibid., 30.

23. Ibid., 63.

24. For an analysis of this development within the official teachings, see Ellen Van Stichel, "Global Justice as Participation," in *Catholic Social Conscience: Reflection and Action on Catholic Social Teaching,* ed. Keith Chapell and Francis Davis (Leominster, UK: Gracewing, 2011), 21–44.

25. See, respectively, Third General Conference of the Latin American Episcopate, *Final Document: Evangelization in Latin-America: Present and Future* (1979), nos. 209–19; United States Conference of Catholic Bishops, *Economic Justice for All: Pastoral Letter on Catholic Social Teaching and the U.S. Economy* (1986), no. 64.

26. Cambón, *Trinità,* 63.

27. Ibid., 115.

28. Ibid.

29. Ibid., 117.

30. Ibid., 40.

31. Brendan Purcell et al., "Editor's Preface," in Lubich, *Essential Writings*, xxvi.

The Future of Catholic Public Theology

Mediating the Church and the World in Pluralistic Societies

GONZALO VILLAGRÁN, SJ

This essay, presented in the context of the fifty years since the beginning of the Second Vatican Council, will not address particular ethical issues that require the attention and response of the church today but will deal with a prior foundational issue: How should Catholics approach the public when we want to share our theological-ethical views on a social issue, given the societies in which we live? It may sound abstract, but it is a question of fundamental importance to Catholics today, given the tremendous growth in moral, cultural, and religious pluralism.

In this essay I first present the main traits of the Second Vatican Council's understanding of the relationship between Christian faith and society. I then present the development of (Catholic) public theology in the United States, which developed out of the council. Finally, I suggest the application of this "style" of theology to other contexts and what this means for the development of this style of theology.

THE CHURCH AND THE WORLD
IN THE SECOND VATICAN COUNCIL

The Second Vatican Council's documents reflect a general attitude of openness and dialogue from the Catholic Church toward the world. Jesuit historian John O'Malley sees this new view of the relationship between the church and the world as the main element of the spirit of the council. This new view is expressed, for him, in the inviting literary style of the council's documents.[1] We can trace the theological roots of this new understanding by approaching the pastoral constitution *Gaudium et Spes* (GS), the document that directly deals with the relationship between the church and the world.

As the Spanish theologian Juan Luis Ruiz de la Peña asserts, one of the major dogmatic affirmations of the Second Vatican Council is the christological assertion of Christ as "the perfect man" *(homus perfectus)*[2] in *Gaudium et Spes* no. 22.[3] This christological assertion implies an acknowledgment of the necessary integration between the natural and supernatural dimensions of the human being. The council's view has consequences at many levels in terms of a call for a renewed awareness of created reality's enormous value and integrity,[4] as well as of its fulfillment in Christ. In the case of human beings, there is a preeminence of Christ in any effort to understand them because of his redemption of humanity.[5] This explains why the council, in the decree *Optatum Totius*, asks to put the mystery of Christ and scripture at the center of moral theology (OT, 16). This preeminence of Christ is integrated with the traditional Catholic respect for human nature, because nature is assumed but not annulled in Christ and thus "has been raised up to a divine dignity in our respect too" (GS, 22). Therefore, in contrast with a pre–Vatican II view of nature and grace as compartmentalized, the council expresses the relationship between divine and human reality, between natural and supernatural, in a way that integrates them without diminishing created reality's integrity or Christ's redemptive work.

These christological and anthropological perspectives determine the council's understanding of church-world relationships because these relationships are ultimately a corollary to our views on the human being. Human nature is necessarily social and political (GS, 25); the social and political dimensions, as other earthly realities, have an autonomy of their own (GS, 36); human dignity leads us to honor human conscience and liberty (GS, 16–17) and to respect and value social pluralism (GS, 28). The council sees modern societies as enlightened by Jesus Christ, who helps them to reach their major ideals. Jesus Christ's life, as reflected in revelation, enlightens our social life (GS, 32), no matter how plural it is. The church, the sacrament of unity with God, sheds the light of Christ on humanity (LG, 1), helping to structure the human community as a function of the Lord's will (GS, 42). But because it accompanies humanity in its struggles throughout history (GS, 40), the church can also receive help from the human community (GS, 44). Therefore, the relationship between the church and the world, interpenetrative and reciprocal (GS, 40), reflects the council's understanding of the natural-supernatural relationship.

Gaudium et Spes stresses, thus, two poles that should be integrated: the priority of Christ as key to understanding created reality, and the autonomy and integrity of created reality itself. These two poles imply, in the field of social ethics, the Christian faith and the church, on the one hand, and social realities, on the other. These two poles require a complex and fine mediation in order to harmonize them.

Because the constitution's role was not to develop a systematic theology, we should understand its assertions as a path for theologians to tread. The council asserts the close integration of these two poles without developing further this integration. Since then, theologians have tried to develop concrete ways to mediate these two poles as a function of their contexts. Therefore, different answers have been developed in different contexts to respond to this issue; political theology and liberation theology are part of this effort. In the United States, a society marked by moral, cultural, and religious pluralism, Catholic public theology represents this effort in the field of theological ethics.

PUBLIC THEOLOGY IN THE UNITED STATES

The Protestant Origins of Public Theology in the United States

Public theology is an answer to a particular concern among US theologians. While the reception of Vatican II was occurring in the Catholic Church in the 1970s, in the United States there existed a common concern among scholars of religion about the strong claim that religion should be considered a private issue as an answer to the increasing social pluralism. This claim is present in most Western societies up to the present day. One of the first to voice this concern was the Lutheran historian Martin Marty. Reacting to Robert Bellah's concept of civil religion and inspired by the work of Reinhold Niebuhr, Marty suggested that some particular religions may assume more direct influence on the public forum for the sake of the common good through some kind of "public theology."[6] Instead of reducing all religions to some kind of minimum common denominator or removing them from public life, a public theology may be the best answer to a situation of social pluralism. This reaction spread over different denominations and theological positions, and today we can find different scholars claiming to do public theology from different angles and origins.

Harold Breitenberg's very comprehensive article on public theology reflects the heterogeneity of the set of theologians who affirm they are doing public theology.[7] This heterogeneity of approaches requires that we consider public theology as consisting more in a style of theology than in a school or method.[8] Public theology is, then, theological reflection on social issues rooted in a particular theological tradition that aims to speak publicly in a pluralistic society in ways that are intelligible for all societal actors. Breitenberg speaks of "theologically informed discourses about public issues, addressed to the church, synagogue, mosque, temple, or other religious body, as well as the larger public or publics, argued in ways that can be evaluated and judged, by publicly available warrants and criteria."[9] Breitenberg's definition stresses then two elements in public theology: a certain presence of theological insights and publicness in the discourse.

Understood like this, it is possible to include under the umbrella of the term *public theology* a wide array of theologians interested in social issues in spite of the plurality of their methods. However, we can be more concrete in our approach to public theology. Paying close attention to the American context, we can identify a unique method of theology in the particular way that US Catholic theologians appropriated the insights behind public theology. Within the Catholic tradition, this method represents an incarnation of the Second Vatican Council's insights in the US pluralistic context.

The Catholic Variant of Public Theology

American Catholic social thought until the Second World War was not very relevant because of the minority status of the Catholic Church. It focused not so much on social reform but mostly in helping to Americanize poor Catholic immigrants. It was suspicious of any social change and therefore tended to focus on personal conversion.[10] After the Second World War the situation changed: on the one hand, there was a much better integration of Catholics in America, symbolized by the election of John F. Kennedy as president; on the other hand, the work of John Courtney Murray and the Second Vatican Council showed the full compatibility between Catholicism and American values.[11] This empowered the Catholic Church to have a stronger public voice in society. This voice was first channeled through the traditional natural law argument, as witnessed by the work of John Courtney Murray.

Nevertheless, the growing social pluralism, which made the traditional understanding of the natural law argument more difficult to agree upon, and the council's call to develop a more scripturally based theology (OT, 16) showed the need of a new way of arguing in American Catholic social thought. The idea of a public theology was then well received in the Catholic intellectual milieu.[12] Since 1976, Catholic theologians like John Coleman and David Hollenbach have explicitly sought to develop a Catholic understanding of this idea of theology speaking publicly on social issues.[13] These Catholic authors developed this idea by bringing in other important sources of modern Catholic theology. These new sources are the insights of the Second Vatican Council, the thought of John Courtney Murray (who had introduced the complementary term *public philosophy*),[14] and official Catholic social teaching.[15] The idea of a public theology became, for many Catholic theologians in the pluralistic US society, a very appropriate way to mediate between Christian faith and secular social issues, with the integration and distinction between divine revelation and human knowledge that the council demanded. On the one hand, the preeminence of Christ for understanding the human being was reflected in taking the Christian symbols and narratives as starting points for the reflection on social issues. On the other hand, the differentiation and autonomy of created realities was reflected in the effort to convey the religious inspiration of our discourse in a public way, that is to say, in a way that is understandable and persuasive to a pluralistic society.

David Tracy developed a theoretical framework to sustain this approach to theology in his 1981 book *The Analogical Imagination*. Tracy proposed a theological paradigm of "mutually critical correlations between an interpretation of the event (and the traditions and forms mediating the event in the present) and an interpretation of the situation (and the traditions and forms mediating that reality)."[16] The term *correlation* denotes a correspondence between two series of data, two poles in this case. Thus, one pole of Tracy's critical correlation would be the event of Jesus Christ, that is to say, Jesus Christ as the here-and-now manifestation of God's own self as he is mediated through scripture and tradition.[17] The other pole would be what Tracy calls the human situation, that is to say, the interpretation of contemporary human existence, an interpretation that includes socioeconomic circumstances.[18] Tracy understands this correlation as taking the form of an analogy, that is to say, to discover, beyond the actual differences, ordered relationships of the self and the world to a focal point, God.

This rather simple scheme has become a major tool to think through the relationship between faith and social realities inside the public theology tradition. This scheme is ultimately hermeneutical because its focus is the necessary interpretation of the two poles of the correlation, the meanings of which are not univocal. These interpretations are then put into dialogue in a way similar to a human conversation. Thus, Tracy understands his method of critical correlation as the back-and-forth movement of a conversation, a joint reflection upon the main human questions and concerns that are the subject matter of the theological inquiry.[19] The correlation is mutually critical because we interpret the religious symbols from a particular human situation, and we interpret the human situation in light of particular religious symbols.[20]

This conversation is possible because the religious pole of the correlation is intelligible for any person, even if that person does not belong to the particular religious tradition. Tracy identifies some of the religious symbols and narratives in which the Christ-event is interpreted as classics. The term *classics* is applied by Tracy to "certain expressions of the human spirit [that] disclose a compelling truth about our lives."[21] In saying this, he is asserting that we experience them as teaching us new dimensions and nuances of human life, which we recognize as true. *Classics* are therefore addressed to everyone and are public. Because the effect of an encounter with a classic, either cultural or religious, happens primarily at the level of experience, classics need to be interpreted in order to be shared. Therefore, Tracy affirms in *The Analogical Imagination* that "the theologian's task must be primarily hermeneutical," that is, his role is to interpret and convey the experience of the encounter with the religious classic.[22]

We may consider Tracy's paradigm as a method with which to develop a "fundamental political theology" in service to the public theology effort and in answer to the previous request formulated by David Hollenbach.[23] Various Catholic social ethicists have applied Tracy's method to different situations, giving it the practical approach that Tracy lacks.[24] Tracy's paradigm has been thus fleshed out and applied to actual situations by these other public theologians. The combination of these two efforts represents the particular way in which US Catholics, in the light of the concerns of their society, have implemented the intuitions of the Second Vatican Council.

A specific example of this public theology is the 1986 document of the US bishops entitled *Economic Justice for All*. This document is the fruit of the work of some of the major Catholic public theologians of the day. This document first presents biblical considerations, which it then interprets for society through ethical principles. Drawing from these principles the document then proposes possible policies for particular problems like unemployment, poverty, food and agriculture, and the role of the United States in the global economy. The document describes the goal of the bishops as proposing prudential judgments which are the fruit of interaction between moral values, based on Christian symbols, and empirical data (134). This document thus contains the conversation that Catholic public theology was proposing between Christian symbols and narratives, on the one hand, and the social situation, on the other. Moreover, the way in which the document was drafted (asking for public feedback at different moments), and the way in which it was conveyed to society (presenting it directly in different social forums), are probably the best expressions of the public character of theology that the document reflects.

Since the publication of *Economic Justice for All*, public theologians have continued to employ this particular theological method in their approach to social realities.[25] However, the presence of this current has been more discreet because, on the one hand, the Catholic Church's magisterium has looked for forms of argumentation that offer a stronger certainty,[26] and on the other hand, public theology has been confronted by an alternative theological model, which wants to be more radical and prophetic.[27] This alternative model springs partly from the work of the philosopher Alisdair MacIntyre and has been developed by authors like Stanley Hauerwas and John Milbank.

In spite of these challenges, public theology, perhaps incorporating some new insights, continues to be a privileged way to understand the relationship between Christian faith and social issues. Public theology reminds us of an important dimension of theology that was being forgotten because of the process of privatization: the public role of theology beyond the community of believers. The threat of a privatization of religion helped Catholics rediscover this public role of theology. And this is truly a rediscovery, since there are other examples in the Catholic tradition of a similar effort in the midst of parallel situations of pluralism dating back at least to Augustine in his letters to non-Christian Romans on issues related to the common good.[28]

Public theology, therefore, is this effort to develop a theology that, while remaining a discourse about God, is intelligible for and addressed to every member of a religiously pluralistic society. The goal of this discourse is to contribute to the common good of society. For Catholics, this effort becomes a mediation between the two poles that *Gaudium et Spes* stressed—the primacy of Christ and the autonomy of earthly realities—in a context marked primarily by moral and religious pluralism.

PUBLIC THEOLOGY IN OTHER CONTEXTS

Public theology is not foreign to other cultural contexts outside the United States. Understood in an inclusive sense, as Breitenberg's definition suggests, we could consider other non-US Catholic authors who have tried to enlighten social issues from theological grounds as public theologians, even if they have never used the term. Among these authors we can include Paul Valadier in France and Olegario González de Cardedal in Spain.[29]

However, the present historical circumstances make even more interesting the insights that public theology has to offer. The religious and moral pluralism that has long shaped US society, and which became more politically relevant in the 1960s and 1970s, is today common throughout the world. The effects of increased migration, the phenomenon of globalization, the revolution in media and information technologies, as well as the extended presence of non-Western cultures in the global forum, have increased immensely the pluralism of human societies at the beginning of the twenty-first century. Fifty years after Vatican II, a growing moral and religious pluralism can be considered a main trait of contemporary human societies. This trait of the present global situation makes the insights of public theology developed in the US context relevant for many other nations. Accordingly, there are many studies of public theology that try to adapt the methods developed in the United States to other environments like India or different countries in Europe. Felix Wilfred's 2010 book, *Asian Public Theology,* is an example of this expansion.[30] In these new contexts public theology may need to address new questions, for example, how should Christians share their views on healthcare in a country as religiously pluralistic as India?[31] Or in what ways can we share our Christian understanding of the option for the poor in order to renew the welfare societies of now pluralistic Western Europe?[32] Or how can we reach a common understanding of the dignity and role of women in a society which comprises unbelievers, Christians, and Muslims?[33]

In all these cases Catholics are developing concrete ways to mediate between the Christian faith and the present social challenges in the integrated but differentiated way that *Gaudium et Spes* suggested in light of the present fact of social pluralism.

However, when approaching other cultural contexts, public theology is confronted with new challenges that were not necessarily present in the United States. For example, a public theology in the religiously pluralistic Indian contexts requires a much more developed framework to include the necessary interreligious dialogue.[34] Moreover, in secularized European societies, public theology should overcome a widespread rejection of the presence of religion in public life. This rejection in some cases is well embedded in the culture, as in the case of the French understanding of laicity.[35] When public theology is taken out of its home in the US context and brought into foreign lands, we perceive some dimensions that may be underdeveloped and that may need to be thought through.[36]

Concretely, the present debate between a public theology approach and a more radical-prophetic one to social issues can be enlightened when approached from a particular context: secularized European society. The point of development in public theology I want to suggest is the concern for the identity of the subject and the community elaborating public theology.

After public theology appeared in the 1970s and early 1980s, Alasdair MacIntyre published his *After Virtue* and Stanley Hauerwas started to develop MacIntyre's intuitions theologically. The work of these two authors represents one of the major trends in contemporary theological ethics and has many times been seen as opposed to public theology. The theologians in this line of thought focus their reflection on Christian identity and Christian community as an answer to the dangers of fragmentation they identify in modern pluralism. When confronted with this current, public theology's main asset is its willingness and ability to address society outside the church while keeping the Christian identity of the message. However, I believe we should learn something from this other theological current: the subject that argues is as important as the way of arguing itself.[37] Especially in contexts of strong secularism like European societies, public theologians can be accused of being very much concerned with the way they address the other but forgetting about the identity of the one who dialogues. This way, they may seem to lose their own footing in the dialogue and be unable to reaffirm Christian faith in secularist contexts. An example of such a critique is the one expressed by the Spanish theologian Daniel Izuzquiza. That author, speaking about Christians wanting to promote more social concern in political forums, puts those Christians on guard against highly sophisticated technical discussion that can blur the Christian inspiration. He then invites them to create actual alternative styles of living clearly inspired by the Christian faith.[38]

The strong need to clarify the root sources of personal and communal identity, which the European secularized contexts suppose, helps us to find resources already present in the public theology approach to face this critique. Ultimately, public theology is more than a useful method to participate in public discussions on social issues. Properly developed, public theology's approach entails a strong claim about ourselves: ultimately, we only get to know ourselves by opening to others. Our identity is shaped by our relationships with others, including the stranger. The discovery of our identity ultimately requires our reaching out beyond our own community.[39] We can find this claim very clearly in David Tracy's thought. Tracy, in the conclusion

of *The Analogical Imagination*, speaks of a back-and-forth movement between self-respect and self-exposure when approaching the
other. We can understand this movement as an articulation of two
different elements in Christian life: identity and dialogue.[40] He also
speaks of how the communities and traditions to which we belong,
whether religious or non-religious, shape our pre-understandings and
confront our interpretations of the religious classics we encounter.
Therefore, Tracy agrees with Hauerwas upon the role of Christian
communities and traditions in shaping our Christian life. However,
Tracy shows how these pre-understandings and communal interpretations necessarily have to be interpreted again by each Christian as
he or she encounters other persons who think differently and other
communities with different pre-understandings.[41] Insights like these
reveal that Christian identity is based not only on the intramural life
of the church but also on outward dialogue and encounter with the
other. Christian identity is also public.

Public theology's great insight about the publicness of theology is
an important intuition about the way to mediate between Christian
faith and social realities as Vatican II called Catholics to do. It offers
a concrete method for integrating, on the one hand, the priority of
Christ and revelation in order to understand the human being and,
on the other hand, the autonomy and value of created realities and
human society. This public understanding of Christian identity I am
proposing here (putting the encounter with the other at the center of
Christian identity) would extend the way public theology mediates
between faith and social realities from the way Catholics may argue
and dialogue with others to a foundational understanding of the human being. Such a public understanding of Christian identity honors
the concern of the radical-prophetic current in contemporary theology
for the Christian identity of the subject. But a Christian public identity
integrates also into Christian identity the dignity and autonomy of all
created realities, including human nature, through their influence in
shaping that identity. This other pole of the council's great intuition
many times is not sufficiently present in the radical-prophetic current.
In accordance with the critical-correlational scheme, this development
would simply require taking into consideration what the historical circumstances of more secularized contexts pose for public theologians.[42]

Public theology, as a way to present theological ideas in pluralistic
societies, embodies the understanding of the relationship between
church and society that the Second Vatican Council proposed. As
public theology implies this understanding of the church-society
relationship, it also implies a view of the human being, what I have

called Christian public identity. By unfolding this public identity we would continue to develop Vatican II's insights, particularly *Gaudium et Spes* no. 22's assertion that Christ, the Word of God, sheds light on the mystery of the human being. It is desirable that Christian symbols and texts be the source of our understanding of the human being, but it is also desirable that they be able to address every human being in an understandable way. We need them to be public.

NOTES

1. See John W. O'Malley, *What Happened at Vatican II* (Cambridge, MA: The Belknap Press of Harvard University Press, 2008), 47ff. James F. Keenan identifies this style particularly with Bernard Häring's style of theology ("Bernard Häring's Influence on American Catholic Moral Theology," *Journal of Moral Theology* 1, no. 1 [2012]: 23–42).

2. The official English translation of *Gaudium et Spes* does not use inclusive language. The original Latin term *homo* refers to both genders.

3. See Juan Luis Ruíz de la Peña, *Imagen de Dios: Antropología Teológica Fundamental* (Santander: Sal Terrae, 1996), 186. Massimo Faggioli asserts that the constitution *Sacrosanctum Concilium* is the lens through which we should read the council in order to get its full theological meaning. We can, therefore, find the roots of *Gaudium et Spes* no. 22 in the centrality of Christ for liturgy as stated in *Sacrosanctum Concilium* nos. 5 and 7. See Massimo Faggioli, "*Sacrosanctum Concilium* and the Meaning of Vatican II," *Theological Studies* 71, no. 2 (2010): 437–52.

4. "He thought with a human mind, acted by human choice, and loved with a human heart. Born of the Virgin Mary, He has truly been made one of us, like us in all things except sin" (GS, 22). In the same sense we can understand the affirmation of the autonomy of earthly realities (GS, 36).

5. "Only in the mystery of the incarnate Word does the mystery of man take on light. . . . To the sons of Adam He restores the divine likeness which had been disfigured from the first sin onwards" (GS no. 22). Cf. Peña, *Imagen de Dios*, 186.

6. See Martin E. Marty, "Two Kinds of Civil Religion," in *American Civil Religion*, ed. Russell E. Richey and Donald G. Jones, 139–57 (New York: Harper and Row, 1974).

7. See E. Harold Breitenberg, Jr., "To Tell the Truth: Will the Real Public Theology Please Stand Up?" *Journal of the Society of Christian Ethics* 23, no. 2 (2003): 55–96. Breitenberg highlights four authors: two are of Lutheran origins (Thiemann and Benne), one is Catholic (Tracy), and one comes from a Catholic background but has more recently adopted a more secular approach (Cady). See David Tracy, *The Analogical Imagination: Christian Theology and*

the Culture of Pluralism (New York: Crossroad, 1991); Ronald F. Thiemann, *Constructing a Public Theology: The Church in a Pluralistic Culture* (Louisville, KY: Westminster/John Knox Press, 1991); Robert Benne, *The Paradoxical Vision: A Public Theology for the Twenty-First Century* (Minneapolis, MN: Fortress Press, 1995); and Linell Elizabeth Cady, *Religion, Theology, and American Public Life* (Albany: State University of New York Press, 1993).

8. I use the term *style* as John O'Malley uses it to identify the spirit of the Second Vatican Council (see O'Malley, *What Happened at Vatican II*, 47ff.).

9. Breitenberg, "To Tell the Truth," 66.

10. See Charles E. Curran, *American Catholic Social Ethics: Twentieth-Century Approaches* (Notre Dame, IN: University of Notre Dame Press, 1982), 20–25.

11. See ibid., 172–75.

12. "In the contemporary context of the United States, the dominant stance in Catholic social ethics remains a 'public church' model, albeit with differing methodologies and a degree of internal pluralism." Kristin E. Heyer, "Bridging the Divide in Contemporary US Catholic Social Ethics," *Theological Studies* 66, no. 2 (2005): 401.

13. See John A. Coleman, "Vision and Praxis in American Theology: Orestes Brownson, John A. Ryan, and John Courtney Murray," *Theological Studies* 37, no. 1 (1976): 3–40; David Hollenbach, "Public Theology in America: Some Questions for Catholicism after John Courtney Murray," *Theological Studies* 37, no. 2 (1976): 290–303.

14. John Courtney Murray, *We Hold These Truths: Catholic Reflections on the American Proposition*, ed. Walter J. Burghardt, with a critical introduction by Peter A. Lawler (Lanham, MD: Rowman and Littlefield, 2005).

15. In fact, some parts of modern Catholic social teaching can be considered examples of public theology in themselves, for example, the principle of solidarity as a way to propose Christian charity to society (see John Paul II, *Sollicitudo Rei Socialis*, no. 40).

16. Tracy, *The Analogical Imagination*, 406. Tracy struggled at some point with critiques coming from more practical theologies on his approach; see ibid., 69ff. In later books Tracy will fully assert his hermeneutical approach to the issues; see David Tracy, *Plurality and Ambiguity: Hermeneutics, Religion, Hope* (San Francisco: Harper and Row, 1987), 3ff.; and idem, *Dialogue with the Other: The Inter-religious Dialogue* (Grand Rapids, MI: Eerdmans, 1990), 3ff.

17. Tracy, *The Analogical Imagination*, 234ff.

18. Ibid., 340ff. In his understanding of theology as a critical correlation and of the human situation, Tracy is very much inspired by Paul Tillich (see Paul Tillich, *Systematic Theology*, vol. 1 (Chicago: University of Chicago Press, 1973), 3–68.

19. Also see Tracy, *The Analogical Imagination*, 421ff. The central role of conversation became even more important in his following book, *Plurality and Ambiguity*. Cf. Tracy, *The Analogical Imagination*, 101.

20. Tracy, *The Analogical Imagination,* 58–62.

21. Ibid., 108.

22. Ibid., 67.

23. David Hollenbach, "Editor's Conclusion: A Fundamental Political Theology," in "Theology and Philosophy in Public: A Symposium on John Courtney Murray's Unfinished Agenda," *Theological Studies* 40, no. 4 (1979): 713–15.

24. We can include here the work of John Coleman, Michael and Kenneth Himes, and David Hollenbach. For example, Hollenbach's 2002 book *The Common Good and Christian Ethics* can be seen as a critical correlation between the Catholic understanding of the concept of common good and the present situation of moral and religious pluralism (Cambridge, UK: Cambridge University Press, 2002). See also David Hollenbach, "The Common Good Revisited," *Theological Studies* 50, no. 1 (1989): 70–94; John A. Coleman, *An American Strategic Theology* (Mahwah, NJ: Paulist Press, 1982); Michael J. Himes and Kenneth R. Himes, *Fullness of Faith: The Public Significance of Theology* (Mahwah, NJ: Paulist Press, 1993).

25. Major works of public theology have been produced after 1986, for example, Hollenbach's *The Common Good and Christian Ethics* in 2002.

26. This shift toward a greater certainty, and therefore toward a natural law argument, is evident in John Paul II's pontificate with the publication of the encyclicals *Veritatis Splendor* (1993) and *Evangelium Vitae* (1995).

27. Kristin Heyer studies the two theological currents in social ethics, looking for relations and similarities between them. See Heyer, "Bridging the Divide in Contemporary US Catholic Social Ethics."

28. See Augustine, Letters 90ff., in *Augustine: Political Writings*, ed. E. Margaret Atkins and Robert Dodaro, 1–21 (Cambridge, UK: Cambridge University Press, 2001).

29. See Paul Valadier, *Détresse du politique, force du religieux* (Paris: Seuil, 2007); and Olegario González de Cardedal, *España por pensar: Ciudadanía hispánica y confesión católica* (Salamanca: Ediciones Universidad Salamanca, 1985).

30. Felix Wilfred, *Asian Public Theology: Critical Concerns in Challenging Times* (Delhi: ISPCK, 2010); Patrick Gnanapragasam, "Public Theology in the Indian Context: A Note on Its Prospects and Challenges," presented at the Conference of Catholic Theological Institutions, Bangalore, India, 2011; Gerrit de Kruijf, "The Challenge of a Public Theology," in *Theology Between Church, University, and Society*, ed. M. E. Brinkman, 139–48 (Assen: Van Gorcum, 2003).

31. For a glimpse on this debate, see Jayati Ghosh, "'Publicness' of Health," *Frontline: India's National Magazine* (September 29, 2009). Available on the frontlineonnet.com website.

32. One good example is the advocacy work of several Catholic non-governmental organizations (NGOs) against reducing healthcare coverage for undocumented immigrants. See María Sahuquillo, "Las organizaciones católicas, contra el 'apartheid sanitario,'" *EL PAÍS* (June 10, 2012), available on the sociedad.elpais.com website.

33. Particularly interesting is the reflection produced by women from inside the Islamic tradition in order to develop their proper understanding of feminism. See, for example, "International Congress on Islamic Feminism" (2008), available on the feminismeislamic.org website.

34. "Asian Public Theology will be one that will be inherently interreligious in nature" (Wilfred, *Asian Public Theology*, xi).

35. For a good critical approach to the origins of the particular laicity model of the French republican tradition, see Valadier, *Détresse du politique, force du religieux*, 110ff.

36. For example, a more historical understanding of pluralism, a more robust reflection on its connection with interreligious dialogue, and a better articulation with the natural law tradition.

37. Kristin Heyer, discussing George Lindbeck's views, has reflected on the way the critical-correlational approach has introduced a greater concern for identity ("How Does Theology Go Public? Rethinking the Debate Between David Tracy and George Lindbeck," *Political Theology 5*, no. 3 [2004]: 307–27; see also Heyer, "Bridging the Divide in Contemporary US Catholic Social Ethics").

38. Daniel Izuzquiza, "De la liberación a la resistencia: Una mirada a la teología de la liberación desde el corazón del imperio," *Revista de Fomento Social 59*, no. 235 (2004): 544.

39. For example, "Jesuit identity is relational; it grows in and through our diversities of culture, nationalities, and languages, enriching and challenging us" ("General Congregation 35 of the Society of Jesus," Decree 2, Paragraph 19, in John Padberg, *Jesuit Life and Mission Today: The Decrees of the 31st–35th General Congregations of the Society of Jesus* [Saint Louis: The Institute of Jesuit Sources, 2009]: 740–41). For similar reflections, see Paul Valadier, *Jésus-Christ ou Dionysos: La foi chrétienne en confrontation avec Nietzsche* (Paris: Desclée, 2004), 18.

40. "With the self-respect of that self-identity, the Christian should be released to the self-transcendence of genuine other-regard by a willing self-exposure to and in the contemporary situation" (Tracy, *The Analogical Imagination*, 446).

41. Ibid., 115ff.

42. I believe my proposal of a Christian public identity goes in the same direction that Kristin Heyer suggests for the development of public theology in the future. She writes, "A more fully theological and fully public approach will help to avoid a false opposition between charity and structural justice and between embodiment and advocacy" ("Bridging the Divide in Contemporary US Catholic Social Ethics," 440).

What Does *Gaudium et Spes* Have to Say toward Contemporary Issues of Racism?

KRISTA STEVENS

In *American Catholic Revolution*, Mark Massa compares the Catholic Church in the years between the Council of Trent and the Second Vatican Council to Miss Havisham, the jilted widow in Charles Dickens's *Great Expectations*. Just as Miss Havisham withdrew into a world where time stopped at 8:40 a.m., the Tridentine Church hunkered down in a "hermetically sealed brand of Counter-Reformation belief and practice that had defined Roman Catholicism for four centuries."[1] John XXIII's call for Vatican II put into motion the council that would set the church's clocks moving once again. Leaving an indelible mark on Catholic identity and practice, the council, in the words of Gary Wills, "let out the dirty little secret . . . that the *church changes*."[2] The most profound effect of the council, then, may not have been changes in liturgy or authority but the realization that "the gospel message should be understood and proclaimed in a sea of history that was now seen to touch and shape everything."[3]

Against this background of change, a question must be asked. If the church—and history—can and does change, what contributions can the Second Vatican Council make to contemporary questions of justice and Catholic social thought? Can Catholic social thought, drawing on the insights gained during Vatican II, offer a unique perspective to pressing contemporary ethical questions? Specifically, the goal of this chapter, then, is to apply these questions to the continuing and increasingly complex problem of racism in the United States.

THE PROBLEM OF RACISM AND THE CATHOLIC CHURCH

First, the need for the church to address racism in a more profound and explicit way is clear. To quote black Catholic priest Bryan Massingale,

"The conclusion is obvious and inescapable: the moral aspects of race relations have not been, and still are not, a major concern . . . of American Catholics."[4] Massingale's quotation is representative of recent critiques leveled against the US Catholic Church for failing to address adequately the systemic reality of racism still pervasive in US society. Massingale and others accuse the Catholic Church of being entrenched in and reflecting a history of white privilege and inhospitality to those deemed "other" by race. These critiques often are bolstered by historical examples of the church's acting to maintain the status quo of white privilege by accepting (and sometimes contributing to) the existence and the effects of racism, both within the church and in society at large.[5]

At the same time, however, these critics note that, first, the Catholic Church *does* condemn racism, and second, the church *does* have the tools and resources necessary to analyze, diagnose, and enact remedies for racial justice. Modern church teachings on social sin and solidarity with the poor *should* equip the church to offer an adequate response to racism. Over more than a century of modern social teaching, the official church has developed various themes and concepts relevant to social analysis, action, and solidarity.[6] However, with respect to the issue of race and racism, the US Catholic Church has failed to use these resources either to analyze or to condemn racism in any systematic or effective way. The United States Catholic Bishops' 1979 pastoral letter "Brothers and Sisters to Us" took tentative steps toward identifying racism as a structural problem comprising not just interpersonal relations but economic, political, cultural, and educational issues. "To struggle against [racism]," this document contends, "demands an equally radical transformation, in our minds and hearts as well as in the structure of our society."

Nonetheless, a decade later the US Bishops' Committee on Black Catholics, marking the tenth anniversary of "Brothers and Sisters to Us," declares: "The promulgation of the pastoral on racism was soon forgotten by all but a few. A survey . . . revealed a pathetic, anemic response from archdioceses and dioceses around the country. . . . The pastoral on racism had made little or no impact on the majority of Catholics in the United States."[7] Furthermore, Massingale points out that "Brothers and Sisters to Us" was the last pastoral on racism written in the name of the US bishops as a whole. He goes on to survey a variety of statements released by individual US bishops on racism, concluding that "these episcopal statements . . . implicitly convey an understanding that reduces racism to demonstrable manifestations of personal prejudice. Substantively, these prelates understand racism as the racially pejorative beliefs of individuals that are expressed in interpersonal actions and omissions."[8] With few exceptions, over the last thirty years, the church's treatment of racism has focused on the individual, with racism understood to be a display of person-to-person animosity that can be overcome through moral suasion and personal conversion. According to this view, if you change people's hearts, you will eradicate racism.

While there can be no doubt that these person-to-person displays of individual bigotry and hatred do exist, if we are to talk about justice that is truly *social*, it seems that the US bishops are missing the mark. To draw again from Bryan Massingale, twenty-first century racism goes well beyond individual manifestations of harmful and negative acts toward a person of color. Instead, racism needs to be understood as a

> *cultural* phenomenon, that is, a way of interpreting human color differences that pervades the collective convictions, conventions, and practices of American life. Racism functions as an ethos, as the animating spirit of US society, which lives on despite observable changes and assumes various incarnations in different historical situations.[9]

Recognizing that definitions of culture are manifold and complex, Massingale goes on to make four observations about culture: Cultures are "*shared* or group realities. . . . Cultures are *learned* communal beliefs and values. . . . Cultures are *formative*, that is they shape the personal identities of a community's members. . . . A group's set of meanings, values, and beliefs about life are expressed *symbolically*."[10]

Crucially, given Massingale's presentation of culture, if racism functions as a culture, then racism functions as a "set of shared beliefs and assumptions that undergirds the economic, social, and political disparities experienced by different racial groups." Furthermore, racism as culture "provides the ideological foundation for a racialized society, where society's benefits and burdens are inequitably allotted among the various racial groups."[11] This culture of racism pervades every aspect of our society, often in unconscious and unintentional ways. The result is nothing less than a system of white privilege that subjects people of color to oppressive economic, political, and educational policies and regulations that are undoubtedly social in their inescapable and widespread reach. Eradicating racism, then, cannot rest solely on overcoming personal animosity through individual moral suasion. Instead, racism must be recognized as a fundamentally *social* problem that permeates the social fabric of American society and culture. In this larger discussion of Catholic social thought, what is fundamentally at stake is how Catholics, guided by Catholic social teaching, understand the relationship between individuals and society as well as how we understand the root causes—and thus remedies—of injustices like racism.

WHAT DOES *GAUDIUM ET SPES* HAVE TO SAY?

If, as Mark Massa points out above, the realization of the Second Vatican Council was that "the gospel message should be understood and proclaimed in a sea of history that was now seen to touch and shape everything," then *Gaudium et Spes* (GS) is the council document that most profoundly addresses how the Catholic Church should identify itself and its obligations in light of this new realization.[12] *Gaudium et Spes* makes its purpose clear early on:

> The Church seeks but a solitary goal: to carry forward the work of Christ himself. . . . To carry out such a task, the Church has always had the duty of scrutinizing the signs of the times and interpreting them in the light of the gospel. Thus . . . she can respond to the perennial questions which men ask about this present life and the life to come, and about the relationship of the one to the other. We must therefore recognize and understand the world in which we live, its expectations, its longings, and its often dramatic characteristics. (GS, 3–4).

This document—one that frequently appears in compilations of Catholic social thought—is tasking itself and its members with the responsibility of discerning God's presence in the "signs of the times" in order to respond adequately and justly to the reality around us.

This reality, according to *Gaudium et Spes*, is one in which "never before has man been so keenly aware of freedom, yet at the same time, new forms of social and psychological slavery make their appearance" (GS, 4). These "new forms of social and psychological slavery"—perhaps manifested in what we could call structural de facto racism and de facto Jim Crow segregation—suppress human freedom and urge us to recognize that racism in the United States demands attention as a social reality. *Gaudium et Spes* presents an understanding of the relationship between person and society that, almost fifty years later, offers a refreshing way of addressing this problem of racism as an issue of social justice. The document brings a unique anthropological dimension to questions of social justice by offering a twofold, theologically based understanding of the human person. The person, while individually important, is inherently social and thus cannot be separated from his or her social surroundings.

Drawing from the Genesis creation story, *Gaudium et Spes* takes note of the nature of humanity's creation. The person, as an individual, is created in the image and likeness of God (GS, 12). By virtue of this creation, humans are imbued with human dignity that must be fostered, protected, and promoted. *Gaudium et Spes* spends much of its first chapter—titled "The Dignity of the Human Person"—discussing the dignity of the human person, the dignity of the human mind, and the dignity of moral conscience (GS, 12–16). The document also recognizes that humanity's shared creation in God's image grants all people "the same divine calling and destiny," such that "the basic equality of all must receive increasingly greater recognition" (GS, 29). At the same time, this document insists that "God did not create man as solitary. . . . For by his innermost nature man is a social being, and unless he relates himself to others he can neither live nor develop his potential" (GS, 12). This insistence is crucial to critiquing the US Catholic Church's approach to racism.

Gaudium et Spes avows that "the subject, and the goal of all social institutions is and must be the human person, which for its part and by its very nature stands completely in need of social life. The social life is not something added to man. Hence, through his dealings with others . . . he develops all his gifts and is able to rise to his destiny" (GS, 25). The document continues: "The social order and its development must unceasingly work to the benefit of the human person. . . . This social order requires constant improvement. It must be founded on truth, built on justice, and animated by love" (GS, 26). People and social institutions, therefore, are intimately interdependent.

This assertion is important for a couple of reasons. How people interact with one another informs how society functions. How society functions affects how people flourish. In a de facto racially stratified society, both aspects are negatively affected. Interaction between members of the white dominant culture and the "racialized other" are few, thus limiting opportunities for learning and growth. This, in turn, helps perpetuate economic, political, educational, and institutional racism that hinders the flourishing of all people. If the function of society is to uphold and protect the human dignity of *all* people, then a racist society fails miserably at this task.

By recognizing that the person and society are intricately connected, it seems that *Gaudium et Spes* would agree with Massingale's above understanding of racism as something that could function "as an ethos, as the animating spirit of US society."[13] As such, it offers something of a corrective to the US bishops' recognition of racism that, as noted above, often approaches the problem as only an individual one. *Gaudium et Spes* contends that people cannot content themselves "with a merely individualistic morality. . . . The obligations of justice and love are fulfilled only if each person, contributing to the common good . . . also promotes and assists the public and private in situations dedicated to bettering the conditions of human life" (GS, 30). Ethics and virtue are cultivated in society and community. There is no room for individualistic notions of ethics. Eradicating racism will take more than individual persuasion and moral conversion. It will require a full-scale evaluation and adjustment of society.

CONCLUSION

Finally we must ask, so what? What can we do? After all, as we all know, ethics, "*to be ethical*, must end in action."[14] Crucially, in addition to identifying the social nature of the person—and thus of justice—*Gaudium et Spes* also makes clear that the Catholic Church cannot limit its ethics and work to the level of discussion. The church can and must address and combat social injustice on the levels of culture and society. The document's discussion on human dignity, community, and activity lays the very "foundation for the relationship between the Church and the world" (GS, 40). If the church lives and acts in the world, then the church cannot withdraw from its challenges. Social life cannot be disconnected from faith and worship. In order to find answers, several questions must first be raised to address how we combat racism both in our churches and in our classrooms and academic institutions.

In the Church

How might the US Catholic Church, led predominately by white clergy, address racism both within the broader public spectrum and within its own ranks, increasingly made up of people of color? Can the church create space for the voices of racial minorities to be heard? How might these voices positively contribute to the church's ever changing identity and practice? As noted above, the church does have the resources to address these questions embedded in its very identity. Bryan Massingale identifies three *practices* of solidarity that, central to the Catholic Church's very being, call for a radical equality and inclusiveness that has significant implications for addressing racism: conversion, baptism, and Eucharist.

Conversion causes a "fundamental shift in one's paradigm of understanding, interpreting, and acting upon reality."[15] Conversion into the church should shift one's frame of reference from an understanding of a world built on possessions, competition, and division to one built on giving, love, and solidarity. As Massingale points out, this shift in focus is crucial to eradicating racism. He says, Christianity "offers a faith-based narrative that makes the process of racial conversion—the journey through indifference, complicity, simplicity, empathy, and solidarity—comprehensible and worthwhile."[16] Jesus' life narrative was one of embracing those deemed "other" by the powers-that-be, a narrative that those within the Catholic Church must fully live. Conversion to this narrative creates space for the "radical conversion" called for above by the US Catholic bishops.

Baptism places a similar emphasis on solidarity in its insistence on the equality of all, gained through baptism in Christ. Again from Massingale: "Baptism does not result in a monochrome faith community; rather the social significance of skin color is redefined and indeed undetermined. The social meanings of skin tone cannot—and must not—compromise the fundamental equality of the baptized through Christ."[17] This baptism—immersion—into the life of Christ signals a new life for believers in which racial barriers are nonexistent.

The Eucharist manifests Jesus' radically inclusive table fellowship that is "foreign and peculiar to the ways of the world. Jesus did not discriminate when he broke bread, eating with all people regardless of gender, race, or social class. In doing so, his table fellowship "stretches our social imaginations, and challenges the boundaries we give to our inclusion and acceptance."[18] What might happen if those in the church—both clergy and laity—stretched their social imaginations to truly embrace a radically inclusive table fellowship in which all are invited to the table?

In the University

Finally, for those of us who currently find ourselves at institutions of Catholic higher education, or for those of us who foresee a future there, perhaps we start by questioning our own institutions. What are our admissions policies? What types of communities and students do we serve? Where and whom do we recruit? If our institutions are located within urban settings, where our neighbors are predominantly people of color, do we recruit from local high schools? If not, why? Is it assumed that students at these schools are not capable of success?[19]

In our classrooms do we talk about racism at all? If we do, how do we talk about it? Do we address it in a nuanced and respectful way that recognizes current racial concerns? Tim Wise, in his book *White Like Me*, suggests that educators often fail to deal with race in any meaningful, contemporary way, focusing only on well-known past movements and people—the civil rights era and Martin Luther King, Jr., for example. While these things undoubtedly are important when discussing racism, the danger in making them our sole focus is that of presenting history as an "uninterrupted string of linear progress, where things were really bad, but slowly got better, and are always improving when it comes to race."[20] In other words, if we end our discussions with the positive aspects of the civil rights movement, we risk ignoring the negatives of the racist reality in which we currently live.

Finally, do we urge students to reflect upon not only racism but also social injustice in general? Do we challenge them to identify social structures that create and perpetuate oppression? Do we create a safe space for them to have these discussions? How do we creatively lead them to truthful and honest discussions about the continued existence of racism as a social issue? As Wise points out, "The truth a person comes to on their own (even if they had a little help being led there) is always more lasting than the truth you transmit to them directly."[21]

I do not presume to know the answers to these questions, but I do think that the Catholic Church can help society in profound and effective ways. Bound by no temporal laws and beholden to no particular group or culture, a Catholic Church that strives to be truly universal can and should serve as a bridge among different people. A church that really believes it has an important religious and ethical function in the modern world must act on these convictions.

NOTES

1. Mark Massa, *The American Catholic Revolution* (Oxford: Oxford University Press, 2010), 1.

2. Garry Wills, *Bare Ruined Choirs: Doubt, Prophecy, and Radical Religion* (Garden City, NY: Doubleday, 1971), 21.

3. Massa, *The American Catholic Revolution*, 13. Here Massa is drawing from Bernard Lonergan's "The Transition from a Classicist Worldview to Historical Mindedness," in *Law for Liberty: The Role of Law in the Church Today*, ed. James Biechler, 126–33 (Baltimore: Helicon, 1967).

4. Bryan Massingale, "The African American Experience and US Roman Catholic Ethics: 'Strangers and Aliens No Longer?'" in *Black and Catholic: The Challenge and Gift of Black Folk*, ed. Jaime T. Phelps (Milwaukee: Marquette University Press, 2002), 86.

5. A number of black scholars have named the problem of racism and have called upon, or attempted to use, the Christian and Catholic traditions to resist it: James H. Cone, "A Theological Challenge to the American Catholic Church," in *Speaking the Truth: Ecumenism, Liberation, and Black Theology* (Grand Rapids, MI: Eerdmans, 1986); idem, "Black Liberation Theology and Black Catholics: A Critical Conversation," *Theological Studies* 61, no. 4 (2000): 731–47; idem, *A Black Theology of Liberation*, 40th anniv. ed. (Maryknoll, NY: Orbis Books, 2010); M. Shawn Copeland, "Tradition and Traditions of African American Catholicism," *Theological Studies* 61, no. 4 (2000): 632–55; Bryan N. Massingale, "James Cone and Recent Catholic Episcopal Teachings on Racism," *Theological Studies* 61, no. 4 (2000): 700–730; idem, *Racial Justice and the Catholic Church* (Maryknoll, NY: Orbis Books, 2010); idem, "*Vox Victimarum Vox Dei*: Malcolm X as Neglected 'Classic' for Catholic Theological Reflection," *Proceedings of the Annual Convention of the CTSA* 65 (2010): 63–88; Traci C. West, *Disruptive Christian Ethics: When Racism and Women's Lives Matter* (Louisville, KY: Westminster John Knox Press, 2006). A number of white Catholic and non-Catholic scholars have accepted the challenge of racism and are working in the areas of whiteness/white privilege and the Christian tradition. See Laurie M. Cassidy and Alex Mikulich, eds., *Interrupting White Privilege: Catholic Theologians Break the Silence* (Maryknoll, NY: Orbis Books, 2007); Christopher Pramuk, "'Strange Fruit': Black Suffering/White Revelation," *Theological Studies* 67, no. 2 (2006): 345–77; Jennifer Harvey et al., eds., *Disrupting White Supremacy from Within* (Cleveland: Pilgrim Press, 2004); Mary Elizabeth Hobgood, *Dismantling Privilege: An Ethics of Accountability* (Cleveland: Pilgrim Press, 2009).

6. See, for example, Pope John XXIII's encyclicals *Mater et Magistra* (1961) and *Pacem in Terris* (1963), and John Paul II's encyclical *Sollicitudo Rei Socialis* (1987).

7. Bishops' Committee on Black Catholics, *For the Love of One Another: A Special Message on the Occasion of the Tenth Anniversary of Brothers and Sisters to Us* (Washington, DC: United States Catholic Conference, 1989), 39, 41.

8. Massingale, "James Cone and Recent Catholic Episcopal Teaching on Racism," 706.

9. Massingale, *Racial Justice and the Catholic Church*, 15.

10. Ibid., 16–17.

11. Ibid., 24, 24–25.

12. Massa, *The American Catholic Revolution*, 13. Here Massa is again drawing from Bernard Lonergan, "The Transition from a Classicist Worldview to Historical Mindedness."

13. Massingale, *Racial Justice and the Catholic Church*, 15.

14. James F. Keenan, "Virtue and Identity," in *Creating Identity: Biographical, Moral, Religious*, ed. Hermann Häring, Maureen Junker-Kenny, and Dietmar Mieth, *Concilium* 2000/2 (London: SCM Press, 2000), 70.

15. Massingale, *Racial Justice and the Catholic Church*, 121.

16. Ibid., 122.

17. Ibid., 123.

18. Ibid., 124, 125.

19. Timothy Wise, a white activist, explores this question in *White Like Me: Reflections on Race from a Privileged Son* (Berkeley, CA: Soft Skull Press, 2008).

20. Ibid., 62.

21. Ibid., 108.

VI.

THE FUTURE OF ECCLESIOLOGY

STEPHEN OKEY

The theme of ecclesiology and the future of the church is perhaps the most fundamental concern of this entire project. Reflections on the future of dialogue, ethics, liturgy, and ministry each presuppose some idea of the church and its trajectory. In the ecclesiology section many of the implicit concerns and assumptions of these other sections were made explicit in a series of investigations into how the role of relationality within the church.

Rooted in the documents of the Second Vatican Council, particularly the dogmatic constitution *Lumen Gentium*, the papers on ecclesiology in this volume look to the future of the church. That document's tension between the church as the people of God and the church as hierarchical provides a fertile ground for investigating the wide variety of relationships that builds up the community of the church. The relationships between laity and bishops, universal and local churches, and the present community and its conditional future provide a compelling case for mining the Catholic theological tradition in order to strengthen communication and solidarity among the members of the faithful and between the church and the wider world.

Amanda Osheim discusses the relationships among lay ministers, lay theologians, and bishops, particularly in the context of the local church. She advocates for what she calls an "orthopraxis of reception," in which members of these groups try to discern the work of the Holy Spirit in dialogue with one another. Central to this dialogue is the effort toward genuine reception of the other that takes account of the integral yet different vocations of each. Since all are called to witness to God's revelation in the world, living out that call must be performed in community. In light of the current modes of interaction

177

among these three groups, Osheim believes that developing an ortho-praxis of reception will require both reworking what *consultation* means and then developing a spirituality of dialogical consultation. Through this, the church will be best enabled to discern the work of the Holy Spirit through the *sensus fidelium*.

Kevin Brown looks at the relationship between the local and universal churches with a focus on their mutual reciprocity. Brown looks especially at the debates between Cardinal Kasper and Cardinal Ratzinger following the council about the relationship between the local and universal church, a debate that highlights the tension within the council between the roles of communion and jurisdiction. Kasper claims that the universal and local churches are historical realities that exist simultaneously, while Ratzinger argues for an ontological and temporal priority to the universal church, with local churches being particular instances thereof. Brown advocates for an inductive ecclesiology that begins with a historically aware understanding of the experience and practice of local churches and then builds outward to an understanding of the universal church. He maintains that the local church in Rome is important in affirming the mutual reciprocity of universal and local churches, but he claims that Rome could better effect this by acting as a facilitator for the collegiality of bishops. Toward this end, Brown advocates for several concrete practices that can encourage this mutual reciprocity: smaller dioceses, local input on the selection of bishops, the end of translating bishops between dioceses, greater efforts to build communion between local churches and their bishops, and more effective inculturation of the liturgy. These practices would strengthen the communion within and among local churches and thus, by extension, the communion of the universal church.

Eduardo Gonzalez takes on the very framework of the conference by raising the question of the crucified future. While many assume the future as a given, Gonzalez highlights the growing sense that the future is a fragile possibility that is dependent on contemporary human activity. Ecological devastation serves as the primary example of how he thinks humanity is crucifying the future. Gonzalez connects this crucified future with Ignacio Ellacuría's "crucified peoples," arguing that we are called to concern ourselves with the victims of environmental devastation and work to "bring the future down from the cross." Informed by Johann Baptist Metz, Gonzalez advocates for an "apocalyptic eschatology" that takes seriously the role of the Holy Spirit in ecclesiology as presented in *Lumen Gentium*. The Spirit guides the church, and in fact all of creation, toward perfect union with Christ that is only realized in the fullness of time. The crucified future, therefore, serves as a "sign of the times" that the documents of the council call us to attend to.

During the ecclesiology-working-group session, the focus revolved around both *ad intra* and *ad extra* issues facing the church. In particular, there was a desire for building and improving structures within the church that would enable the faithful to express lament, experience healing, and pursue discernment together. The relationship between lament and discernment was especially pertinent, as it was seen that creating space for the faithful to express concerns about the church and the wider world was necessary for the church's authentic discernment of how the Holy Spirit might be guiding the community. The process of discernment must take account of both the church's grounding in the gospel and the church's historical and cultural situation, as only in light of these can a way forward be developed.

The essays presented here serve as an important starting point for the ongoing conversation about what it means to be church in the twenty-first century. Building on the work presented here, we hope that young theologians and church leaders will continue to participate in this work of building up the church. It will only be through the forging of strong relations of praxis and solidarity that we can continue to witness to the revelation of God in Christ and the guidance of the church by the Holy Spirit.

The Local Church in Dialogue

Toward an Orthopraxis of Reception

AMANDA C. OSHEIM

While dialogue is often cited as an important factor within current approaches to ecclesiology, the practice of dialogue in the life of the church requires further reflection and development. Discernment of the *sensus fidelium* highlights multiple voices of authority and calls the faithful to receive one another in a dialogue reflective of diverse baptismal vocations. The need for dialogue among lay ecclesial ministers, lay theologians, and bishops offers the opportunity for critical reflection on the structures and principles necessary for an orthopraxis of reception in the life of the local church.

The *sensus fidelium* is rooted in baptism and the Eucharist, sacraments in which the faithful enter into the paschal mystery and become members of Christ's body. The apostle Paul indicates that "having the same love, being in full accord and of one mind" is characteristic of Christ's body; it is the unity that results from allowing "the same mind be in you that was in Christ Jesus" (Phil 2:2, 5). Thus, the indwelling of the Holy Spirit within believers not only orients the faithful to action as the body of Christ, but also cultivates what might be described analogously as the "muscle memory" of Christ's body. This living memory allows believers to discern those articulations and enactments of faith that cohere with God's revelation in Christ.

Arising from union with Christ and the indwelling of the Holy Spirit, the *sensus fidelium* has an epistemological character. Francis Sullivan describes the *sensus fidei* as both an instinct and a disposition, and compares it to the virtue of faith; Zoltán Alszeghy indicates it is "an experiential knowledge based on what has been lived," in contrast to an intellectual knowledge.[1] This instinct for faith is not merely reactive; rather, it both forms the basis for and is influenced by the believer's spiritual life, and it is a knowledge that is gained through the active reception and return of God's love mediated by history and the community of faith.[2] The church comes into being and discovers its mission through the faithful reception of God's self-disclosure within history embodied and enacted in the *sensus fidelium*.

The presence of the Holy Spirit in all church members means that the church as a whole is the bearer of the apostolic tradition; thus there are multiple "authorities" within the church, that is, people who share in the "mind of Christ." Nicholas Lash writes, "The human quest for truth is irreducibly pluralistic. We employ, and we need to employ, a rich variety of languages and explanatory frameworks in our efforts to hear the truth and respond to it. (Or if a more explicitly theological formulation is preferred, the one word of God, the God who is one word, speaks to us in a variety of voices.)"[3] To engage in dialogue with the variety of voices that speaks in the church is to enter into a process of authentication in which the faithful receive God's self-revelation from one another and discern revelation's meaning together. Ormond Rush describes this as "*dialogic orthodoxy* in which the truth is discovered 'from below' through a process of dialogue."[4] Dialogical discernment of the *sensus fidelium* is a means of both perceiving and receiving God's truth. For dialogical orthodoxy to flourish in the local church, an orthopraxis of mutual reception and dialogue between all believers is necessary.

Focusing on dialogue among lay ecclesial ministers, lay theologians, and bishops is not a replacement for ongoing dialogical discernment of the *sensus fidelium* amid all believers; yet two sets of reasons prompt attention to reception among these persons. The first reasons are practical. The growing number of lay theologians coupled with the extraordinary increase of lay ecclesial ministers following Vatican Council II marks a new opportunity for dialogical orthodoxy among lay persons and the local bishop. These two groups of laity are relatively easy to identify, and due to their ecclesial vocations one would expect to encounter individuals with experience of critical, faithful reflection who are aware of both the time commitment and the purpose of practicing dialogical orthodoxy through the mutual reception and discernment of the *sensus fidelium*. In order to cultivate these new ecclesial realities, however, formal structures for dialogue with these two lay groups need to be established.

The second set of reasons is more inherently theological and pastoral: lay ecclesial ministers, lay theologians, and bishops have a particular call to dialogue within the local church. For example, *Christus Dominus* (CD) notes that dialogue, initiated and promoted by the bishop, "should be marked by clarity of expression as well as by humility and courtesy, so that truth may be combined with charity, and understanding with love"; dialogue is also to be "characterized by due prudence allied . . . with confidence. This, by encouraging friendship, is conducive to a union of minds" (CD, 13). Rooted in dialogue between the US bishops and lay ecclesial ministers, the USCCB's *Co-Workers in the Vineyard of the Lord* defined lay ecclesial ministry in part by the lay ministers' "*close mutual collaboration* with the pastoral ministry of bishops, priests, and deacons" (10).

The call to dialogue is present with regard to the theological vocation as well. In a 1975 document on magisterial-theological relationships, "Theses on the Relationship Between the Ecclsiastical Magisterium and Theology," the International Theological Commission suggested that tensions between the roles of theologians and bishops "can be seen as a vital force and an incentive to a common carrying out of [their] respective tasks by way of dialogue (thesis 9). More recently, in the 2012 document "Theology Today: Perspectives, Principles, and Criteria," the commission not only described the *sensus fidelium* as a "criterion for Catholic theology" but also recognized the contribution of lay theological voices to the church, noting:

> Especially with the expanded number nowadays of lay theologians who have experience of particular areas of interaction between the Church and the world, between the Gospel and life, with which ordained theologians and theologians in religious life may not be so familiar, it is increasingly the case that theologians give an initial articulation of "faith seeking understanding" in new circumstances or in the face of new issues. (36, 47)

Taken together, these two documents suggest that lay theologians have particular contributions to make to dialogical orthodoxy.

STRUCTURES FOR DIALOGICAL DISCERNMENT

The communion of the church as a sacrament of salvation comes to fruition through the active, mutual reception of each person's baptismal vocation, in other words, the person's embodiment of the church's mission. Thus discernment of the *sensus fidelium* is mediated through the way each member of the faithful fulfills his or her apostolic call. *Lumen Gentium* (LG) affirmed: "To the extent of their knowledge, competence or authority the laity are entitled, and indeed sometimes duty-bound, to express their opinion on matters which concern the good of the church. Should the occasion arise this should be done through the institutions established by the church for that purpose" (LG, 37). What are the structures that allow the members of the laity to fulfill their obligation and that manifest the laity's empowerment? Further, how do these structures take into account the particular authority—knowledge base or experiential expertise—of lay ministers and theologians? In other words, how is the lay ecclesial minister's or lay theologian's understanding and practice of faith discerned in light of his or her apostolic role?

The reality of many local churches is advancing more quickly than our ecclesial structures. A few examples highlight the need for structuring spaces of mutual dialogue. First, presbyteral councils are canonically required in each diocese.[5] In 2005 there were 28,702 diocesan priests and 30,632 lay ecclesial ministers in the United States.[6] Yet there is no canonically required structure that facilitates the local bishop's regular consultation with lay ecclesial ministers in light of their apostolic mission. While the number of diocesan pastoral councils seems to be increasing,[7] such councils are not required by canon law, are not composed only of lay ecclesial ministers, and are not conceived as venues for dialogical discernment but rather as consultative groups who assist in implementing the bishop's pastoral vision.[8] The immediately practical, rather than the dialogically discerning, character of diocesan pastoral councils points to the need for dedicated structures that facilitate dialogue between lay ecclesial ministers and the local bishop apart from a particular pastoral agenda.

Second, dialogue between bishops and theologians is an ongoing and at times divisive question within the church. The 1989 document "Doctrinal Responsibilities: Approaches to Promoting Cooperation and Resolving Misunderstandings Between Bishops and Theologians" notes: "Bishops and theologians involved in ongoing collaboration are likely to grow in respect and trust for one another and thus to assist and support their respective service to the gospel."[9] As Bradford Hinze points out, however, the ecclesial status shift among theologians from primarily priests to lay persons means "there is no context for these predominantly laypeople to form good relationships, living relationships, with [bishops.]"[10] The lack of informal structures points to the need for creation of regular opportunities for dialogue between bishops and theologians in order to develop the authentic personal relationships that ground discernment within the local church.

Finally, lay ecclesial ministers and lay theologians should also have the opportunity for dialogical discernment. While these groups may encounter each other in the educational context of ministry formation, opportunities for more mutual forms of dialogue that transform the power dynamic of the student-teacher relationship in favor of recognizing the value of both practical and theoretical expertise are needed.[11] Consistent, shared reflection between these two lay groups creates the possibility for mutual reception and critique that is based in their common baptismal vocation and is reflective of the perspectives provided by their diverse ecclesial vocations.

PRINCIPLES OF DIALOGICAL DISCERNMENT

Structures require animating principles: the body of Christ is no mere skeleton and requires the breath of the Spirit to be a living reality. Two principles are necessary for the embodiment of reception: a redefinition of consultation, and a spirituality of dialogical consultation.

Redefining Consultation

Canon law describes several of the structures of the local church, such as presbyteral and pastoral councils, as consultative rather than determinative bodies. The distinction is important, though, in order to gauge how it might affect new structures for dialogical orthodoxy within the local church, the question of what *consultation* means must be considered. When John Henry Newman urged the consultation of the faithful, he used the analogy of consulting a clock for the time: the faithful's opinion was not consulted, but rather their belief was consulted in an objective manner.[12] While Newman's suggestion was controversial in its time, additional development of our understanding of consultation is necessary in our own. It is one thing to consult through observation in quest of factual information and another to consult through dialogue in search of understanding. Dialogical consultation presumes a growing ability to enter into another's world, to empathize with another's personal experiences and interpretations, and thus to thicken our shared account of lived faith in its richness and complexity. This may help to avoid the temptation of projecting our own meanings onto another's lived faith. Such consultation almost certainly involves conversion, though it may not necessarily demand surrender of our own perspective.[13] Rather, it asks that our own experiences be re-viewed in light of another's experience. To borrow from Newman, dialogically based consultation provides an illative grasp of the *sensus fidelium* that implicates not only how you understand your faith and I understand my faith, but how we understand our faith together.

The relational quality of consultation in dialogical orthodoxy is highlighted when Newman's analogy of the clock is pressed. When the face of a clock is consulted, I may make a determination that it is not telling the time well; when I dialogically consult another person, I may no longer treat that person simply as an object that can be manipulated into "telling the correct time" but rather must encounter that person as another "thou" in the church's personal relationship with the triune God. In dialogical consultation the apostolic vocation of the lay ecclesial minister, lay theologian, and bishop is viewed as essential to the ecclesial relationship rather than as circumstantial. Recognition of personal context is necessary for learning and teaching to be mutual and in order to acknowledge the diverse forms of authority present in ecclesial dialogue.

Spirituality

It is difficult to conceive of an empathetic entry into another's experience, a dialogical consultation that may result in conversion, or a true acknowledgment of context and mutuality, without a spirituality that empowers it. First, the dialogical and mutually receptive aspects of our personal and ecclesial spiritualities need to be consciously fostered. This can be done by returning to a traditional spirituality with these aspects in mind, or it can involve emerging spiritualities that consciously center on dialogue and reception. In either case these spiritualities should be easily adapted to or arise out of the vocational context of lay ecclesial ministers and lay theologians.[14]

Conscientious development of these spiritualities should incorporate both the unitive and apostolic aspects of the church, which is patterned on trinitarian life, lest the dynamic between these two marks of the church be lost by prioritizing the church's communion over the church's mission or vice versa. Ecclesial spiritualities that aid dialogical orthodoxy engage the church's mission, preventing the church's communion from becoming narrowly parochial; in turn, these spiritualities should recognize that the bonds of love and justice that unite the church also propel the church's mission. Spiritualities informed by the reciprocal relationship between the church as "one" and "apostolic" create holiness through the integration of union and mission and manifest a catholicity that avoids both the contraction of the communal into sectarianism and the diffusion of apostolic purpose into a vague humanism. Further, in order to navigate constructively the tensions between the ecclesial marks, these spiritualities will need to consciously address conflict as potentially creative for dialogue rather than as inherently destructive.[15]

Second, in order for dialogical consultation to flourish, those in dialogue with each other should engage in common spiritual practices. Eucharistic liturgy is the foundation for these practices, which should also include common reflection on scripture and tradition, and common social action. Shared spiritual practices help to create and sustain spiritualities that are truly catholic: coherent with the faith of the universal church while also expressive of the faith context of the local church.

Third, while groups engaged in dialogical orthodoxy may find a particular spirituality most fruitful for their orthopraxis, the temptation to prize one spirituality over another or to think that dialogue is not possible among persons and communities of diverse spiritualities must be avoided. Rather, critical awareness of the spiritualities that undergird the praxis of dialogical orthodoxy should enable us to recognize that diverse spiritualities are necessary in order to discover continually what it means to be a church that is one, holy, catholic, and apostolic.

CONCLUSION

Dialogically based discernment of the *sensus fidelium* is ultimately the praxis of receiving the revelation of Christ through the power of the Holy Spirit. Therefore the orthopraxis of reception is both a call and a responsibility shared by all the faithful and manifested in a particular way in the apostolic vocations of lay ecclesial minsters, lay theologians, and bishops. The process of reception is organically connected to baptism and the Eucharist and yet requires conscious planning, personal conversion, and communal fortitude in order to be engaged continually and fully. While orthopraxis is undertaken in relation to our present context, there is hope in the realization that the task is not ours alone: Paul's encouragement that "the same mind be in you that was in Christ Jesus" (Phil 2:5) is the task of the church in all times and places.

NOTES

1. Francis A. Sullivan, "The Sense of Faith," in *Authority in the Roman Catholic Church*, ed. Bernard Hoose (Burlington, VT: Ashgate, 2002), 86. Zoltán Alszeghy, "The *Sensus Fidei* and the Development of Dogma," in

Vatican II Assessment and Perspectives, ed. R. Latrourelle, vol. 1 (New York: Paulist Press, 1988), 139.

2. "For what we call the *sensus fidelium* is rooted precisely in this lived margin, this space of truth that emerges between the received Word and what it becomes through the power of the Spirit for the believer who tries to conform himself to it. . . . Thus life itself is a commentary which renders explicit the Word that is received, and this unfolding adds to the understanding of the objective data themselves" (J.-M.R. Tillard, "*Sensus Fidelium*," *One in Christ* 11, no. 1 [1975]: 15).

3. Nicholas Lash, *Voices of Authority* (Shepherdstown: Patmos Press, 1976), 27.

4. Ormond Rush, "Determining Catholic Orthodoxy: Monologue or Dialogue," *Pacifica* 12, no. 2 (June 1999): 126.

5. *Code of Canon Law* in *New Commentary on the Code of Canon Law*, ed. John P. Beal et al. (New York: Paulist Press, 2000), canon 495, §1.

6. For diocesan priests, see "Frequently Requested Church Statistics," Center for Applied Research on the Apostolate. For lay ecclesial ministers, see United States Conference of Catholic Bishops, *Co-Workers in the Vineyard of the Lord,* 13. "Today, 30,632 lay ecclesial ministers work at least twenty hours per week in paid positions in parishes. An additional 2,163 volunteers work at least twenty hours per week in parishes. The number of paid lay parish ministers has increased by 53% since 1990, while the percentage of parishes with salaried lay ecclesial ministers has increased from 54% to 66%. In 2005, the percentage of lay women is 64%; laymen, 20%; religious women, 16%. Religious educators (41.5%) and general pastoral ministers (25%) account for two thirds of all parish ministers." The document draws its statistics from David DeLambo, *Lay Parish Ministers: A Study of Emerging Leadership* (New York: National Pastoral Life Center [NPLC], 2005).

7. "Sixty percent of responding dioceses have a diocesan pastoral council. This is a substantial increase from the 44 percent report in a 1997 CARA study co-sponsored by the USCCB Committee on the Laity and the USCCB Committee on Pastoral Practices" ("Dioceses and Parishes Making More Use of Pastoral Councils," *The CARA Report* 10, no. 1 [Summer 2004]: 1).

8. See canons 511 and 512 with commentary by Barbara Anne Cusack in Beal et al., *New Commentary on the Code of Canon Law,* 658–59.

9. National Conference of Catholic Bishops, "Doctrinal Responsibilities: Approaches to Promoting Cooperation and Resolving Misunderstandings Between Bishops and Theologians," in *Origins* 19, no. 7 (June 29, 1989): 103.

10. Bradford Hinze, interview, College Theology Society annual convention, Iona College, New Rochelle, New York, June 2–5, 2011. Reported in Joshua J. McElwee, "Religion Professors' Convention Shows Theology's New Lay Face," *National Catholic Reporter* (June 20, 2011).

11. "The number of lay ecclesial ministry candidates enrolled in degree and certificate programs in 2009–2010 is 17,935, of whom 12,462 (69 percent) are working toward a certificate in ministry and 5,473 (31 percent) are working toward a graduate degree in ministry. This represents a 2 percent increase over the 17,538 candidates reported in 2008–2009" ("Lay Ministry Formation Programs Profiled," *The CARA Report* 16, no. 19 [Summer 2010]: 9).

12. John Henry Newman, *On Consulting the Faithful in Matters of Doctrine*, ed. John Coulson (New York: Sheed and Ward, 1961), 54–55: "Thus we talk of 'consulting our barometer' about the weather:—the barometer only attests the *fact* of the state of the atmosphere. In like manner, we may consult a watch or a sun-dial about the time of day. . . . Doubtless [the laity's] advice, their opinion, their judgment on the question is not asked; but the matter of fact, viz. their belief *is* sought for, as a testimony to that apostolical tradition, on which alone any doctrine may be defined."

13. "Empathy does not mean agreement; it does not require that I accept the other's point of view as my own or even as 'best' or 'right' for that person. The goal of empathy is to understand; as such it precedes evaluation. Evaluation and decision are not necessarily secondary in communication, but they follow on accurate understanding" (James D. Whitehead and Evelyn Eaton Whitehead, *Method in Ministry: Theological Reflection and Christian Ministry*, rev. and updated [Lanham, MD: Sheed and Ward, 1995], 70).

14. "This lay spirituality will take its particular character from the circumstances of one's state of life—married and family life, celibacy, widowhood—from one's state of health and from one's professional and social activity. . . . Similarly, lay people who have followed their particular vocation and become members of any of the associations or institutions approved by the church aim sincerely at making their own the forms of spirituality proper to these bodies" (*Apostolicam Actuositatem*, 4).

15. "[Conflict's] destructive effects sear our memories: we have seen friendships destroyed and partnerships broken. But our experience holds another conviction: conflict sometimes brings grace. . . . Sometimes conflict arises between good and evil, challenging us to abandon selfishness or cowardice and choose the righteous path. But conflict also erupts around competing goods" (Evelyn Eaton Whitehead and James D. Whitehead, *The Promise of Partnership: A Model for Collaborative Ministry* [Lincoln, NE: iUniverse, 2000], 90–91).

The Local and Universal Churches

Expressing Catholicity Through Their Reciprocity

B. KEVIN BROWN

The Second Vatican Council, its subsequent reception, and the theological and pastoral debates surrounding that reception have significantly shaped the life of the Catholic Church for the last half-century. Among the most public of these debates is that between Cardinal Walter Kasper and Cardinal Joseph Ratzinger (now Pope Benedict XVI). At the heart of their debate is how each understands the relationship between the universal and local churches in light of the ecclesiology presented in the documents of the council. The debate is significant for several reasons, not the least of which is that it demonstrates that Vatican II holds in tension both a universalistic ecclesiology and one based upon the communion of the local churches.

Throughout Christian history the relationship between the universal and local churches has revealed how the Christian Church, as a whole, understands both its catholicity and the communion in which it participates. Today, there is a contentious debate in the Catholic Church over how this relationship ought to be expressed. At the local level many voice concerns over a recentralization of decision making and doctrinal authority in Rome resulting from the prioritization of the universal church over the local churches by hierarchical and curial officials. In contemporary theological discourse there exist multiple understandings on the nature of this relationship in a contemporary *communion ecclesiology*, which has been used to describe the ecclesiologies stemming from the documents of Vatican II.[1] Recently, many Roman officials have used the term to describe an ecclesiological praxis that prioritizes the universal church over the local churches. I reject the notion that such an understanding is the correct expression of communion ecclesiology. Instead, engaging an inductive methodology, I argue that while the current practice of many church officials reflects a theology that prioritizes the universal church, the Catholic Church must practice a true communion ecclesiology, rooted in the documents of the Second Vatican Council, that recognizes the simultaneity of the universal and local churches in order to express more fully its catholicity.

To address this problem and develop my argument, I begin by briefly examining the inductive ecclesiological method and how it may be adapted to address the relationship between the universal and local churches. Second, I recount several major historical shifts in the understanding of this relationship, culminating in the teachings of Vatican II. Third, I engage the observations of several local church leaders and ecclesiologists to demonstrate that, while Vatican II laid the groundwork for an ecclesiology that recognizes the simultaneity of the local and universal churches, the practice of Roman authorities reflects those aspects of Vatican II's ecclesiology that are more universalistic. Finally, building upon post-conciliar ecclesiologies, I offer several practical proposals to make visible the reciprocal nature of the local and universal churches. Such practices acknowledge that neither the local churches nor the universal church could exist without the other by paying deference to both culture and ecclesial communion and more fully express the catholicity of the whole church.

INDUCTIVE ECCLESIOLOGY AND THE LOCAL AND UNIVERSAL CHURCHES

In the last decade the inductive method of ecclesiology has been seen, in Catholic theology, most prominently in the works of Roger Haight, Gerard Mannion, and Paul Lakeland.[2] With roots in the theological method of Bernard Lonergan and the historical ecclesiology of Joseph Komonchak, an inductive ecclesiology begins with the lived experience and practice of a local church and moves outward to the development of constructive ecclesiological proposals and models.[3] In the years following Vatican II, Lonergan observed that a new empirical theology, which embraces a philosophy of each individual "as incarnate subject," was emerging.[4] Lakeland argues that an inductive ecclesiology views the church as a "collective incarnate subject, moved and changed by the same forces that affect the human person."[5] Therefore, he writes that "inductive ecclesiology has to begin from the Church that actually exists. . . . Although the end product of all ecclesial reflection is to arrive at some generalizable sense of what the Church is, inductive method approaches that point through reflection upon a definite local context."[6] By beginning at the local level and moving outward toward broad ecclesiological concepts, the theologian is able to call the church to "be attentive, be intelligent, be reasonable, be loving, and, if necessary, change."[7] Similarly, Mannion writes, "Any postmodern 'ecclesiology' [should] confront the challenges of the age in an open and positive fashion. Part of its task would be to influence the development of new and effective forms ecclesial practice, organization, ministry, and leadership."[8] The theologian, then, must make an argument, based on empirical observations at the local level and contemporary theological reflection, of what constitutes the present situation of the church in its relation to the tradition and, from it, develop constructive, theological proposals for future praxis.

However, the aim of this essay is not to develop an ecclesiological portrait of the church but instead to argue for an ecclesiological praxis that reflects the simultaneity of the local churches and the universal church. As a result, the point of departure is not an examination of the experience of the people in a given church, but rather one of the experiences of Catholic local churches in relation to the local church at Rome. Admittedly, by beginning with the experiences of churches rather than people, this method forfeits some of its inductivity and begins with several hermeneutical presuppositions. First, it begins with the assumption that local churches are, in fact, churches. Additionally, in the Catholic context with which this essay deals, these local churches may be assumed to be eucharistic, possessive of an episcopal form of leadership, and in communion with the See of Rome, to which they grant a form of primacy. Furthermore, it is written in the historical context of a post–Vatican II church still engaged in debate and discussion over how the council's documents should be reflected in the life of the church. However, by beginning at the local level, with the experiences of local churches in their relationship with the church of Rome, it remains inductive.

Finally, Haight makes it clear that any inductive ecclesiology should be historically conscious and begin with a description of the historical context. He writes: "Historical consciousness involves one in a dialectic across temporal distance. The church is bound to the past and freed from its particularity: but one must study the data of the historical church to be within it for its future."[9] Addressing Haight's work, Mannion writes, "An ecclesiology 'from below' bears the promise that, in its attentiveness to historical context and in its historical consciousness, it can better adapt itself to meeting the challenges of the postmodern age."[10] Therefore, an examination of the historical relationship between the church of Rome, whose jurisdiction and authority has often come to represent the universal church, and those other local churches in communion with it throughout Christianity's history is essential to the question at hand.

HISTORICAL OVERVIEW

The scriptural account of the Pentecost event in Acts 2 is among the earliest writings to address, at least implicitly, the relationship of the local and universal churches (Acts 2:1–13). Christopher Ruddy, in his work on Jean-Marie Roger Tillard's theology of the local church, argues that the Lukan account of the gift of the Spirit to the primitive post-Easter community communicates an important ecclesiological principle. Ruddy writes, "The church's foundation in Jerusalem shows that the church is inherently both local and universal: announcing a salvation destined for all the nations, the church does so only through particular histories and places."[11] The church at Jerusalem is local because it is made manifest "in and through a given place's history and culture, a place that is, in fact, at the center of salvation history."[12] In Tillard's interpretation of the Pentecost event the localness of the church at Jerusalem, then, is essential. Ruddy writes that for Tillard "the church's foundation at Jerusalem is not accidental, but historically and eschatologically necessary" as it is the location which represents for both Jews and Christians "the realization of human destiny."[13] However, the church of Pentecost is simultaneously universal as the Jerusalem community, compelled by the Spirit's gift of communion, is immediately drawn outward to share the Gospel with the Jewish diaspora gathered at Jerusalem (and eventually beyond).[14] Ruddy argues, "As the miracle of the Jerusalem community's common understanding of many languages shows, the unity brought by the Spirit is not uniformity, but a communion of differences bonded together."[15] Put differently, at Pentecost the universal gospel preached did not triumph over the local, but the universal was made manifest locally in each hearer's particular language. Tillard, therefore, according to Ruddy's analysis, argues that investigations into the relationship between the local and universal churches should explore how this relationship expresses the catholicity of the whole church in a given historical context rather than arguing for one's historical priority over the other.[16]

Much of Christianity's first millennium was marked by a practice and theology of communion between local churches and the emergence of Rome as a primatial local church.[17] Klaus Schatz writes, "Key to the ancient Church's self-understanding is the word *communio* [communion]."[18] Representing the church's catholicity (or universality), communion, among its many meanings at the time, referred to the bond each local church shared with one another in the universal church. This was symbolized in a number of ways, including the participation of neighboring bishops in the ordination of a new bishop, the participation of bishops in councils and synods, and the exchange of pastoral letters.[19] As Christianity spread, certain local churches emerged as primatial or metropolitan churches through which their respective neighboring local churches maintained communion in the universal church. These "hubs of communion" and their respective bishops settled regional disputes, oversaw regional structures of communion, and held a symbolic but practical role in maintaining its region's communion with local churches of other areas.[20] Among these churches was Rome.

Since the first generation of Christianity the local church at Rome has maintained a certain pride of place among all other local churches.[21] In the first millennium, communion with Rome represented communion with the whole of the universal church and was thus a sign of a local church's catholicity.[22] Eventually, Rome's influence grew, particularly in the West, and, by the fifth century, "parties increasingly turned to Rome" to settle church disputes.[23] While Rome did not hold the same influence in the East, it was nevertheless "acknowledged as the ultimate norm of ecclesial communion."[24] During the second half of the first millennium Rome's influence in the West slipped from the peak it had reached in the fifth century, then rose to greater levels as Roman practice began to be seen as the ultimate ecclesial norm.[25] Additionally, in the late first millennium Rome assumed a greater role in maintaining the communion of the whole church since "the ancient episcopal collegial structures no longer existed or had ceased to function" and were replaced by imperial and royal episcopal courts built around local civil leaders.[26] The Petrine ministry of the pope, named for Peter, who was by then remembered as the first bishop of Rome, had thus begun to include an aspect of universal jurisdiction. By the time of the split between the Christian East and West in the eleventh century, the bishop of Rome had developed into a quasi-monarchial role over the West.[27]

The first half of the second millennium—roughly bookended by the split of the Christian East and West in the eleventh century and the Protestant Reformation in the sixteenth century—marked a further centralization of Roman authority and a decline in the importance of the local churches in the West. Richard Gaillardetz notes that an originally unintended consequence of the Gregorian reforms in the late eleventh century, which sought to fight episcopal corruption resulting from political interference, was a coalescing of ecclesial power in Rome.[28] As a result, the reforms elevated Rome to the status of a mother church and source of life for each other local church in its communion.[29] This, subsequently, contributed to a belief that the catholicity of the whole church was expressed not by the communion shared within the universal church, but rather by the universal jurisdiction of Rome.[30] It reflected a shift toward a "Roman-centric" ecclesiology (often termed universalistic) that prioritized the universal church over the local churches. As a result, councils of bishops, which had been symbols of the equal communion among the heads of each local church, became instruments and signs of Roman control over the college of bishops and the universal church. This was further seen in the pope's appointment of bishops in churches that were considered particularly important.[31]

The period from the Protestant Reformation until just before Vatican II was characterized by a continued centralization of papal power and an even greater emphasis on Roman control as representative of the universal church. While the factors that led to this further centralization of Roman power and authority (the fractured nature of Western Christianity in the wake of the Protestant Reformation, the Council of Trent, the French Revolution, and the Enlightenment, to name a few) cannot be explored in detail here, the definitions of Roman primacy defined at the First Vatican Council should be noted. Though Vatican I, in *Pastor Aeternus* (PA), reaffirmed the jurisdiction of the ordinary bishop in each local church, it also stated that the pope's authority is "'ordinary' and 'immediate' both over all and each of the Churches and over all and each of the pastors and faithful" (PA, chap. 3, 9). Furthermore, that council taught that the pope speaks infallibly in matters of faith and morals when speaking "as shepherd and teacher of all Christians" (PA, chap. 4, 9). As a result of these definitions, "Rome ruled the Church in a much stronger fashion and intervened in its life everywhere to a much greater degree than had been the case [prior to Vatican I]."[32] Additionally, during this period the selection of bishops was concretely reserved as a right of Rome rather than the local community.[33] The catholicity of the Catholic Church was not identified with the communion present among local churches in the universal church, but rather with the authority of Rome over all other local churches.

VATICAN II

Written just nine decades after the suspension of the First Vatican Council, the documents of the Second Vatican Council signal a turning point in the Catholic Church's understanding of the relationship between the local and universal churches. Holding in tension both communion and jurisdiction, they lay the foundation for an orthopraxis of catholicity based on communion but remain hindered by the universalistic and juridical ecclesiology they inherited. The four documents that deal most directly with the relationship between the local churches and the universal church are *Sacrosanctum Concilium* (SC), *Lumen Gentium* (LG), *Christus Dominus* (CD), and *Ad Gentes* (AG).

In these documents one is able to discern four major themes that emphasize communion rather than universal jurisdiction. First, the council affirms that each local church possesses the gift of catholicity and contributes to the catholicity of the universal church through its engagement with the culture in which it finds itself. As a result, the council calls on the bishop of Rome to ensure that the unique expressions of catholicity present in the local churches are protected so that they may promote and not hinder unity (LG, 13). The council writes of the unique value of each culture in which a local church manifests itself, stating that Christians must experience their faith "in their own society and culture and in a manner that is in keeping with the traditions of their own land" (AG, 19). Second, the council acknowledges the simultaneity of the local and universal churches, stating that local churches are "modeled on the universal church" and that the universal church exists "in and from" the local churches (LG, 23). Third, the council emphasizes that the college of bishops, with the bishop of Rome at its center, is representative of the communion shared among the local churches. The bishops were not conceived as vicars of the pope but as heads of their respective local churches (LG, 27; CD, 3). Fourth, Vatican II develops a strong eucharistic ecclesiology, stressing that the whole church is fully present and made visible when a local church gathers around its bishop (or other presidential minister) in the communal celebration of the Eucharist (LG, 26; SC, 41; CD, 11).

The writings of the council, however, vacillate between these themes of communion and those that affirm a top-down, universalistic ecclesiology. In each of the documents cited above the First Vatican Council's teachings on the pope's universal, juridical authority are affirmed through direct reference or implication.[34] Komonchak argues that these seemingly contradictory statements reflect the ecclesiological tension that is present throughout the documents of Vatican II.[35] Due to this tension, Ruddy identifies several faults with Vatican II's ecclesiology, particularly as it relates to the local church: that it remains largely universalistic, that it prioritizes the bishop's role within the college of bishops over that in the local community, and that while briefly recognizing the simultaneity of the local and universal churches, it provides no theological justification for the statement.[36] Ruddy therefore calls the ecclesiology presented by the council "a transitional one" attempting to move from the juridical to the "communional" but remaining largely universalistic.[37] The experience of the Catholic Church in the last half-century has reflected this tension.

ACCOUNTS OF CURRENT ECCLESIAL PRACTICE

In the years since Vatican II, the actions of many curial officials have reflected an understanding of Vatican II's ecclesiology as one that prioritizes the universal church over the local churches, attempting to reign in control at nearly every level of ecclesial governance. Yet, many bishops, theologians, and members of the Catholic Church from all walks of life have expressed a desire for the church to practice the communion ecclesiology toward which Vatican II points. Kasper, writing from his experience as bishop in a local church in Germany, observes that many local churches have seen a further centralization of ecclesial power in Rome with fewer powers of self-determination being granted to individual local churches. He argues that this is not only caused by curial officials in Rome, but also bishops who are happy to let Rome make decisions for their local churches despite its disconnect from the local reality.[38] Kasper writes, "Many laypersons and priests can no longer understand universal church regulations, and simply ignore them."[39] Rembert Weakland, the retired archbishop of Milwaukee, recounts throughout his memoir the struggles that he and other bishops, who welcomed Vatican II's step toward a communion ecclesiology, had with Pope John Paul II, curial officials, and bishops who prefer a juridical, universalistic model of church. Describing the divergent ecclesiologies, Weakland recounts a dispute with Cardinal John O'Connor, whom Weakland counts among the latter category:

> O'Connor was a military man: the pope is the commander-in-chief giving orders, we bishops are the generals (the cardinals being those with four stars), the priests are the minor officers, lay people are the combat troops. My model of the Church was much more like the United States of America with a federal government and states' rights.[40]

Weakland's metaphor, while by no means perfect, describes how many leaders of local churches see these two models functioning, or at least attempting to function as they come into conflict in the last fifty years.[41]

Moreover, these concerns are not limited to Western Europe and North America. The late Francisco Claver, a Jesuit bishop in the Philippines, wrote of a recent desire in the curia to return to pre–Vatican II models of ecclesial practice. He argues that the local churches of the Philippines and their bishops embraced and began to practice the communion ecclesiology of Vatican II but encountered great resistance during the pontificate John Paul II.[42] He maintains that several steps suggested either at the council or in the years that followed that would have allowed for a fuller expression of the catholicity of the local churches and the communion they share with one another had their teaching and deliberative authorities not been curtailed. These include the synod of bishops, regional and national episcopal conferences, and the role of local churches in determining the norms for the translation of liturgical texts from Latin to the vernacular.[43] There are also concerns over Rome's increasing influence on the Eastern Catholic Churches. At the 2010 synod of bishops several bishops of these churches complained of a "Roman imperialism" that threatens the survival of the distinct identities of the twenty-two Eastern Catholic Churches in communion with Rome.[44] These examples from Kasper, Weakland, Claver, and the Eastern Catholic Churches are all instances of a growing sense that local churches are not afforded appropriate levels of self-determination in a global church guided by ecclesial communion.

The Roman priority of the universal church over the local churches is also seen in documents produced by Rome since the close of Vatican II. The preeminent example of this is the Congregation for the Doctrine of the Faith's (CDF) letter "Communio Notis" (CN). The letter states that in a proper understanding of communion ecclesiology, the universal church "is not the result of the communion of the Churches, but, in its essential mystery, it is a reality *ontologically and temporally* prior to every *individual* particular Church" (CN, 9). While the document reiterates *Lumen Gentium's* statement that the universal church is formed "in and from" the local churches, it adds that such a claim cannot be understood apart from John Paul II's contention that the local churches are "in and formed out of the [universal] Church" (CN, 9). Drawing upon the writings of "the Fathers" (citing the Shepherd of Hermas and Clement of Rome specifically), the CDF holds that the universal church "precedes creation, and gives birth to the particular Churches as her daughters" (CN, 9). The understanding of communion ecclesiology presented in "Communio Notis" is also found in John Paul II's apostolic letter on episcopal conferences, "Apostolos Suos." In the letter the late pope states that a bishop's role in the universal college of bishops "precedes the office of being the head of a particular Church" (AS, 12). Such claims have led to a great deal of theological discussion over the relationship between the local and universal churches in recent years.

RECENT THEOLOGICAL THOUGHT ON THE RELATIONSHIP

As was noted above, the most public of the debates regarding the relationship between the universal and local churches since Vatican II is that between Ratzinger and Kasper, sparked by Kasper's response to "Communio Notis." Kasper is concerned that the CDF's letter is not a development of Vatican II's theology of the relationship but a reversal of it. He argues that the presentation of the universal church as ontologically and historically prior to the local churches is unfaithful to the reality of the one church of Christ.[45] In addition, he worries that by prioritizing the universal church, the local church of Rome (specifically the pope and curia) is "de facto identified" with the universal church. This identification, he argues, perpetuates "an attempt to restore Roman centralism, a process which is already an actuality" and dismisses Vatican II's teachings on the communion of the church.[46] Moreover, while Kasper does not deny the pre-existence of the church, he argues it cannot be used to argue for an ontological priority of the universal church or the local churches as they are both earthly manifestations of this reality, occurring simultaneously.[47] Drawing upon the Lukan account of Pentecost, he argues that the church at Jerusalem is "universal and local in its single reality."[48] Kasper maintains that the "concrete historical universal Church" present in the Jerusalem community and the local church at Jerusalem cannot be separated from one another. He contends that the universal church must be understood in this situation to be a concrete reality, simultaneous to the local church, lest the universal church be seen as an ahistorical, ideal abstraction.[49]

Ratzinger's position is primarily a defense of the assertion in "Communio Notis" that the universal church historically and ontologically precedes the local churches. Killian McDonnell writes, "Ratzinger defends the ontological and temporal priority of the universal Church by reference to the teaching of the Fathers that the one and only Church precedes creation and gives birth to the particular churches."[50] Like Kasper, Ratzinger turns to the Pentecost narrative to support his argument. Highlighting the significance of the Twelve gathered with the Jerusalem community, he argues that "the narrative is a 'theological declaration'" of the ontological and historical priority of the universal church.[51] For Ratzinger, the Pentecost event, at which the preexistent mystery of the church is born into temporal being, communicates the precedence of the universal church primarily by establishing the earthly manifestation of the church upon the Twelve as the New Israel. The miracle by which the Jewish diaspora was able to understand the preaching of the Twelve, Ratzinger asserts, "shows forth the oneness of the New Israel, a unity which spans all times and all places, and this even before it comes to a question of forming a local Jerusalem community."[52] Responding to Kasper, Ratzinger rejects the claim that that prioritizing the universal church over the local churches seems to support Roman centralism since the universal church is identified solely with the pope and curia. While recognizing the particular ministry of the church of Rome to care for the universal church, he argues that such identification expresses "a growing inability to imagine the one, holy, catholic, and universal Church in any concrete way."[53] Rather, Ratzinger argues, the universal church ought to be understood in light of "the christological and trinitarian formulations of *Lumen Gentium* nos. 2–4," in which the communion that unites the whole church is compared to that which unites the Triune God.[54]

Since Vatican II, much of the theological reflection on the relationship between the universal and local churches has resonated with the concerns of Kasper, Weakland, Claver, and the Eastern Catholic bishops mentioned above.[55] For example, Mannion demonstrates that the vision of a communion ecclesiology presented in the CDF's letter has been used to justify a centralization of power in Catholicism and hurts the identity of the local churches as manifestations of the one church of Christ.[56] Likewise, Thomas Rausch notes the need to find the proper balance between the local and universal churches. Rausch argues that, while the CDF's letter may have some basis for warning against an overemphasis on the autonomy of local churches, such an argument cannot be taken to the point of prioritizing the universal church by means of ecclesial uniformity.[57]

Today, many theologians argue that a communion ecclesiology rooted in the documents of Vatican II ought to recognize the simultaneity of the local and universal churches. Richard Gaillardetz writes, "Only a theology of the church that asserts the simultaneity of the local and universal dimensions of the church can avoid the centralization of authority that has haunted Catholicism for the most of the second millennium."[58] Similarly, Joseph Komonchak writes that the ecclesiology of Vatican II should be understood to "guarantee that the relationship between the whole Church and the individual

Churches is seen as one of reciprocal or mutual inclusion."[59] It is Tillard, however, who has addressed this topic most comprehensively. Tillard states, "The church is catholic by uniting [the local churches] within the communion of Christ Jesus, which integrates the diversities (having their source in creation) into the space salvation and the new creation opened by the cross. The church is a communion of churches, themselves made of communions of persons enriching one another through diversity."[60] Tillard argues that diversity is at the heart of the communion that unites each local church in the universal church. Ruddy writes the following of Tillard's ecclesiology of communion:

> Tillard rejects the question of priority as a mistaken one, arguing that the universal church is a communion (not a confederation) of local churches, a communion of communions, a church of churches: each local church exists only in communion with that universal church of churches, and the universal church exists only in, through, and from the local churches.[61]

Tillard's emphasis on the mutual dependence of the local and universal churches is characteristic of the above-cited theologians. The argument of each is for a balanced theology of the relationship between the local and universal churches.

EXPRESSING CATHOLICITY IN THE LOCAL AND UNIVERSAL CHURCHES

The above survey of the current state of the relationship between the local and universal churches, in the Catholic Church, reveals that there is a great deal of tension not only in ecclesial practice but also in the theological understanding of this relationship. Vatican II's documents marked a change in Catholic ecclesiology by emphasizing both communion and jurisdiction. This tension seemed to invite the church to express its catholicity by putting the local churches on equal footing with the universal church in ecclesial practice and recognizing the interdependence of the local and universal churches upon one another. However, in the fifty years since Vatican II, the practices of many Roman and hierarchical officials have reflected only the more universalistic elements of Vatican II's ecclesiology. This has caused a number of local church leaders and theologians to express concern that such a limited reading of Vatican II's ecclesiology unduly justifies practices of Roman centrism in a church marked by great cultural diversity. I concur with these concerns and argue that the Catholic Church ought to adopt an ecclesial praxis that is reflective of Vatican II's movement toward a communion ecclesiology—one that recognizes the simultaneity of the local and universal churches by inviting them to enter into a reciprocal relationship with each other. This final section offers several proposals through which the reciprocal nature of this relationship would be made more visible in the life of the church and more fully express its catholicity, particularly when these proposals are practiced collectively.

If a local church is to express its catholicity, it must first fully express the faith and life of the one church of Christ in its own culture through the practice of inculturation. Edward Schillebeeckx writes, "Universality—which in Greek is 'catholicity'—means that Christian faith is open (critically) to all, to every people and to every culture."[62] Inculturation is the organic method through which the church expresses its universality by engaging each culture it encounters so as to become truly local in every historical, cultural context it finds itself. It is not limited to lands where the gospel has not yet been preached but is a necessary action for every local church in every age. Peter Schineller writes that inculturation "represents the efforts of Christians in particular places to understand and celebrate their Christian faith in a way peculiar to that situation or context."[63] That which begins from below as the church in each place responds to the needs of its times and makes known the gospel. Nathan Mitchell writes: "Inculturation is never a one-way street, but a real give and take, a genuine dialogue in which the church is simultaneously teacher and student, eager to learn what the student has to teach. . . . 'In effect, inculturation must involve the whole people of God, and not just a few experts, since the people reflect the authentic *sensus fidei* which must never be lost sight of.'"[64] Inculturation, therefore, does not suggest that the local church should be entirely transformed by culture so as to lose its identity as a church, but rather, it calls the church to embed itself in its surrounding culture so as to be sign of God's kingdom in that particular place.[65] Using Tillard's language, Ruddy argues that the local church must "sink its roots" into the culture so as to "incarnate the Gospel in the 'fleshly earth' of its region." He contends that "locality does not compete with catholicity, but instead expresses it fully."[66] By embracing the practice of inculturation, the catholicity of the universal church is not expressed in its ability to be a homogenous church spread across the earth but in its ability to be a communion of local churches, each engaged with its own culture and united in the communion of the universal church. Gaillardetz writes: "Inculturation names the process of the gospel being received in a specific local context. For Tillard, it is inculturation that preserves the catholicity of the church."[67] Inculturation allows a church to express the catholicity of the whole church by its very practice being local. Such an expression of the church's universality, however, is only possible if the local church also maintains strong bonds of communion within the universal church.

The Catholic Church, then, must also find renewed means through which the local church of Rome and its bishop may exercise their ministry of unity. Rome's role as the center of communion has been an important reality in the church throughout its history—a fact that Vatican II reiterates (LG, 22, 25, and 27). Theologians such as Tillard, Ruddy, Lakeland, Gaillardetz, and Rausch, as well as bishops including Kasper and Claver, all acknowledge the importance of Rome's primatial nature.[68] For example, Lakeland writes, "Without Rome, the local communities would be shorn of their sense of unity of purpose and devoid of presence to the world beyond the local context."[69] However, each of these theologians also notes that Roman primacy cannot amount to Roman absolutism. Rausch writes that, while Rome must remain a strong center of communion, an emphasis must be placed on being in communion "with Rome" rather than "under Rome."[70] The primatial ministry of Rome must be reimagined in such a way that it enables the communion shared between the local churches of the universal church. Its primary function ought to be ensuring that the communion of the universal church is strong and visible through various practices of collegiality and frequent collaboration of local churches. Such an endeavor has important consequence both for the present life of Catholic Church and for its ecumenical future. John Paul II, in his encyclical *Ut Unum Sint*, has noted that if the Catholic Church is to take its ecumenical future seriously, the Petrine ministry of the Roman pope must be reformed to facilitate communion among the reconciling churches. Gaillardetz writes that a renewed Petrine ministry ought to be both "facilitative and interventionist"—facilitating communion between the local churches within the universal church and intervening only in extreme circumstances when a local church has proven incapable of handling the situation.[71] Kasper, who suggests a similar exercise of the Petrine ministry, responds to concerns that such a model of primacy would result in a weakened papacy and weakened center of communion by arguing that it would in fact require a vigorous exercise of Rome's unitive ministry in order to facilitate communion effectively through collaboration and collegiality.[72]

One example of how such a renewed Petrine ministry might facilitate ecclesial communion between the local churches of the universal church is by enabling an effective practice of episcopal collegiality. Vatican II emphasized that each bishop has a dual role as both head of the local church and as a member of the college of bishops, which, with the pope as its head, has a particular concern for the care of the universal church (LG 18–20; LG 27; CD 3). Episcopal collegiality, therefore, represents not only an exercise of the bishops' ministry to the universal church, but also the cooperation and collaboration of the local churches they oversee since "the bishops represent their churches and not themselves."[73] Renewing the synod of bishops as a truly deliberative body with a particular care for the life of the universal church, rather than continuing its current practice of offering recommendations, seemingly predetermined by the curia, to the pope, would allow local churches throughout the world to work more collaboratively through the persons of their bishops. Similarly, episcopal conferences present a unique opportunity through which the church is able deepen its catholicity. Ruddy writes that Tillard sees episcopal conferences not only as an exercise of communion but also as an instrument through which the catholicity of the whole church is expressed. Citing Tillard, Ruddy writes, "Episcopal conferences, as servants of catholicity, therefore have as their mission the task of ensuring that the various enfleshments or inculturations of the Gospel remain in communion with the church of Pentecost."[74] Episcopal conferences, then, as representatives of the college of bishops in particular national (or sometimes multinational) regions, ought to work with one another and the pope, who is responsible for ensuring that local churches are able to engage their own culture (LG, 13), to maintain the communion of the universal church. Others, including Hans Küng, have suggested that the Catholic Church should facilitate a vigorous practice episcopal collegiality at an even more local level by reappropriating some form of a metropolitan system. While archbishops do hold symbolic roles of maintaining unity as the metropolitan of their ecclesial province, there are no formal structures that allow the churches in a given province to work together to address the issues facing them—whether particular to their region or wider in nature. Küng also notes the importance of allowing for similar structures in the church's ecumenical future so local churches occupying some form of primatial role in their own ecclesial context (for example, Canterbury in the Anglican Communion) may continue to do so if (or when) they are reconciled with Rome and those local churches in communion with it.[75]

Additionally, the people of each local church must enter into a renewed sense of communion with their bishop if episcopal communion and collegiality are to represent the communion shared among local churches. Lakeland argues that most Catholics today find it difficult to share communion beyond the parish level.[76] Additionally, Ruddy notes that the Roman habit of prioritizing a bishop's role in the college of bishops over his role as head of a local church, as is seen in "Communio Notis" and "Apostolos Suos," "severs the ancient, intrinsic link between bishop and church."[77] In order to strengthen the communion between a local church and its bishop, the episcopal office must be exercised in a consultative and collegial manner at the local level—just as Roman primacy must be exercised at the universal level. A bishop must consult the people of his diocese in pastoral and temporal matters and invite them to collaborate with him in his ministry.

While canon law affords several opportunities for such collaboration, including diocesan-wide pastoral councils and diocesan synods, steps must first be taken to make such collaboration possible. First, both Küng and Tillard argue that the size of dioceses ought to be reduced. Ruddy contends that by reducing the size of dioceses, the need for titular auxiliary bishops will also be reduced (or, ideally, eliminated) as more dioceses would be formed at sizes able to be led by one bishop rather than several.[78] Küng notes that shrinking the size of dioceses would allow bishops more time to minister to and with the people of a local church rather than coordinating the logistical and bureaucratic aspects of managing a diocese that is too large for one person to lead.[79]

Second, both Gaillardetz and Rausch argue that the local church ought to be given a greater voice in the selection of its bishop.[80] This is not to say that bishops should be chosen solely on the basis of a democratic vote, but it does mean that Rome should not be the principal actor in selecting bishops. Rather, the Catholic Church ought to develop a process of discernment to select and appoint bishops—one that includes both the people of the local church (perhaps in consultation with neighboring bishops) and Rome. By actively involving the people of a local church in the selection of their bishop, the people are invited into the process of collaboration from the start of their bishop's ministry. In this respect the Catholic Church is able to look both to its past and to the examples of other Christian traditions, such as the churches of Anglican Communion, who have included the faithful in the selection of their bishops.

Third, Gaillardetz suggests that ending the practice of translating bishops from diocese to diocese would encourage greater communion between a local church and its bishop. Bishops would be able to work for the good of the local churches that they serve without worrying about what effect a given decision may have on potential promotions to more prominent or larger local churches. Likewise, the people of the local church would be more willing to collaborate with a bishop they know is there to stay.[81] By enacting practical reforms such as the three just mentioned, a local church and its bishops would more easily be able to enter into a collaborative relationship, and episcopal collegiality would more concretely represent the communion shared between each local church and just that between individual bishops.

The catholicity expressed in the reciprocal nature of the relationship between the local and universal churches, however, is ideally seen in the celebration of the Eucharist. Massimo Faggioli suggests that one is more easily able to discern the eucharistic ecclesiology of Vatican II if its documents are read through the hermeneutical lens of the council's first document, *Sacrosanctum Concilium*.[82] In it, the council calls the eucharistic assembly "the preeminent manifestation of the Church" (SC, 41). Through this statement, the bishops of Vatican II underscore the importance of the most basic experience of church for most Christians: the gathering of a local community at table with its presidential minister to celebrate the Eucharist as a memorial of the paschal mystery. Tillard writes, "The Eucharistic community is not a fragment of the mystery of the universal Church, but an appearance of this Church in communion with the Father and in the communion of brotherhood, through the Spirit of Christ the Lord."[83] Ruddy suggests that the communion offered in the Eucharist makes real the catholicity of the local church by affirming and affecting its own internal communion, divine communion with God, eschatological communion with all who have previously celebrated the Eucharist and will in the future, and ecclesial communion with those celebrating "the same eucharist" in their own cultures.[84] Through its gift of communion in the person of Christ, the Eucharist makes real the universal church's catholicity at the local level, bringing those gathered at table into communion with all other local churches who celebrate the Eucharist in their own communities.

Among the many liturgical reforms of Vatican II was the endorsement of liturgical inculturation (SC 37–40). John Baldovin defines liturgical inculturation as the "adaptation of Catholic liturgy to the various cultures in which it finds itself celebrated."[85] Inculturation of the liturgy, then, entails appropriately incorporating various symbols and rituals of the local culture into the liturgy while still maintaining its essential eucharistic nature and ritual shape. The celebration of an inculturated Eucharist allows a local church to celebrate the communion it and all other local churches share within the universal church while also celebrating its own unique expression of being church. It manifests the unity of faith in a diversity of expressions that is central to any understanding of the church's catholicity as a gift reliant upon the reciprocity and simultaneity of the local and universal churches. As Tillard notes, the practice of inculturation is reminiscent of the Pentecost event, for Acts 2 does not state that Peter and those with him were heard in one language, but rather that each person gathered from the Jewish diaspora heard the gospel proclaimed in his or her own tongue.[86] If the gospel of Christ was simultaneously manifested locally while being proclaimed universally at its first proclamation by the Twelve and their companions, so too should the one church of Christ be understood in a way that recognizes the reciprocal nature of universal and local churches.

CONCLUSION

The church's self-understanding of its own catholicity has manifested itself in the relationship between the universal and local churches since Christianity's first generation. Throughout the tradition, however, this relationship has been understood and expressed in myriad ways. When an overemphasis is placed on the universal church, the church's catholicity is too easily identified with the spread of ecclesial uniformity under the jurisdiction of Rome. If an overemphasis were to be placed on the local church, the catholicity of the church would be damaged by failing to acknowledge the importance of real and visible structures of communion. In the current situation of the Catholic Church, there have been attempts to renew an ecclesiology reminiscent of, but not identical to, Christianity's first millennium—one that recognizes the reciprocal nature of the universal church and the local churches. However, the practice of authorities in Rome, in large part, remains that of the second millennium, in which the universal church was prioritized through Roman control. As a result, the Catholic Church must find new ways, such as inculturation, a renewal of Rome as the center of communion, and a renewal of the communion between the local church and its bishop, to express better the reciprocity of the local and universal churches, and in the process, more fully express its catholicity.

NOTES

1. Dennis Doyle identifies six competing and complementary notions of communion ecclesiology. See Dennis M. Doyle, *Communion Ecclesiology: Vision and Versions* (Maryknoll, NY: Orbis Books, 2000), 15–21.

2. See Roger Haight, *Historical Ecclesiology*, vol. 1 of *Christian Community in History* (New York: Continuum, 2004); idem, *Comparative Ecclesiology*, vol. 2 of *Christian Community in History* (New York: Continuum, 2005); idem, *Ecclesial Existence*, vol. 3 of *Christian Community in History* (New York: Continuum, 2008); Paul Lakeland, *Church: Living Communion* (Collegeville, MN: The Liturgical Press, 2009); and Gerard Mannion, *Ecclesiology and Postmodernity: Questions for the Church in Our Time* (Collegeville, MN: The Liturgical Press, 2007). Haight prefers the phase "ecclesiology from below," while Mannion refers to the method as an "ecclesiology from below" and a "postmodern ecclesiology." In this essay—because it is Lakeland's appropriation of the inductive lens that guides my own use of the method—I use his "inductive ecclesiology."

3. Lakeland, *Church*, 121–26; Neil Ormerod, "'The Times They Are A-Changing': A Response to O'Malley and Schloesser," *Theological Studies* 67 (2006): 835.

4. Bernard Lonergan, *A Second Collection* (Philadelphia: Westminster, 1974), 60.

5. Lakeland, *Church*, 123.

6. Ibid., 121.

7. Bernard Lonergan, *Method in Theology* (New York: Herder and Herder, 1972), 231.

8. Mannion, *Ecclesiology and Postmodernity*, 27.

9. Haight, *Historical Ecclesiology*, 27.

10. Mannion, *Ecclesiology and Postmodernity*, 36.

11. Christopher Ruddy, *The Local Church: Tillard and the Future of Catholic Ecclesiology* (New York: Herder and Herder), 59.

12. Ibid.

13. Ibid.

14. Ibid., 55, 61.

15. Ibid., 61.

16. Ibid., 106–7.

17. For the paradigmatic work on this subject, see Ludwig Hertling, *Communion: Church and Papacy in Early Christianity*, trans. Jared Wicks (Chicago: Loyola University Press, 1972).

18. Klaus Schatz, *Papal Primacy: From Its Origins to the Present*, trans. Linda A. Maloney and John A. Otto (Collegeville, MN: The Liturgical Press, 1996), 17.

19. Ibid.

20. Ibid., 17–18.

21. Ruddy writes that the most fundamental, theological reason for the primacy of Rome "is its foundation upon the apostolic faith and martyrdom"

of Peter, the apostle to the Jews and first among the Twelve, and Paul, the apostle to the Gentiles (Ruddy, *The Local Church*, 117).

22. Hertling, *Communion*, 53–55.

23. Schatz, *Papal Primacy*, 19. See also Hertling, *Communion*, 73–75.

24. Schatz, *Papal Primacy*, 60.

25. Ibid., 63–68.

26. Ibid., 71–72.

27. Ibid., 78–85.

28. Richard Gaillardetz, *Ecclesiology for a Global Church: A People Called and Sent* (Maryknoll, NY: Orbis Books, 2008), 259–60.

29. Schatz, *Papal Primacy*, 85.

30. Ibid., 85–87.

31. Ibid., 96–99.

32. Ibid., 168.

33. Thomas P. Rausch, *Towards a Truly Catholic Church: An Ecclesiology for the Third Millennium* (Collegeville, MN: The Liturgical Press, 2005), 204–5.

34. Ruddy, *The Local Church*, 51.

35. Joseph Komonchak, "The Ecclesiology of Vatican II," available on the publicaffairs.cua.edu website.

36. Ruddy, *The Local Church*, 51–52.

37. Ibid., 46.

38. Walter Kasper, *Leadership in the Church: How Traditional Roles Can Serve the Christian Community Today*, trans. Brian McNeil (New York: Herder and Herder, 2003), 161.

39. Ibid., 159. See also Rausch, *Toward a Truly Catholic Church*, 203–4.

40. Rembert Weakland, *A Pilgrim in a Pilgrim Church: Memoirs of a Catholic Archbishop* (Grand Rapids, MI: Eerdmans, 2009), 337.

41. For similar comments, see Geoffrey Robinson (a retired auxiliary bishop from Australia), in Geoffrey Robinson, *Confronting Power and Sex in the Catholic Church: Reclaiming the Spirit of Jesus* (Collegeville, MN: The Liturgical Press, 2008).

42. Francisco F. Claver, *The Making of a Local Church* (Maryknoll, NY: Orbis Books, 2008), 25–26. See also Rausch, *Towards a Truly Catholic Church*, 175–77.

43. Claver, *The Making of a Local Church*, 140–42.

44. John Allen, "Protests Against Roman Imperialism at Middle East Synod," *National Catholic Reporter*, October 12, 2010, available on the ncronline.org website.

45. Killian McDonnell, "The Ratzinger/Kasper Debate: The Universal Church and Local Churches," *Theological Studies* 63, no. 2 (June 2002): 230–31.

46. Ibid., 231.

47. Walter Kasper, "On the Church: A Friendly Reply to Cardinal Ratzinger," *America* (April 23–30, 2001), 13.

48. Walter Kasper, "Zur Theologie und Praxis des bischoflichen Amtes," *Auf neue Art Kirche Sein: Wirklichkeiten—Herausfoderungen—Wandlungen* (Munich: Bernward bei Don Bosco, 1999), 44, quoted in McDonnell, "The Ratzinger/Kasper Debate," 231.

49. McDonnell, "The Ratzinger/Kasper Debate," 231.

50. Ibid., 234.

51. Joseph Ratzinger, "On the Relation of the Universal Church and the Local Church in Vatican II," *Frankfurter Allgemeine Zeitung*, December 22, 2000, 46, quoted in McDonnell, "The Ratzinger/Kasper Debate," 236.

52. McDonnell, "The Ratzinger Kasper Debate," 236.

53. Ratzinger, "On the Relation of the Universal Church and the Local Church in Vatican II," 46, quoted in McDonnell, "The Ratzinger/Kasper Debate," 237.

54. McDonnell, "The Ratzinger/Kasper Debate," 237.

55. Ratzinger's most ardent supporter during and after the debate has been Cardinal Avery Dulles. See Avery Dulles, "Ratzinger and Kasper on the Universal Church," *Inside the Vatican*, May 2005, 101.

56. Mannion, *Ecclesiology and Postmodernity*, 67–69.

57. Rausch, *Towards a Truly Catholic Church*, 178.

58. Gaillardetz, *Ecclesiology for a Global Church*, 119.

59. Komonchak, "The Ecclesiology of Vatican II," available on the publicaffairs.cua.edu website.

60. Jean-Marie Roger Tillard, *The Flesh of the Church, Flesh of Christ: At the Source of the Ecclesiology of Communion*, trans. Madeleine Beaumont (Collegeville, MN: The Liturgical Press, 2001), 10.

61. Ruddy, *The Local Church*, 100.

62. Edward Schillebeeckx, *Church: The Human Story of God*, trans. John Bowden (New York: Crossroad, 1990), 169.

63. Peter Schineller, *A Handbook on Inculturation* (New York: Paulist Press, 1990), 1.

64. Nathan D. Mitchell, "Cultures, Inculturation, and *Sacrosanctum Concilium*," *Worship* 77 (2003): 172–73, quoting *Redemptoris Missio* no. 54.

65. Ruddy, *The Local Church*, 68.

66. Ibid., 69.

67. Richard Gaillardetz, "The Office of the Bishop Within the *Communio Ecclesiarum*: Insights from the Ecclesiology of Jean-Marie Tillard," *Science et Espirit* 62, no. 2–3 (May 2009): 187.

68. Ruddy, *The Local Church*, 117–18; Lakeland, *Church*, 50; Gaillardetz, *Ecclesiology for a Global Church*, 284–89; Rausch, *Towards a Truly Catholic*

Church, 219–20; Kasper, *Leadership in the Local Church*, 163–67; Claver, *The Making of a Local Church*, 40–41.

69. Lakeland, *Church*, 50.

70. Rausch, *Towards a Truly Catholic Church*, 219.

71. Gaillardetz, *Ecclesiology for a Global Church*, 286–87.

72. Kasper, "On the Church," 14; McDonnell, "The Ratzinger/Kasper Debate," 249.

73. Ruddy, *The Local Church,* 111.

74. Ibid., 112.

75. Hans Küng, *The Church* (New York: Doubleday, 1976), 549–50, 608.

76. Lakeland, *Church*, 49.

77. Ruddy, *The Local Church*, 138.

78. Ibid.

79. Küng, *The Church*, 549–50.

80. Gaillardetz, *Ecclesiology for a Global Church*, 277–78; Rausch, *Towards a Truly Catholic Church*, 206.

81. Gaillardetz, *Ecclesiology for a Global Church*, 277–78.

82. Massimo Faggioli, "Quaestio Disputata: *Sacrosanctum Concilium* and the Meaning of Vatican II," *Theological Studies* 71, no. 2 (June 2010): 445, 450.

83. Jean-Marie Roger Tillard, *The Bishop of Rome*, trans. John de Satgé (Wilmington, DE: Michael Glazier, 1983), 81.

84. Ruddy, *The Local Church*, 70.

85. John F. Baldovin, *Reforming the Liturgy: A Response to the Critics* (Collegeville, MN: The Liturgical Press, 2008), 6.

86. Ruddy, *The Local Church*, 55–57.

Timelessness, Solidarity,
and the Crucified Future

Attuning Ecclesial Praxis to a Theology of Fragility

EDUARDO GONZALEZ

The challenges concerning the ongoing reception of the Second Vatican Council entail the question of the future. The importance of this question is reflected not only in the theme of the present book, but also in its various sub-themes: the future of Catholic ethics, the future of dialogue, the future of ecclesiology, and so forth. The vicissitudes of context that characterize reception as a hermeneutical event incessantly introduce new problems into these areas, rendering the question of the future as indispensable not only to responsible theological reflection, but also, and more important, to responsible praxis. It is a question that offers the necessary space for addressing current and possible directions of the reception of the council. The importance of remaining attentive to changing realities is reinforced by the conciliar documents themselves. This is true not simply regarding the task of discerning the "signs of the times," but also in terms of the pneumatological significance that endows such a task with its proper ecclesiological depths.[1] The activity of the Holy Spirit is constitutive of the church as a living dynamism, involving constant renewal and thereby enabling and guiding its engagement with new situations. The question of the future underlies every reflection on the ongoing process of receiving Vatican II in light of the challenges that accompany shifting contexts.

This fundamental status of the future signals the necessity to consider the adequacy of every dialogue concerning the reception of the council whose point of departure is not a direct confrontation with the questions that the theme of the future silently harbors. What is the status of the implicit understanding of the future that is operative in such discussions? What is the relationship between this surreptitiously accepted meaning of the future and the process of reflection on the reception of the council? In what sense does the former affect the latter? Is it possible to pursue an analysis that involves the question of the future without explicitly addressing the significance of that question in a critical manner? How does such a situation affect the task of discerning the signs of the times? Is it possible for the church to listen to and interact with its contemporary realities in the absence of an adequate understanding of the future? What does this signify for the pneumatological dimension of ecclesiology? Such questions highlight the importance of engaging a certain preapprehension of the future as a condition for discussing the current challenges in the reception of the council.

It is the task of this essay to identify, analyze, and reframe critically the conception of the future that tends to remain operative in such discussions. Attending to the question of the future in an analytical and evaluative manner is an indispensable point of departure for addressing the future of ecclesiology and other areas of theology. As such, the essay first considers the meaning of the future that emerges in light of the challenges posed by the contemporary world. This meaning of the future will designate a concrete historical standpoint from which to rethink the otherwise implicitly operative notion of the future. Finally, the interruptive theological significance of the critically reframed future will reorient the discussion of the ongoing reception of the council toward the cultivation of a mystical-political ecclesial praxis within the framework of ecological justice.

THE FUTURE: FORMULATING THE PROBLEMATIC

The aim of this section is neither to provide a comprehensive survey of contemporary understandings of the future nor to introduce an entirely new manner of thinking about the future. It is not a matter of articulating the meaning of possible, probable, or unforeseeable trajectories of history. Rather, the question of the future will be formulated in a way that highlights the *tragic sense of its conditionality*, thereby departing from the certainty and imperturbable presence of a landscape upon which different or currently inconceivable historical trajectories will eventually concretize.

Toward the end of a 1998 pastoral statement on the environment, "NMCCB Statement on the Environment: Partnership for the Future," the New Mexico Conference of Catholic Bishops mentions that "if there is to be a future" in light of current ecological destruction, then conversion is necessary. It is precisely this *if* that radicalizes the question of the future; indeed, the question of the future, insofar as it is no longer preapprehended as unconditional, becomes the problem of a *questionable* future. Thomas Berry expresses this questionability concisely, "In the twentieth century the glory of the human has become the desolation of Earth. The desolation of Earth is becoming the destiny of the human." Such a destiny signals the disquieting uncertainty that characterizes the future itself: "The viability of the human is in question."[2]

It is not possible here to offer a detailed discussion of the scientific data concerning ecological devastation. The literature on the topic is extensive and does not require repetition. It will be helpful, however, to mention a few points in order to communicate the exigencies and severity of the situation. In her discussion of the Fourth Assessment Report of the United Nations Intergovernmental Panel on Climate Change (IPCC), Sallie McFague notes its "'unequivocal' confidence that global warming is under way, and 'very high confidence' (90 percent) that human activities are the cause." The reliability of the IPCC report resides in the fact that it presents not its own climate science but rather "the consensus view of hundreds of scientists who study articles on climate change published in peer-reviewed journals." The urgency of the report lies in the recognition that climate change "is now an issue of human—indeed, of planetary—security."[3] Although the scientific consensus presented by the IPCC is, as McFague and others observe, inherently conservative, since it amounts to "lowest-common-denominator conclusions" and thus tends to underestimate the situation, "it is still frightening in its predictions."[4] The disconcerting image of the future offered by such underestimations is only indicative of the reality of the threat currently confronting human history.

This urgent sense of insecurity is forcefully articulated by the biologist Edward O. Wilson. Toward the end of his otherwise joyous open letter to Henry David Thoreau, Wilson offers a bleak update to his transgenerational friend:

The natural world in the year 2001 is everywhere disappearing before our eyes. . . . No one in your time could imagine a disaster of this magnitude . . . An Armageddon is approaching at the beginning of the third millennium. But it is not the cosmic war . . . foretold in sacred scripture. It is the wreckage of the planet by an exuberantly plentiful and ingenious humanity.[5]

It is no longer possible to accept the certainty and unconditionality of the future. The challenges of the contemporary world put into question the inexorability of the historical process. Wilson continues his portentous forecast: "The living world is dying; the natural economy is crumbling beneath our busy feet. We have been too self-absorbed to foresee the long-term consequences of our actions, and we will suffer a terrible loss unless we shake off our delusions and move quickly to a solution."[6] Thus it is not simply a matter of reframing the future as vulnerable and threatened, but of doing so in a manner that highlights the causal relationship between that vulnerability and human activity. The destructive character of the (in)human orientation toward the world signals the *dialectical* nature of the future as uncertain. The future viewed from the standpoint of ecological destruction does not merely exhibit weakness and fragility but receives such features as a result of human activity; that is, the future is *inflicted* with fragility. To understand the future itself as conditional means to attend to the dialectical constitution of that conditionality.

Paleontologist Peter D. Ward is disturbingly clear about the necessity to rethink our ingenuous projections of a placid future in light of contemporary climate science:

> Greenhouse gases strongly affect planetary temperature. As carbon dioxide levels rise, so will planetary temperature. . . . The rule of thumb used by climatologists is that each doubling of the carbon dioxide level can be expected to increase global temperatures by about 2 degrees Celsius. Thus the projected carbon dioxide level even for a century from now would be expected to increase the global temperature between 3 degrees and 4 degrees Celsius. Today that temperature is estimated to be between 15 degrees and 16 degrees Celsius. It would climb to just beneath 20 degrees Celsius. The effect of that would be Earth-changing, conceivably bringing about the greatest mass death of humans in all of history.[7]

It is no surprise, then, that a 1988 pastoral letter on the environment by the Catholic bishops of the Philippines, "What Is Happening to Our Beautiful Land?" compares the future to the devastation of a nuclear war: "We know that a nuclear war would turn the whole earth into a fireball and render the planet inhospitable to life. We tend to forget that the constant, cumulative destruction of life-forms and different habitats will, in the long term, have the same effect." It is important to note here that such comparisons and Wilson's usage of apocalyptic imagery in the quotation above should not be uncritically dismissed as exaggerated, overly dramatic, doomsday madness. Reframing the question of the future in terms of radical fragility and uncertainty is no rhetorical exercise or theoretical dramatization; rather, it is an effort to qualify and intensify the conception of time that governs our thinking in light of concrete history. As McFague observes, "Climate is our planet's largest, most important, and most vulnerable interlocking system: it allows for and sustains life. . . . Therefore, a sober, prudent assessment of our situation behooves us to take action now. It is not apocalyptic or radical to do so, but simply common sense."[8]

The dialectical meaning of fragility, albeit highlighting the severity of the question of the future, is irreducible to the future. That is, the destructive activity that puts the future into question is *already* effective in the present. Ward offers an example of how the consequences of climate change are currently claiming lives:

> There is already significant human mortality from the current greenhouse-induced global warming of Earth. A 2004 study by scientists at the World Health Organization and the London School of Hygiene and Tropical Medicine determined that 160,000 people die every year from the effects of global warming, from malaria to malnutrition, children in developing nations seemingly the most vulnerable. These numbers could almost double by the year 2020.[9]

The contemporary situation, then, challenges one to rethink the future not only in light of the predictions made by climatologists but also in relation to the fact that victims of ecological destruction already exist. Furthermore, as Ward indicates, the victims are primarily the poor. The ecological crisis brings to the surface a more expansive network of structural injustice with which it is inextricably linked. McFague highlights this dimension of the problem:

> North America and Western Europe have contributed two-thirds of carbon dioxide emissions, while only 3 percent has come from Africa. However, the northern, richer countries will suffer fewer adverse consequences, and they are also better able to pay for expensive adaptive measures to reduce the impact. These countries are already turning seawater into drinking water, erecting flood barriers, cultivating genetically altered drought-resistant seeds. Nothing of this sort is happening in Africa and in similar high-risk areas.[10]

The present reality concretely, albeit partially and disproportionately, participates in the tragic violence of a conditional, uncertain future. The unjust structural vulnerability of the poor in the contemporary world reflects the ubiquitous vulnerability of a future humanity, irrespective of the differences perpetuated by power and marginality.

The unsettling effects of the ecological crisis on the current global situation expose the dehumanizing presence of such differences. During the 2011 United Nations Climate Change Conference in Durban, South Africa, for instance, Nnimmo Bassey, executive director of Environmental Rights Action in Nigeria and chair of Friends of the Earth International, expressed the partiality with which the current disproportionate impact must be addressed:

> We are here to send a solid, strong message . . . to the leaders and negotiators at the climate change conference that this is no time to play around. This is a time for a real commitment to cut emissions, a legally binding agreement to cut emissions, as such that rich, polluting countries should understand that their inaction . . . will destroy the planet, will cook Africa, and will put poor, vulnerable people in jeopardy. We can't accept that.[11]

The role of global power dynamics in climate change signals the structural nature of the change required in order to respond effectively. The leaders of the privileged countries seek to postpone any meaningful engagement with concrete change until the year 2020. Bassey's response highlights the relationship between the urgency of the situation and the historical marginality of the victims: "Eight years from now is a death sentence on Africa. . . . Everything about Africa is about extracting resources to power industry, to make life comfortable for people outside of Africa."[12] It is no surprise that Pablo Solón Romero, Bolivia's former ambassador to the United Nations and chief negotiator on climate change, describes the situation in terms of "climate apartheid," noting that the primary victims of ecological devastation will be "the developing countries, the poor nations, and the poor people around the world, even in the United States."[13] The uncertainty currently imposed upon the world of the poor and historically oppressed peoples chiefly as a result of the ecologically irresponsible activity of the richer countries exemplifies the tragic fragility of the future of humanity.

It is important to clarify what *fragility* signifies in this context. The category of fragility does not designate a particular feature of an anticipated or possible future. This is true not only because of the manner in which ecological degradation is already affecting the world, and more specifically historically oppressed peoples, but primarily because such a mode of thinking continues to take for granted the eventuality of the future and the imperturbable continuity of the historical process. That is, it reproduces the conception of the future as a certainty and simply inscribes it with the significance of a regional fragility. The foregoing discussion on the ecological crisis signals an understanding of fragility that departs radically from the relentless historicism—in all its ahistorical irony—of an unconditional future. It is not a mere fragility *in* the future that forms the challenge of the contemporary situation, but a fragility *of* the future itself.

Reframing the future in terms of fragility strikes at a more fundamental level than does the fragile qualification or modality of an otherwise persistently unfolding and essentially undisturbed historical process; it signals the possible discontinuity of time as such. On the other hand, the category of fragility, insofar as it identifies historical discontinuity as a *possibility* and the future as *uncertain*, prevents the emergence of catastrophic fatalism and the defeatism that results from the certainty and inevitability of destruction.

Fragility, exhibiting an openness to both continuity and discontinuity while recognizing the latter possibility as the current trajectory, preserves the space for a critical, hope-filled, transformative praxis. The meaning of that space is rooted in the disruptive reverberations of a departure from the unconditionality of the future. The increasingly tragic sense of fragility resides in the real, albeit not yet irreversible, vulnerability that characterizes time in light of such a departure.

THE FUTURE: TIMELESSNESS AND IDEOLOGICAL IDENTITY

The challenge posed by the contemporary situation concerning the future is twofold. It is not simply a question of the insecurity of time in the wake of the departure from the notion of the future as unconditional. The inverse side of this challenge presents a greater difficulty: the degree to which such a departure has been internalized and engenders the necessary praxis in response to a threatened future. Indeed, the present historical context obliges one to consider whether a departure from the unconditionality of the future has occurred at all. Where are the signs that the menacing possibility of historical discontinuity has catalyzed an interruption of the present moment? Does not a fundamental certainty of continuity govern the current understanding of time? Does not the contemporary world betray the failure of fragility to penetrate its orientation toward the future? Is it not an ironic abstraction and an idealist construction to thematize this departure? The interruptive meaning of the future that emerges in the present situation entails the challenge of accounting for the conception of the future that remains operative.

In addressing the conditions that have contributed to the absence of an adequate apocalyptic eschatology in Christian theology, Johann Baptist Metz describes *the spell of timelessness* as a kind of neo-metaphysics left over from the Enlightenment project that continues to haunt not only theological discourse but also society in general. Although Metz describes this vestige of modernity within the framework of rehabilitating an apocalyptic consciousness, his analysis of timelessness provides a helpful lens for considering the implicit understanding of the future that concerns this essay. He identifies an "evolutionistic logic" that preserves and nourishes a sense of time as an "infinite continuum . . . devoid of surprise," and which thereby results in a humanity that feels absorbed "into the waves of an anonymous evolution that mercilessly rolls over everything from behind." This understanding of time, Metz remarks, "has its efficacy by the fact that it has already deeply rooted itself in prereflective consciousness as a sort of 'feeling for life' and shapes the form in which everyday 'modern persons' experience themselves."[14]

Metz's earlier work contains the initial efforts to engage the dominant ways of thinking about the future that would eventually find their most fully developed expression in his description of the spell of timelessness. In *Theology of the World*, for instance, Metz recognizes the "hiddenness of the problem of the future in metaphysics," noting that it is rooted in "a tacit, unquestioned assumption, namely, that history is the history of the origin of the particular present." He writes, "The future appears exclusively as the correlate of the present, but not as a reality grounded in itself and belonging to itself, which precisely does not have the character of what exists and is present and therefore cannot be—in the classical sense—ontologized." The metaphysics of presence conceals the future insofar as it amounts to a transposition of the present into a future which precisely does not exhibit the lineaments of presence. The possibility of the future as such is precluded from the outset. The future as "what is not yet, what has never been, . . . what is really 'new'" remains inaccessible to a thought wherein "another perspective of time operates, namely, the 'always' of a present that is constant and always has been."[15]

It is only the future, then, that "can free us for something truly new . . . an absolute *novum* which cannot be understood merely as an evolutionary extension of our own possibilities."[16] The deployment of presence that characterizes an ontologizing orientation toward the future ipso facto abandons the possibility of the new. Metz eventually develops this critical engagement with the metaphysical concealment of the future in terms of "the dominion of time," that is, the "elemental, relentless, and unfathomable majesty of time." Continuously transposing the contours of the present into the future results in a sense of time as an endlessly unfolding historical process; a time that offers nothing other than more of itself, "more eternal than God, more deathless than all the gods."[17] This notion of time as eternal does not anticipate or even allow for anything other than the perpetual self-giving of presence. It is a "time without a finale," which thereby signals "the rule of time, the elementary, inexorable, and impenetrable sovereignty of time . . . as the last remaining monarch" that casts humanity under the "mythical spell" of its "divinity."[18]

The irony of the unyielding self-giving of time lies in its de-temporalizing effects. That is, the eternally unfolding historical process that results from the enthronement of time ultimately amounts to the profound loss of time. The ostensible abundance of time is de facto a spell of timelessness that, as Metz observes, generates resignation and defeatism. He writes that "an image of time as an empty continuum, expanding evolutionarily into infinitude, mercilessly encompassing everything . . . casts out every substantive expectation and so engenders that fatalism that is eating away at the souls of modern men and women." The juggernaut temporality that constitutes this sense of time precludes any interruption or inbreaking of alterity. It is for this reason that Metz describes timelessness as "an ersatz metaphysics, a new quasi metaphysics," noting that it is "the virtually mythical universalization of the symbol of a directionless evolution."[19] The impenetrability of time leaves no option for humanity but to assume a de-temporalized position of fatalistic complacency.

As already noted, Metz develops the analysis of timelessness in relation to his theology of the apocalyptic God. He discusses two opposing ways of thinking about time: (1) the eternal dominion of unbounded time; and (2) the interruptive apocalyptic time with a finale.[20] How does the future as fragile relate to this binary of the sovereignty of time and apocalyptic time? Does the alternative offered by these two opposing temporal horizons adequately reflect the challenges of the contemporary world? The exposure to historical discontinuity that fragility signifies is incommensurable with the impenetrable eternity of time. Moreover, the openness to averting desolation and ensuring continuity does not amount to the potential vindication of unbounded time; indeed, the very openness itself, expressive of a disastrous finale as a currently real possibility, effectively dethrones time and unmasks the myth of its endlessness. On the other hand, the tragic sense of vulnerability that accompanies a departure from the unconditionality of the future interrupts the eternal unfolding of time otherwise than as apocalyptic finale. The fragility of the future, although not requiring the exclusion of apocalyptic consciousness, yields a possibility of the finale of time that is not confined to apocalyptic eschatology. As such, the present historical context disturbs the timelessness-apocalyptic binary with the introduction of a third moment. The task is to rethink the end of time in a manner that takes seriously the horrific insecurity of the future by resisting a cursory recourse to the enclosure of apocalyptic time as the solitary interruption of timelessness.

The internalization of timelessness, however, means that the future is preapprehended within the framework of inexorability. This orientation toward the future does not result from an explicit thematization in such terms. The fundamental mode of this neo-metaphysics occurs not as a conceptual construction of timelessness but as a kind of lived metaphysics. It allows for a situation wherein prereflective, practical fatalism and theoretical advocacy of unqualified freedom can coexist harmoniously. Such is the embodied manner in which ideology functions. As Slavoj Žižek notes, "Ideology is not constituted by abstract propositions in themselves, rather, ideology is itself this very texture of the lifeworld which 'schematizes' the propositions, rendering them 'livable.'"[21] The implicitly operative conception of the future as unconditional and imperturbable exhibits the ideological structure of the spell of timelessness.

It is important to highlight this deeply internalized sense of time in order to engage the societal inability to appropriate an understanding of the future as seriously threatened and fragile.[22] The ideological spectacle of sovereign time amounts to a lived dissimulation of the vulnerability of the future. The prereflective apprehension of continuity inscribes itself in every reflective recognition of potential discontinuity. Hence Žižek remarks that "we *know* the (ecological) catastrophe is possible, probable even, yet we do not *believe* it will really happen."[23] There remains the fatalistic presence of an ideologically rooted, and thus privatized, future. The term *spell* is entirely appropriate.

It is not difficult to identify the spell of timelessness in contemporary society. The notion of time as eternally unfolding is expressed in its purest form in the recently aired television series *Terra Nova*. The plot of the series concerns the uninhabitable conditions of earth in the year 2149. The planet can no longer support the destructive practices of humanity. However, the vast majority of the series does not take place in 2149. The setting—made possible by the scientific discovery of time travel—is Terra Nova, a human colony that is being built by former inhabitants of 2149 who have been sent eighty-five million years into the past, allowing humanity to begin anew and thereby secure its viability. Thus even in a future that threatens humanity with imminent extinction, even in a situation wherein the tragic possibility of discontinuity concretizes as an inevitability—the certainty of unconditionality allows history triumphantly to march onward, humanity continues, time continues, a future remains. The juggernaut temporality is invincible, even if it means relocating eighty-five million years into the past.

Similarly, the lived experience of timelessness finds expression—often in subtle and unintentional ways—in contemporary theological discourse. It serenely reconciles a reality characterized by the insecurity of time and, for instance, the importance for a theological classic to appear in a new edition "every half century."[24] As indicated in the previous section, it is imperative for one to rethink what can be taken for granted even a century from now. Nonetheless, the preapprehension of an unconditional future from a position rooted in the unsettling path toward the destructive finale of history results in conceptual frameworks and practical orientations that inadvertently dissemble that context. Time continues to unfold imperturbably, vitiating the increasing fragility of the future by the rumbling spectacle of its divinity. In order to consider the challenges involved in the ongoing reception of the Second Vatican Council, then, it is necessary to attend to the ideological structure of timelessness. The inexorability of time remains operative in such efforts. It enables, for example, a reflection on the reception of the council and tendencies in the church today that indicate its direction "in the coming centuries" of the third millennium.[25] The question of reception challenges contemporary theologians not only to engage the insecurity of the future as a critical methodological concern, but also to address its meaning from a theological standpoint.

THE MYSTAGOGICAL SIGNIFICANCE OF THE FUTURE

The foregoing discussion concerns the challenges posed by the contemporary situation. As David Tracy observes, "To name our contemporary idols is often the first step demanded by a serious theological assessment of our complex and troubling situation."[26] Remaining attentive to the questions and difficulties of the present context prevents theology from withdrawing into the disembodied tranquility of ahistorical seclusion. Resisting the idealist enclosure of "situationless theologies," Metz notes, means to be "nourished by a certain uneasiness, indeed a certain shock, an experience of nonidentity," which awaits every entrance into concrete history. The previous sections of the chapter discern a troubling experience of nonidentity confronting contemporary theological reflection in the interruptive fragility of the future. Theology, then, must "take this situation into its conscience and formulate a theological concept in and from it, with all intellectual integrity."[27] Jacques Derrida describes Emmanuel Levinas's writing as moving along the "cracks" on the surface of the totality of philosophical language.[28] Contemporary theology finds itself in a similar situation, moving along certain cracks, or at least confronted with the urgency of doing so if it seeks to preserve its integrity; these are not primarily the cracks of language, however, but the tragic cracks of time, openings to a negation in which the cry on the cross can be heard.

To think theologically from the cracks of a fragile historical process means to enter into the world of the victims whose cries resound through those very cracks. The theologian is confronted not only with the victims of the current effects of ecological destruction, but also with the future victims of a vulnerable humanity. In his own efforts to respond theologically to the horrific reality of the victims of history, Ignacio Ellacuría introduced the prophetically charged language of "the crucified peoples." He describes this image, which was central both to his theology and to the praxis of solidarity that oriented his life, as follows:

> What is meant by crucified people here is that collective body, which as the majority of humankind owes its situation of crucifixion to the way society is organized and maintained by a minority that exercises its dominion through a series of factors, which taken together and given their concrete impact within history, must be regarded as sin.[29]

The expression, Kevin Burke mentions, refers to a "reality that embraces a communion of victims," and thus it does not concern suffering in a general sense but the suffering of "those whose historically inflicted torments are tantamount to crucifixion."[30] Similarly, Jon Sobrino observes that the language of the crucified peoples is "useful and necessary" since "*cross* means death," and more specifically it "expresses a type of death actively inflicted. To die crucified does not mean simply to die, but to be put to death; it means that there are victims and there are executioners."[31] The reality of crucified peoples designates a situation of dialectical suffering. The usage of such language signals a refusal to forget that "Jesus did not end his life 'in the fullness of days' but as a 'victim,' and that his resurrection did not consist in giving life back to a corpse but in giving justice back to a victim."[32]

Burke notes that Ellacuría employed the image of crucified peoples in order to "uncover and condemn historical mortal sins such as poverty, persecution, and violence against innocent peoples."[33] The reality of victims "shows us what we are," Sobrino remarks, and thus we "can and must look at ourselves reflected in the crucified people in order to grasp our deepest reality. As in a mirror, we can see what we are by what we produce."[34] This highlights the concretely salvific character of the crucified peoples.[35] The "light" that is offered by the victims of history, unmasking "the existence of enormous sin" and thereby demanding conversion, "is an important element of salvation."[36] As such, the oppressive reality of historical crosses both exposes the sin of the world and contributes to its salvation.[37] The crucified peoples make present "sin and grace, condemnation and salvation, human action and God's action."[38] The dialectical situation of crucifixion gratuitously confronts one with the question of participation in the structurally complex process of inflicting suffering and death on others. To encounter the victims is to receive a disruptive cry for humanization in the graced form of an imperative inflected by one's own sinful condition.

In discussing the theme of the crucified peoples, Sobrino writes, "It may be said that things have changed, and that Ellacuría himself would be on guard against the mimetic repetition of concepts; he would prompt us to historicize them."[39] Indeed, things have changed. To be sure, the reality of crucified peoples persists and continues to expose dehumanizing conditions, demanding solidarity and radical structural transformation. However, the challenges of *historicizing*—which Ellacuría understands as the process of assessing the truth of a concept by means of its contextualization[40]—the theme of the crucified peoples are not to be ignored. Such challenges receive concrete expression today in the openness to historical discontinuity that characterizes time.

The depths of dehumanization characterizing the contemporary situation are reflected in the fragility of the future, which thereby unmasks the sinfulness of our destructive disposition toward the world and one another. Fragility is *inflicted* on the future, that is, it originates dialectically, worsening beneath the spectacle of an inexorable historical process that deploys prereflectively. A future world of victims—and not simply the world of the future victims as a reality among others—exposes the ideologically privatized future as the idolatry of the mythic spell of timelessness. That is, the tragic sense of the future penetrates the de-temporalizing transpositions of presence into eternity and identifies its executioners. The vulnerability of time confronts the world today with its own broken condition, displaying the violence and injustice eclipsed by the lived experience of time without a finale. Ideological identity, which always already suspends the interruptive insecurity of the future and thus enables the complacency that nourishes the crisis, is revealed as nonidentity. Among the idols of the present is the furtive idol of presence.

Does not the present context orient humanity, precisely as an inhumanity responsible for the current crisis, toward the future as cross? Is it not time, precisely as a timeless time that offers a pernicious situationless innocence, for a *crucified future* to convict us? Does not the violent entanglement of nonidentity and timelessness carry Ellacuría's questions into the immediacy of one's very skin, questions that renew themselves before a threatened future "by asking, what have I done to crucify them? What am I doing to uncrucify them? What ought I to do so that this people will be raised?"[41] The salvific light offered by the vulnerability of the future highlights the rupture of the idolatrous certainty of historical continuity that conversion must enact. The crucified future confronts the present situation with its sinful complicity in the process of crucifying.

Theological reflection faces the task of addressing its own relationship to these challenges. As Metz notes, "Whoever talks about God in Jesus' sense will always take into account the way one's own preformulated certainties are wounded by the misfortune of others."[42] To do theology from the cracks of the future means internalizing the horrific contradiction to which those cracks open. The cross that is thereby signified obliges theology to engage the meaning and process of that crucifixion in a critical, liberative manner. That is, theology must uncover the crucifying activity hidden in its own discourse. Tracy writes, "To seize the heart of the matter of the Christian gospel in our present moment is to expose the false visions of the present which afflict us."[43] The theologian is charged with the task of exposing the false transpositions of the present that afflict the future. In this sense the primary critical function of theological reflection involves the deprivatization or de-ideologization of the future. It is a response to the exigencies of the crucified future, exposing the sin of the world and contributing to its salvation. This humanizing path of theology is oriented toward a praxis of solidarity that seeks to bring the future down from the cross.

TOWARD AN ECCLESIAL PRAXIS
IN LIGHT OF A THEOLOGY OF FRAGILITY

The interruptive significance of the crucified future highlights the necessity for a praxis of humanization. The exposure of the distorted, destructive anthropological horizon of the present is salvific in that it calls humanity back to itself, de-centering identity beyond the ideological confines of timelessness and thereby enabling the necessary solidarity with the future world of victims. This vision of the future makes it possible to return to the original questions concerning the ongoing reception of the Second Vatican Council. Indeed, the humanizing significance of the crucified future concerns what the council describes as "the most fundamental of all questions," such as the meaning of humanity, suffering, evil, and so forth (GS, 10). The continuing challenges in the reception of the council entail the critical status of such questions in light of the fragility of the future. The present historical situation demonstrates the density of this understanding of the future as a principal sign of the times. As McFague notes, "Climate change, quite simply, is the issue of the twenty-first century. It is not one issue among many, but, like the canary in the mine, it is warning us that the way we are living on our planet is causing us to head for disaster. We must change."[44] The crucified future speaks an urgent and life-affirming word to the reception of the council.

The pneumatological ecclesiology presented in *Lumen Gentium* offers an important dialogical framework for addressing the question of reception. It was noted in the introduction that understanding the church in light of its pneumatological significance highlights its dynamic character. That is, the church is not a static reality. Rather, the presence of the Holy Spirit signals the very life of the church. *Lumen Gentium* no. 4 describes various activities of the Spirit: dwelling in the church and in the faithful, praying, bearing witness, guiding the church into truth, uniting the church in fellowship, bestowing gifts, rejuvenating and renewing the church, and leading it into union with Christ. The pneumatological dimension of ecclesiology, then, does not designate the presence of a theologically significant inertia. The Spirit comprises the very movement of the church; it reveals the church as a living reality. Furthermore, the activity of the Spirit in the church is not described as something that occurs only sporadically or intermittently, but rather as a constant event. The Spirit, for instance, is described as sanctifying "the church continually," and as "constantly" and "unceasingly" renewing it (LG, 4, 7, 9).

Such activity signals the temporal, and fundamentally eschatological, trajectory of the church, or what *Lumen Gentium* refers to as "the pilgrim church" (LG, 7, 8, 48–51). This trajectory of the church is expressed, albeit not in great detail, quite early in the document: "Established in this last age of the world, and made manifest in the outpouring of the Spirit, [the church] will be brought to glorious completion at the end of time" (LG 2).[45] The constant activity of the Spirit in the church is constitutive not only of the church as a living dynamism, but also of the eschatological orientation of that vitality. This temporal orientation provides the necessary framework for understanding ecclesiology as pneumatological. The renewing, guiding, unifying, and sanctifying work of the Spirit always exhibits an eschatological significance.

This feature of pneumatology is expressed most clearly in the chapter titled "The Pilgrim Church." The chapter highlights the eschatological trajectory of the church, whereby it is directed toward perfection as its end. The church will attain this perfection "only in the glory of heaven, when the time for the renewal of all things will have come" (LG, 48). It is possible, then, to recognize the eschatological significance of the Spirit not simply in the *orientation* of its constantly renewing activity—namely, toward the perfection of the church—but also in the very renewals themselves that characterize the church as pilgrim. The church, guided and sanctified by the Holy Spirit, continually experiences eschatologically prefigurative renewals while on a path toward the perfecting renewal of everything.

It is important to recognize that this final perfecting renewal is confined neither to the church nor even to all humanity; rather, it pertains to the entirety of creation. The passage continues, "At that time, together with the human race, the universe itself, which is closely related to humanity and which through it attains its destiny, will be perfectly established in Christ" (LG, 48). The mystery of the church shows its depths in the eschatological orientation of its pneumatological dimension, with all the significance of its reference to creation.

The eschatological activity of the Holy Spirit in the church provides a fruitful point of departure for engaging the reception of the council in light of the challenges of the crucified future. The constantly renewing activity of the Spirit, insofar as such activity exhibits an essential eschatological reference, maintains the significance of all creation at the center of the church. That is, the continuous renewals, which make up the eschatological trajectory of the church, participate in the meaning of the perfecting finality of that trajectory. The inclusion of all creation in that final perfection highlights an opportunity for considering the significance of creation in its currently threatened condition from the standpoint of a pneumatological ecclesiology.

The guiding activity of the Spirit of life in a context marked by the fragility of the future is concretized in the response of conversion as humanizing praxis. The vivifying role of the Holy Spirit signals the nature of its renewals in a situation oriented toward the future as cross. Conversion involves resistance to conditions that prevent the universal flourishing of humanity, and thus conversion amounts to a transformative solidarity with all persons, which takes the form of diachronic solidarity in recognition of a future world of victims. It is only through such a re-temporalized responsibility for the suffering—the salvific de-centering that accompanies the unmasking of the mythic eternity of timelessness—that the future can be brought down from the cross. Derrida articulates this indispensable character of non-contemporaneity as follows: "No justice . . . seems possible or thinkable without the principle of some *responsibility*, beyond all living present, within that which disjoins the living present . . . before the ghosts of those who are not yet born . . . who are not yet *present and living*."[46] Subverting the ideology of sovereign time becomes central to the encounter with the God of justice. The tragic openness to discontinuity that confronts the historical process indicates the gratuitous relationship between the vivifying eschatological orientation of the Spirit and solidaristic resistance to structures perpetuating ecological destruction.[47]

The renewing activity of the Spirit in the church necessarily prevents it from becoming a situationless church. The renewals of the Spirit are constantly transpiring precisely because historical reality unfolds as a process; that is, the renewing activity inherently opposes the withdrawal of the church from history. Thus, the nature of the renewals requires the church to take seriously the interruptions of concrete history. An ecclesial praxis that aims to remain in communion with God, then, retains the historical character of the renewals that structure such praxis. The cry on the cross challenges the church in a new way in the present historical context. The primary challenge is for the cry to be heard at all through the dissimulating idols of inexorable time. Only on the basis of the disruptive attunement to this cry can an ecclesial praxis emerge that embodies the urgency of its historical situation. The crucified future is an expression of the inextricable relationship between salvation and ecological justice. Extricating the concern for salvation from ecology, as Edward Schillebeeckx observes, "is perhaps to dream of a salvation for *angels*" and not for humanity.[48]

The reality of suffering is an essential mediation of the salvific role of the church in history. *Lumen Gentium* states, "Just as Christ carried out the work of redemption in poverty and oppression, so the church is called to follow the same path if it is to communicate the fruits of salvation to humanity" (LG, 8). As mentioned above, the activity of the Spirit involves guidance into "perfect union" with Christ (LG, 4). The service and proclamation of the reign of God that characterize the life of Christ, then, not only establish suffering, oppression, and poverty as the reality into which the church must enter, but also provide a christological horizon for considering its pneumatological significance and salvific praxis. Christ came "to bring good news to the poor," providing the foundation for a church that "encompasses with its love all those who are afflicted by human infirmity and . . . recognizes in those who are poor and who suffer, the likeness of its poor and suffering founder" (LG, 8).

The reality in which the suffering founder of the church can be discerned today inscribes a futural structure into ecclesial praxis. The christological foundation of the pneumatological ecclesiology introduced in *Lumen Gentium* enables the church in the contemporary world to recognize the cross in the fragility of the future. Prophetically exposing the sinful privatizations of a wounded tomorrow signals the first step of a humanizing praxis that embraces victims not simply in a restricted spatial manner, but also temporally. The interruptive meaning of time that characterizes the present historical situation requires a reception of the council that remains attentive to the vivifying and guiding activity of the Holy Spirit. It is through discerning this activity of the Spirit that the church is able to receive the council in a way that allows it to remain rooted in its concrete situation and to address that situation as a salvific mediation through which its union with Christ passes. The cry of the crucified future, as a principal sign of the times, signals the new challenge facing the church today: bringing the future down from the cross.

NOTES

1. See *Gaudium et Spes,* 4–10, 11, 26, 44; *Lumen Gentium,* 4, 7, 48.

2. Thomas Berry, *The Christian Future and the Fate of the Earth*, ed. Mary Evelyn Tucker and John Grim (Maryknoll, NY: Orbis Books, 2009), 117, 118.

3. Sallie McFague, *A New Climate for Theology: God, the World, and Global Warming* (Minneapolis, MN: Fortress Press, 2008), 10, 10–11, 11.

4. See Bill McKibben, "Warning on Warming," *The New York Review of Books* (March 15, 2007); McFague, *A New Climate for Theology*, 10–11.

5. Edward O. Wilson, *The Future of Life* (New York: Random House, 2002), xxii–xxiii.

6. Ibid., xxiv.

7. Peter D. Ward, *Under a Green Sky: Global Warming, the Mass Extinctions of the Past and What They Can Tell Us About Our Future* (New York: HarperCollins Publishers, 2007), 165.

8. McFague, *A New Climate for Theology*, 14.

9. Ward, *Under a Green Sky*, 186.

10. McFague, *A New Climate for Theology*, 20–21. See also James H. Cone, "Whose Earth Is It Anyway?" *Cross Currents* 50, nos. 1–2 (2000); Leonardo Boff, *Cry of the Earth, Cry of the Poor*, trans. Phillip Berryman (Maryknoll, NY: Orbis Books, 1997).

11. Nnimmo Bassey, "Thousands March at UN Climate Summit in Durban to Demand Climate Justice," *Democracy Now!* (December 5, 2011). See also Nnimmo Bassey, *To Cook a Continent: Destructive Extraction and the Climate Crisis in Africa* (Cape Town, South Africa: Pambazuka Press, 2012).

12. Nnimmo Bassey, "At Durban Summit, Leading African Activist Calls US Emissions Stance 'A Death Sentence for Africa,'" *Democracy Now!* (December 6, 2011).

13. Pablo Solón Romero, "The Lost Decade: Bolivian Pablo Solón Decries Climate Deal Postponing New Emissions Cuts Until 2020," *Democracy Now!* (December 12, 2011). See also the New Mexico Conference of Catholic Bishops' denunciation of "actions and policies which perpetuate various forms of environmental racism," in "NMCCB Statement on the Environment: Partnership for the Future."

14. Johann Baptist Metz, *Faith in History and Society: Toward a Practical Fundamental Theology*, trans. J. Matthew Ashley (New York: Crossroad, 2007), 156–65, 24, 26.

15. Johann Baptist Metz, *Theology of the World*, trans. William Glen-Doepel (New York: Herder and Herder, 1969), 98. It is important to note the influential role of Ernst Bloch in the development of the problem of the future in Metz's thought. See James Matthew Ashley, *Interruptions: Mysticism, Politics, and Theology in the Work of Johann Baptist Metz* (Notre Dame, IN: University of Notre Dame Press, 1998), 104–7.

16. Johann Baptist Metz, "The Controversy About the Future of Man: An Answer to Roger Garaudy," *Journal of Ecumenical Studies* 4, no. 2 (1967): 226.

17. Johann Baptist Metz, "God: Against the Myth of the Eternity of Time," in *The End of Time? The Provocation of Talking About God*, ed. Tiemo Rainer Peters and Claus Urban (New York: Paulist Press, 2004), 30.

18. Johann Baptist Metz, "Time Without a Finale: The Background to the Debate on 'Resurrection or Reincarnation,'" in *Faith and the Future: Essays on Theology, Solidarity, and Modernity*, with Jürgen Moltmann (Maryknoll, NY: Orbis Books, 1995), 79, 80.

19. Metz, *Faith in History and Society*, 157–58.

20. See Johann Baptist Metz, *A Passion for God: The Mystical-Political Dimension of Christianity*, trans. J. Matthew Ashley (New York: Paulist Press, 1998), 50–53; Metz, "Time Without a Finale," 79; Metz, "God: Against the Myth of the Eternity of Time," 28–31, 46; Metz, *Faith in History and Society*, 156–65.

21. Slavoj Žižek, *Living in the End Times* (London: Verso, 2011), 3.

22. To be sure, other factors are undeniably involved—for instance, politically and economically motivated views, power interests, the mainstream media narrative, inaccessible or inadequate educational programs, and so forth—and contribute to the problems of awareness and praxis. However, it is insufficient simply to view these factors as accountable for the general lack of concern for the future. "Awareness" of the disastrous consequences of current human practices occurs as a reflective imposition on an already lived experience of time as inexorable.

23. Žižek, *Living in the End Times*, 328.

24. Martin E. Marty, "Foreword," in H. Richard Niebuhr, *Christ and Culture* (New York: HarperCollins Publishers, 2001), xix.

25. Ladislas Orsy, *Receiving the Council: Theological and Canonical Insights and Debates* (Collegeville, MN: Liturgical Press, 2009), 1.

26. David Tracy, *On Naming the Present: God, Hermeneutics, and Church* (Maryknoll, NY: Orbis Books, 1994), xii.

27. Metz, *A Passion for God*, 23–25.

28. Jacques Derrida, *Writing and Difference*, trans. Alan Bass (Chicago: The University of Chicago Press, 1978), 90.

29. Ignacio Ellacuría, "The Crucified People," in *Mysterium Liberationis: Fundamental Concepts of Liberation Theology*, ed. Ignacio Ellacuría and Jon Sobrino (Maryknoll, NY: Orbis Books, 1993), 590.

30. Kevin F. Burke, *The Ground Beneath the Cross: The Theology of Ignacio Ellacuría* (Washington, DC: Georgetown University Press, 2000), 181. See also Kevin F. Burke, "Christian Salvation and the Disposition of Transcendence: Ignacio Ellacuría's Historical Soteriology," in *Love That Produces Hope: The Thought of Ignacio Ellacuría*, ed. Kevin F. Burke and Robert Lassalle-Klein (Collegeville, MN: Liturgical Press, 2006), 175.

31. Jon Sobrino, *The Principle of Mercy: Taking the Crucified People from the Cross* (Maryknoll, NY: Orbis Books, 1994), 50.

32. Jon Sobrino, *No Salvation Outside the Poor: Prophetic-Utopian Essays* (Maryknoll, NY: Orbis Books, 2008), 100.

33. Burke, "Christian Salvation and the Disposition of Transcendence," 175.

34. Sobrino, *The Principle of Mercy*, 49, 53.

35. The English title of Ellacuría's essay on the crucified people omits the key reference to historical soteriology.

36. Jon Sobrino, *Jesus the Liberator: A Historical-Theological Reading of Jesus of Nazareth*, trans. Paul Burns and Francis McDonagh (Maryknoll, NY: Orbis Books, 1993), 262; Sobrino, *No Salvation Outside the Poor*, 5.

37. Ellacuría, "The Crucified People," 603.

38. Sobrino, *The Principle of Mercy*, 51.

39. Sobrino, *No Salvation Outside the Poor*, 1–2.

40. Robert Lassalle-Klein, "Ignacio Ellacuría's Debt to Xavier Zubiri: Critical Principles for a Latin American Philosophy and Theology of Liberation," in Burke and Lassalle-Klein, *Love That Produces Hope*, 109.

41. Ellacuría, translated in Burke, *The Ground Beneath the Cross*, 26.

42. Metz, *A Passion for God*, 2.

43. Tracy, *On Naming the Present*, 5.

44. McFague, *A New Climate for Theology*, 15.

45. *Lumen Gentium*, no. 4, provides a more direct formulation of this meaning of the Holy Spirit: "By the power of the Gospel [the Holy Spirit] rejuvenates the church, constantly renewing it and leading it to perfect union with its spouse. For the Spirit and the Bride both say to Jesus, the Lord, Come!"

46. Jacques Derrida, *Specters of Marx: The State of the Debt, the Work of Mourning, and the New International*, trans. Peggy Kamuf (New York: Routledge, 1994), xix.

47. See also Edward Schillebeeckx's discussion of the essential relationship between human salvation and ecology in terms of anthropological constants in *Christ: The Experience of Jesus as Lord*, trans. John Bowden (New York: Crossroad, 1980), 734–36.

48. Ibid., 736.

Conclusion: Visions of Hope

As this project makes clear, young theologians care deeply about the Second Vatican Council. We believe that Vatican II continues to be a source of hope for the church today. Such hope, in a genuine Christian sense, however, cannot be naive to the real problems facing the church and the world in which it lives. Rather, we are challenged, fifty years after Vatican II, to find creative ways to respond to the *ad intra* and *ad extra* questions facing the church today.

In March 2012 the authors featured in this volume, together with dozens of other promising theologians, gathered in Boston to discuss many of these challenges in light of the council. Rooted in the texts of Vatican II and a commitment to the church, the following are some of the concerns and hopes raised by many of the participants in their final consensus document:

THE FUTURE OF LITURGY

1. Re-Centralization of Scripture

The word of God in scripture, in the years since the Second Vatican Council, has been recovered as liturgically central. This is of course not to say that scripture had no place in liturgy before the Second Vatican Council. Rather, it is simply to point out that a renewed emphasis on scripture is alive and well in the contemporary church, and this is a good thing. Few would try to argue that scripture ought to be sidelined, or (on the other hand) that scripture has always enjoyed its current central liturgical role, and such apparent consensus is a witness to the success of this liturgical current.

2. The Clergy and the Laity

There is a resurgence in the contemporary church of practices that, for good or ill, ritually emphasize the distinction between the clergy and the laity. Instances of lay persons (particularly women) being prevented from serving as extraordinary ministers of the Eucharist, a reemergence of communion under only one species for the laity (withholding the cup), and other similar examples were cited by the group. This is not to say that there is no place for some clarification of liturgical roles, but the consensus was that the bulk of these practices clarifies in a very particular way that the clergy is somehow "above" the laity. Such a view may not be the intent behind re-emphasizing the distinction between the two groups; however, it is undeniably a byproduct. Looking forward, the group was left wondering whether this will ultimately lead to a healthy clarity of roles or to a reinvigorated, zealous, and divisive clericalism.

3. Dialogue About Liturgy

In the years following the Second Vatican Council, lay voices in theological dialogue have increased. However, what may have begun as a healthy dialogue between the magisterium and the laity seems to have morphed into two monologues moving more or less past each other. This is not to say that there is no communication between the magisterium and the laity; it is instead to say that the communication—especially in regard to the liturgy—seems often to be unidirectional. The magisterium seems quite interested in regulating the liturgy (specifically in ways that increasingly center on Rome rather than the local diocese), and this alienates constructive input from the laity—particularly from those in the academy. On the other hand, the magisterium is not always a welcome conversation partner in discussions of liturgical theology, which seems to exacerbate the perceived need to regulate.

THE FUTURE MINISTRY

1. Promotion

We want to see a greater awareness of the many different vocations of ministry—ordained, religious, and lay—present in the church. All of these forms of ministry, whether sacramental, administrative, or academic, should be promoted by those involved in teaching ministry and theology.

2. Invitation

Often someone needs only to be asked to join in opportunities of ministering to others. A teacher can ask students if they would like to come on a service trip. A pastor can ask a parish to join in helping a sister parish in a needed area of the world. For the future of ministry to remain strong, we all need to help to bring new life into our church through invitation.

3. Respect

We found a need for "safe spaces" for dialogue between ministers and those to whom we minister. We envision respectful atmospheres that encourage people to ask for help and that foster new solutions to current problems based on the real needs and experiences of the people.

4. Integral Education

Young adults today need to be more aware of the interrelation between their spiritual and their secular lives. Professors in all fields can play an important role in helping to bridge this divide in their classrooms. Universities and parishes ought to create programs that help promote such integral development.

THE FUTURE OF DIALOGUE

1. Dialogue Is Not Monologue

The relationship and tension between dialogue and proclamation continue to be critical issues for the future of interreligious dialogue. The blurred boundary between these two necessary activities of church has led to confusion and conflation, unease and distrust. We must continue to define dialogue's proper place in the life of the church—a pursuit that promotes hospitality, humility, and mutuality.

2. Dialogue Is Both Religious and Theological

It is not simply an intercultural dialogue—though this is an important component to it—but a dialogue between persons and communities of faith. We must be reminded of the sacramental quality of dialogue, which incorporates people's beliefs, lives, and practices.

3. Dialogue Is Multidimensional

From the formal gathering of religious leaders and experts to the informal fellowship of local lay groups, dialogue occurs in many different contexts. We seek the continued contributions of persons from both groups in helping to shape the future of dialogue.

4. The Foundations of Dialogue

For the promotion of dialogue we shall continue to build upon its biblical and theological foundations. Paul at the Areopagus, Jesus before the Syro-Phonecian woman, the charge not to bear false witness against our neighbors are biblical examples to which we can turn to inform our practice. Furthermore, we can cultivate the virtues of humility, hospitality, charity, and prudence in our relationships with religious others knowing that dialogue leads to greater understanding not just of other faiths but of our own as well.

5. The Hope of Dialogue

We hope that a continued commitment to dialogue will lead to better dialogue, responsible practice, and enlivening encounters. We hope that dialogue becomes a constitutive posture of the church, a church that speaks to, hears from, and learns with persons of other religious faith. And we hope that dialogue will lead to a renewal in pneumatology, a deeper sense of the Holy Spirit's presence and operations in the world, an awareness to the gifts born from the Spirit, and a recognition of the responsibility that accompanies them.

THE FUTURE OF ETHICS

I. Church and World

How shall we be the church *in* the world in the twenty-first century? How shall we enact our commission to live the gospel in a multicultural, cosmopolitan world? Viewing this diversity as an opportunity rather than a threat, we aim to promote a dialogical stance of openness, trust, and humility as a path to fulfilling our baptismal vocation to be the church in the twenty-first century world. Moreover, we affirm—like the council—that there are likely to be traces of the gospel already present even in those parts of the world that seem farthest from the church; therefore, we shall prepare ourselves to receive Truth, wherever it may be found.

2. Structural Injustice

The God in whose image we are created is a God of mercy and justice. Therefore, we consider the manifest structural injustices that plague humanity, both outside and within the visible boundaries of the church, to be grave offenses to human dignity and to the will of the Creator. Aiming to translate our Christian hope into a credible, tangible witness for peace and justice, we seek to coordinate our efforts with persons and organizations at every level of human society in order to become structures of justice and grace in the world.

3. Moral Authority

Being aware that the church's own life is marked by profound division and disagreement concerning moral methodology, the content of normative ethics, and the appropriateness of the actions and omissions of church leaders, we yearn for an open discussion of the nature of moral authority in the church. How do we recognize those persons possessing true authority? How is true authority gained, and how is it lost? What is the status of moral claims proposed by those lacking professional competency in moral theology? How do we know when moral disagreement breaks the bond of communion, and when it need not break it?

4. Integrated Moral Anthropology

The division of labor in applied ethics between sexual ethics and social ethics, while perhaps practically necessary, seems to imply a disjointed moral anthropology. Remaining aware that this disjunction has been addressed in the past by the consistent ethic of life, we seek a more carefully nuanced and more sophisticated approach to integrating the various dimensions of human agency. In particular, we aim to develop a relational moral anthropology, including special attention to the interpersonal level, as a bridge between the established individual and structural levels of moral analysis.

THE FUTURE OF ECCLESIOLOGY

1. Centrality of the Gospel

The good news of the gospel provides the foundational context in light of which and within which the Second Vatican Council must be received and interpreted.

2. Historical Consciousness

One of the movements of the Holy Spirit that has manifested itself in the event and documents of the Second Vatican Council is a self-awareness of the historical consciousness of the church. This awareness includes our own Catholic and communal responsibility to engage the situation of our world today.

3. Lament and Healing

Out of this sense of responsibility we recognize the laments that arise not only from the situation of the world, but also from the situation and structures of our church in that world. These sources and expressions of lament must be allowed real channels of discourse so that they may be heard with greater clarity and incorporated into the authoritative discernment of the church.

4. Discernment

It is necessary for church theologians and the magisterium to uncover sources and models of discernment by which the church can structurally address the pressing laments and social concerns in the church and in the world. By gathering and incorporating new models of discerning the *sensus fidei*, the church will continue to embody the good news of the council and the gospel.

Contributors

Kevin J. Ahern is a doctoral candidate in theological ethics at Boston College and an adjunct professor at Blessed John XXIII National Seminary.

Elizabeth L. Antus is a doctoral candidate in systematic theology at the University of Notre Dame.

Sandra Arenas is a doctoral researcher of the Katholieke Universiteit Leuven, where she is a member of the Center for the Studies of the Second Vatican Council.

B. Kevin Brown is a doctoral student in systematic theology at Boston College. His research interests include ecclesiology, ecumenism, and methods of dialogue.

Christopher Conway is a doctoral candidate in comparative theology at Boston College with a concentration on the Christian and Hindu traditions.

Charles Ochero Cornelio is the international president of the International Movement of Catholic Students (IMCS-Pax Romana).

Anselma Dolcich-Ashley recently completed a PhD in moral theology and is currently a post-doctoral teaching fellow at the University of Notre Dame.

Benjamin Durheim is a PhD candidate in systematic theology at Boston College with a focus on liturgical/sacramental theology, liturgy and ethics, and ecumenism.

Massimo Faggioli, PhD, is an assistant professor at the University of St. Thomas (St. Paul, Minnesota). His most recent books are *Vatican II: The Battle for Meaning* (Paulist Press) and *True Reform: Liturgy and Ecclesiology in "Sacrosanctum Concilium"* (Liturgical Press).

Peter Folan, SJ, is a student in the Master of Divinity and Licentiate of Sacred Theology programs at Boston College's School of Theology and Ministry.

Eduardo Gonzalez is a doctoral student in systematic theology at Boston College with a concentration on liberation and political theologies.

Nathaniel Hibner is an MTS student in theological ethics at the Boston College School of Theology and Ministry.

Gina Ingiosi is a doctoral student at the University of Dayton, where she teaches Catholic theology in the Religious Studies Department.

Michael P. Jaycox is a doctoral candidate in theological ethics at Boston College. His research interests include virtue ethics, feminist ethics, bioethics, and political theology.

Stephen Okey is a PhD candidate and a teaching fellow at Boston College with a focus on fundamental theology, theological anthropology, and the media.

Amanda C. Osheim holds a doctoral degree in systematic theology from Boston College. She is an assistant professor of practical theology at Loras College.

Heather Miller Rubens holds a PhD from the University of Chicago Divinity School and is the Roman Catholic Scholar at the Institute for Christian and Jewish Studies.

Sofia Seguel Ñancucheo holds an STB and an STL from the Pontificia Universidad Católica de Chile and is pursuing a license in canon law at the Pontifical Gregorian University in Rome.

Krista Stevens is a doctoral student in theology at Fordham University with a focus on social ethics and US Catholic studies.

Ellen Van Stichel is a postdoctoral researcher at the Faculty of Theology and Religious Studies at the Katholieke Universiteit Leuven with a focus on Catholic social ethics.

Gonzalo Villagrán, SJ, recently received his doctorate in sacred theology from the Boston College School of Theology and Ministry focusing in theological ethics.

Index

ableism, 30, 33, 35n6
Adam, Karl, 55
Ad Gentes (Vatican II), 197
Ad Pascendum (Paul VI), 87
Africa, climate change's effects
    on, 218
After Virtue (MacIntyre), 159
agency, 41, 56–57
Alberigo, Giuseppe, 15
Alszeghy, Zoltán, 181
altruism-reciprocity, 143
American Catholic Revolution
    (Massa), 167
Americans with Disabilities Act
    of 1990, 25
Analogical Imagination, The
    (Tracy), 155–56, 159–60
Anglican Communion, 206
anthropology
    moral, 239
    personalist, 133, 136–38
    relational, 146
    theological, 130, 133–34,
        139–40, 146–47
    trinitarian, 133–34, 139–44,
        146–47
Antus, Elizabeth, 22–23
apocalyptic eschatology, time-
    lessness and, 222
apostolic call, fulfillment of,
    183–84
Apostolicam Actuositatem (Vati-
    can II), 72, 73, 127

"Apostolos Suos" (John Paul II),
    200, 206
Aquinas, Thomas, 136
Archdiocese of Boston, 69
Arenas, Sandra, 98
Asian Public Theology (Wilfred),
    158
Augustine of Hippo, 28, 157
authority
    breakdown of, 58
    dependent upon mutual jus-
        tice and respect, 58
    feedback to, 58–59
    invention of, 58, 60
    limited by human rights of
        the other faithful, 63
    purpose of, 57
    redefining, 57
    as relationship, 57–58, 60
    reliant upon the governed, 57
    response to, 57, 58
    understood in community, 57

Baldovin, John, 207
baptism
    addressing racism through,
        173
    universal nature of, 116,
        117–18
Barratt, Anthony, 75–76
Bassey, Nnimmo, 218
Bea, Augustine, 112, 113
Beauduin, Lambert, 10

believers, equality of all, 85
Bellah, Robert, 153
Bellarmine, Robert, 11, 15
Benedict XVI, 8, 15, 16. See also Ratzinger, Joseph
Beope, Paulus, 110
Berry, Thomas, 215
Bevilacqua, Anthony, 65n1
bishops
    authority of, 54–55, 59, 60, 63
    college of, 197, 205
    collegiality of, 178
    councils of, 196
    in dialogue with local church and laity, 182–85, 205–6
    office of, 63–64
    papal appointments of, 196
    performance of, in sexual-abuse scandal, 55–56
    relationships of, 63–64
    roles of, 200, 205, 206
    selection of, 206
bodiliness, 40. See also body; mystical body of Christ
    and the Catholic Church, 44
    construction of, 42
    performativity of, 43
body
    attributes of, 47n5
    Christians' resistance to, 29
    as a construction, 42
    dependent on its perfor-mance, 43, 44
    described in terms of compo-sition and capacity, 40
    differing conceptions of, 22
    emphasis on, in sacramental theology, 30
    fluidity of, 42–44
    as interrelation, 41

    as locus of self-expression, 30–31
    value of, 29, 30
    as visible, ordered actor, 40
body capital, 32
body of Christ, reception of, 46
Boff, Leonardo, 134, 140
Boyer, Charles, 113
Breitenberg, Harold, 153–54
"Brothers and Sisters to Us" (USCCB), 168
Brown, Kevin, 178
Buckley, Michael J., 63
Burke, Edmund, 127
Burke, Kevin, 224, 225
Butler, Judith, 22, 39, 40, 41–44, 46

Cambón, Enrique, 141–46
Canada, Muslim-Christian dia-logue in, 126
Caritas in Veritate (Benedict XVI), 139
Catholic Church
    acknowleding significance of intellectually disabled Catholics, 33–34
    acting as church, 44, 45–46
    approaching racism, necessity of, 167–68
    authorities in, 182
    barriers around, removing, 12
    becoming a restorative com-munity, 64
    as body, reconfigured, 39
    as the body of Christ, 22, 23–25, 27
    catholicity of, expressing, 203
    committed to dialogue with culture and other reli-gions, 123–25

communion ecclesiology of, 191–92

conservative stereotypes in, 54–56

councils of, long-term relevance of, 7

dedication of laity in, 49–50

dialogue in, 98, 181

division in, after Vatican II, 15

eschatological trajectory of, 228

evangelical mission of, 101–2

facing global changes at time of Vatican II, 134–35

gendered references to, 42

goal of, 170

governing authority of, 53–55, 57

hierarchical nature of, 40, 53

human rights advocacy in, 60–63

human rights and authority in, 62–63

inclusivity in, 22

institutional crisis in, 147

liberal stereotypes in, 54, 56–57

membership in, 2, 110, 111, 130

ministry in the structure of, 72

mission of, 72

moral authority in, 239

movements in, post–Vatican II, 147

moving toward the modern world, 11–12

multicultural nature of, 130

mystery of, 228

as mystical body of Christ, 22

as the people of God, 54

perfecting renewal of, 228–29

reflecting history of white privilege, 168

relations with non-Christians and nonbelievers, 11

relations with local churches, 178

relations with the world, related to views on the human being, 152

reorienting, around the Gospel, 14

resistance of, to more democratic governance, 56

responding to history's interruptions, 229

salvific role of, 230

self-awareness of, 11, 239–40

sexual-abuse crisis in, 2, 53–54, 59–60, 61, 64

shifting to participation of the governed, 59

structure of, 70, 78

symbols for, 46

using biblical and christological arguments, 147

youth movements in, 123

catholicity

church's expression of, 203–5

church's self-understanding of, 208

eucharistic community and, 207

gift of, local churches possessing, 197

Catholics with disabilities. See also intellectually disabled persons

accommodations for, 25
participating in worship, 25,
    27
privileged place of, 33
Catholic social justice move-
    ments, 39
Catholic social teaching, 61–62,
    168
  anthropology of, 138–39
  justice and participation in,
    144
Catholic social thought, 130
  Gaudium et Spes as shift in,
    133
  relevance to, of trinitarian
    anthropology, 146–47
  theological anthropology for,
    133–34
Catholic theology
  public, 153, 154–57
  vitality of, 8
CCQOe (Conférence Catholique
    pour les Questions Oecu-
    méniques), 113
celibacy, 77–78, 90
Center for Applied Research in
    the Apostolate, 49
Central Board of Bishops (Con-
    silium Centrale Episcopo-
    rum), 11
CEP. See Congregation for the
    Evangelization of Peoples
Chauvet, Louis-Marie, 26–31
Christ. See also Jesus Christ
  communal conformity to,
    27–28
  life of, meaning for the
    church, 230
  living memory of, 181
  preeminence of, 152, 155
  presence of, in history, 141

priority of, as key to under-
    standing reality, 152–53
  redemptive work of, 152
  shedding light on mystery of
    the human being, 161
  three munera of, 94
Christendom, 12
Christianity
  communal identity of,
    159–60
  fragmentation of, 11
  public identity of, 160–61
  reuniting East and West, 13
  sacramentality of, 28
  symbols of, 155–56, 161
  traditions of, 160
Christians, resisting the body
    and the sacraments, 29
Christian unity, 112
"Christian Witness in a Multi-
    Religious World: Recom-
    mendations for Conduct,"
    99, 100, 103–7
christifideles, 85
Christus Dominus (Vatican II),
    11, 72, 73, 182–83, 197
"Church of Christ," 114, 117
CIC. See Code of Canon Law
classicist worldview, 135–36
classics, 156
Claver, Francisco, 199, 201,
    204
Clement VIII, 15
Clement of Rome, 199
clergy-laity distinction, clarify-
    ing, 235–36
clericalism, 81
climate apartheid, 218
climate change. See also ecologi-
    cal crisis
  consequences of, 217–19

global power dynamics and, 218

as security issue, 215

Code of Canon Law, 8, 16, 75, 78, 85

Coleman, John, 154

college of bishops, 197, 205

collegiality, 11, 205, 207

common good, 130, 157

global character of, 146

participation and, 144

protecting, 58

Common Good and Christian Ethics, The (Hollenbach), 163n24

common priesthood, 85

communal relationships, expansion of, 27

communion

in the ancient church, 194–95

between Christians, new mode of, 27

emphasized over universal jurisdiction, 197

Spirit's gift of, 194

communion ecclesiology, 191–92, 198, 199–201

"Communio Notis" (CDF), 199–201, 206

community, 159

moving together toward God, 140–41

people created for, 137, 138

comparative theology, 97

confessionalization, 13

Congar, Yves, 50, 70, 74, 112

Congregation for the Doctrine of the Faith, 199

Congregation for the Evangelization of Peoples, 102, 104

consensus ecclesiarum, 110, 115–18

consensus fidelium, 116

consultation, 178, 185–86

contextualization, 225

control, 32

conversion, 185

addressing racism through, 173

as humanizing praxis, 229

Conway, Eamonn, 76

Cornelio, Charles Ochero, 98

correlation, 155–56

councils

pastoral, meaning of, 12

types of, 7

Council of Trent, 7, 15, 86, 93, 167

Co-Workers in the Vineyard of the Lord (USCCB), 79, 80, 183

creation, value and integrity of, 152

cross, recognizing, in the fragility of the future, 230

crucified future, 178–79

crucified peoples, 224–25

crucifixion, dialectical situation of, 225

culture, racism functioning as, 169–70

Curran, Charles, 135

deacons. *See also* diaconate

functions of, 88

historical context for, 86–87

as married members of the clergy, 88, 89

relations with priests, 88

understanding of, 86

de Certeau, Michel, 39

dehumanization, 225–26
Dei Verbum (Vatican II), 13
De Keyzer, Mauritis, 110
de Lubac, Henri, 39
democracies, paradox of authority in, 56
De Oecumenismo, 112
Derrida, Jacques, 224, 229
de Smedt, Emile Joseph, 110
destiny, human, related to the Earth's condition, 215
development, participation as part of, 144
diaconate, 87. *See also* deacons
  canonical context for, 90–92
  enabling ministry, 90
  female, 86
  ministry of, 87, 92
  sacramental, 87, 94n9
dialogical consultation, 185–87
dialogical discernment, 184–87
dialogical orthodoxy, 182–83
dialogue
  definitions of, 100, 102–3, 104–5
  distinct from evangelization, 102
  enhancing quality of, between church and secular partners, 131
  as evangelization tool, 105
  future of, 237–38
  as peaceful solution, 124, 127
  practice of, in the life of the church, 181
  in tension with mission, 100–102
Dialogue and Proclamation (PCID and CEP), 102, 123

Dickens, Charles, 167
Dignitatis Humanae (Vatican II), 12
diocesan pastoral councils, 184, 206
diocesan synods, 206
dioceses
  reorganization of, 69
  size of, 206
  translating bishops among, 206–7
discernment, 118, 177, 240
  communal process of, 182
  lament and, 179
  ministry of, 116
disciples, 71–72
diversity, unity in, 142–43
dualistic thinking, 146
Dulles, Avery, 98
Dumont, Christophe, 112

Eastern Catholic Churches, 199
Ecclesiae de Mysterio (Vatican), 80
ecclesial action, 41
ecclesial structures, 70
Ecclesiam Suam (Paul VI), 55, 123
ecclesiology
  communion, 191–92, 198, 199–201
  eucharistic, 197
  future of, 214, 239–40
  historical context for, 193
  inductive, 178, 192–94
  pneumatological, 227, 228–29
  Roman-centric, 196
  universalistic, 196
ecological crisis

and the future's uncertainty, 214, 215, 216
structural injustice and, 217–18
salvation and, 229–30
economic injustice, 144–45
Economic Justice for All (US-CCB), 156–57
economic trinitarianism, 145
ecumenism, 8, 11, 13, 99, 113
education, integrating, spiritual and secular, 237
Edwards, Denis, 76
Eiesland, Nancy, 25
elementa ecclesiae, 109, 110, 111
  doctrine of, development of, 113–15
  recognizing Christ's salvation outside the Catholic Church, 117
Ellacuría, Ignacio, 178, 224, 225
embodiment
  expanding the understanding of, 26, 32–34
  importance of, 28
  meaning of, 29
  refashioning, for intellectually disabled persons, 31
Emerson, Ralph Waldo, 124
episcopacy, 63–64, 87
episcopal conferences, 205
equality, 144
ethics, 129
  communal nature of, 172
  future of, 238–39
  liturgy's connection to, 22
  personalist approach to, 133
Eucharist
  active participation in, 25

addressing racism through, 173
centrality of, 9, 10, 26
community of, 207
conformity with Christ, 27–28
inculturated, 207–8
lay participation in, 29
rational comprehension of, 29–30
sacrifice of, 22
eucharistic ecclesiology, 197
Europe, public theology in, 158
evangelization
  dialogue of, 106–7
  push for, 8
Extraordinary Synod of Bishops (1985), 8, 16

Faggioli, Massimo, 3, 21, 207
faith
  instinct for, 181–82
  integrating science and culture with, 124
faithful, membership in, 109, 110
family service, 90
fatalism, 219, 221, 222
female diaconate, 86
Fifth Lateran Council, 7
First Vatican Council. *See* Vatican I
flesh, sacredness of, 28
Focolare movement, 147
  spirituality of, 134, 140
  theology of, 134
  trinitarian anthropology of, 140
Folan, Peter, 50
fragility, 218–19
freedom, 144

future
    concealment of, 221
    conditionality of, 214–16
    crucified, 226, 227, 229–30
    de-ideologizing, 226
    fragility of, 178, 218–19,
        222, 225–26
    questionable outcome of,
        215

Gaillardetz, Richard, 80, 195,
    201, 203–4, 206
Gaudet Mater Ecclesia (John
    XXIII), 13
Gaudium et Spes (Vatican II), 2,
    10, 11–12, 87, 161
    addressing the church's rela-
        tionship with the world,
        151
    christology of, 152
    on the church needing to fol-
        low Christ, 46
    context for, 134–35
    on created reality, 152–53
    on the goal of the church,
        170
    on human dignity, 171
    influence of, 129
    personalist ethic within,
        137
    proclaiming end to antago-
        nism toward modernity,
        130–31
    on racism, 131, 170–72
    on relationship of the church
        to the rest of Christianity,
        45
    relevance of, 131–32, 133
    suggesting link between Trin-
        ity and humanity's unity,
        139

gender
    feminist criticism of, 41
    historicizing, 42
    subversion of, 44
Gender Trouble (Butler), 39,
    41–44, 46
George, Francis, 77
gestures, magisterium through,
    12
globalization, 130, 133, 146
global warming, 215. See also
    climate change; ecological
    crisis
God
    moving toward, as commu-
        nity, 140–41
    revelation of, dictating the
        church's structure, 70
Gonzalez, Eduardo, 178
González de Cardedal, Olegario,
    157
governance
    baptismal charism of, 59
    ideals of, conflating, 55–56
    meta-levels of, 59–60
    requiring accountability,
        55–56
    secular, 56
governed, human dignity of,
    63
grace, 27
Great Expectations (Dickens),
    167
Great Jubilee (2000), 8
Gregory, Wilton, 65n2
Gregory the Great, 55
Gribomont, Jean, 112
"Guidelines for the Celebration
    of the Sacraments with
    Persons with Disabilities"
    (USCCB), 29

Haight, Roger, 192, 193
Hamer, Jêrome, 112, 113
Hampton, Jean, 56–57, 58
Häring, Bernard, 161n1
Hauerwas, Stanley, 157, 159, 160
healing, 64, 179, 240
heterosexism, 41–43
Hinze, Bradford, 184
historical worldview, 136
historicizing, 225
Hollenbach, David, 154, 156
holy orders
    converging with marriage,
        85, 89–90
    degrees of, 87, 88
    as sacrament, 87
Holy Spirit
    activity of, 227–30
    discerning the work of, 116,
        177
    eschatological significance of,
        228–29
    guiding the church, 178–79
    indwelling of, within believ-
        ers, 181, 182
    presence of, signaling the life
        of the church, 227
hospitality, 23, 34
Humanae Vitae, 8
human beings
    social dimension of, 137–38,
        171–72
    vulnerability of, 224
human dignity, 13, 63, 171
    protecting, 58
    traditional Catholic respect
        for, 152
    turn toward, 130
humanization, praxis of, 227
human relations, trinitarian ap-
        proach to, 143

human rights
    claiming of, 61–63
    shared norms for, 62
human situation, 155–56

imago Dei, 138–39
IMCS. *See* International Move-
        ment of Catholic Students
inclusivity, 22
inculturation, 203–4, 207–8
indefectibility, 111
India, public theology in, 158
inductive ecclesiology, 192–94
inequality, economic, 144–45
infallibility, 111
Ingiosi, Gina, 22
injustice, structural, 217–18,
        238–39
intellectually disabled persons.
        See also Catholics with
        disabilities
    disrupting the liturgy, 33–34
    integral to the church, 26–27
    lacking rational mastery of
        the body, 31
    and the liturgy, 23, 26
    participating through their
        presence, 28
    stigmatization of, 32
    understanding the sacra-
        ments, 29–30
    welcoming, 27, 33
interdependence, 171
International Movement of
        Catholic Students (IMCS–
        Pax Romana), 123, 125,
        126–27
International Theological Com-
        mission, 183
interreligious dialogue, scriptural
        basis for, 107

interreligious engagement, 97
interreligious relations, 99–100
IPCC. *See* United Nations Inter-
    governmental Panel on
    Climate Change
Izuzquiza, Daniel, 159

Janssens, Louis, 136–37
Jerusalem, church at, 194,
    200–201
Jesus Christ
    present manifestation of, 155
    resurrection of, 225
    table fellowship of, 173
John XXIII, 12, 13, 62, 134–35,
    167
John Paul II, 8, 12, 16, 54–55,
    66n10, 76, 78, 85, 101–2,
    198, 199, 200, 204
justice
    global, and trinitarian an-
        thropology, 144
    restorative, 64
    separating love from, 144
Justice in the World (Bishops'
    Synod), 144

Kasper, Walter, 178, 191, 198,
    200, 201, 204
Kelly, John, 136
kenosis, 142–43
Kimmerling, Ben, 77, 81
King, Martin Luther, Jr., 125, 174
Komonchak, Joseph, 192, 197,
    201–2
Küng, Hans, 205, 206

LaCugna, Catherine Mowry,
    134, 140
laity. *See also* lay ecclesial minis-
    try; lay theologians

called to be ministers, 80
dialogical discernment
    among, 184–85
empowerment of, 183–84
ministerial task of, 73–74
role of, in the church, 85
secular role of, 85
Lakeland, Paul, 192, 204, 206
lament, 179, 240
Lash, Nicholas, 182
lay ecclesial ministry, 74, 78–82
    in dialogue with local church
        and church authorities,
        182–83
    formation programs for, 79
    negative bearings on, 81
    women in, 81
lay theologians, 8
    bishops' dialogue with,
        184–85
    contribution of, 183
    in dialogue with local church
        and church authorities,
        182–83
leadership, idealization of, 55
Lefebvrites, 16
Leo XIII, 135
Levinas, Emmanuel, 224
Lialine, Clément, 112
liberalism, suspicion of, 135
liberation theology, 153
liturgical theology, 22, 236
liturgy
    connection of, to ethics, 22
    future of, 235–36
    as greatest act of the church,
        46
    participation in, 26, 28
    rebuilding Catholics as the
        body of Christ, 27, 30
    reform of, 9–10, 13, 21–22

supremacy of, 41
understanding of, 29
local churches
  ecclesiology growing from, 192–93
  embedding themselves in local culture, 203–4
  importance of, declining, 195–96
  involved in selection of bishops, 206
  modeled on universal church, 197
  possessing gift of catholicity, 197
  relations with universal churches, 191, 202
  sharing bonds with each other in the universal church, 195
  theology of, 194
Lonergan, Bernard, 192
love
  separating justice from, 144
  trinitarian, 140, 141
Lubich, Chiara, 134, 140, 147
Lumen Gentium (Vatican II), 10, 11, 12, 13, 109, 177, 178, 197
  on the church as the mystical body of Christ, 40
  on the church's institutional authority, 54
  on the church's relation to the entire church of Christ, 114
  on the church's structure, 59
  on common sanctity in the body of Christ, 57–58
  on deacon's gift of vocation, 90
  on the diaconate, 87
  drafting of, and the doctrine of *sensus fidelium*, 110–11
  emphasizing celebrating the sacraments, 45
  on empowerment of the laity, 183–84
  expressing church unity in terms of bodiliness, 40
  on ministry, dimensions of, 71–74
  on the permanent diaconate, 86–87
  on the pilgrim church, 228
  pneumatological ecclesiology of, 227
  on priestly roles, 80
  recasting relationships between members and the church, 41
  on salvation, 230
Luther, Martin, 7

MacIntyre, Alisdair, 157, 159
Mannion, Gerard, 192, 193, 201
Mariapolis, 141
Maritain, Jacques, 136
marriage
  converging with holy orders, 85, 89–90
  sacrament of, 90
  vocation of, 85
Martin, Diarmuid, 64
Marty, Martin, 153
Massa, Mark, 167, 170
Massingale, Bryan, 131, 167–69, 171–73
matter, conversing with meaning, 42–44
McDonnell, Killian, 200
McFague, Sallie, 215, 217, 227

meaning, conversing with matter, 42–44
metropolitan churches, 195
metropolitan system, 205
Metz, Johann Baptist, 178, 220–21, 224, 226
Milbank, John, 157
ministerial education programs, growth of, 49
ministerial priesthood, 85
ministers, as disciples, 71–72
ministry, 49–51, 55, 63
    changes in, 69
    conversation about, after Vatican II, 74–75
    differentiations in, 73
    features of, 71
    invitation to, 236–37
    laity as element of, 73–74, 80
    part of the church's structure, 72
    of priests, 75–78
    as structure, 71
    structures of, 69–70, 71, 74
    tasks and offices of, 72–73
    Vatican II statements on, 71–74
mission
    to non-Catholic Christians, 99
    to non-Christians, 99
    personal embodiment of, 183
    pre–Vatican II notion of, 100, 101, 105
    in tension with dialogue, 100–102
Mitchell, Nathan, 26, 28, 33, 203
modernity, 13, 130–31, 135
moral anthropology, 239
moral authority, 239

moral pluralism, 158
moral theology, Christ and scripture at center of, 152
Mounier, Emmanuel, 136
munera, triple, 63, 88
Murray, John Courtney, 154, 155
Muslim-Christian cooperation, 125–26
mutuality, dialogue of, 106–7
mystical body of Christ
    gender troubles of, 42
    intelligibility of, 40–41
    modern rediscovery of, 39–40
    organization of, 40
    performing itself, 44
    recasting of, 45
    setting boundaries of the church, 45
    supreme act of, 41
    visibility of, 40
mystical body doctrine, 39, 42, 44–45
Mystici Corporis Christi (Pius XII), 22, 40–41, 114

natural law, 136, 137, 147, 154
natural rights, 61, 62
"The Nature and Purpose of the Church" (WCC), 116
neo-atheism, 17
neoclassical natural law, 136
neo-Scholastic framework, 136
Neuhaus, Richard John, 15
new liturgical movement, 9
Newman, John Henry, 185–86
New Mexico Conference of Catholic Bishops, 214–15
Niebuhr, Reinhold, 153

"NMCCB Statement on the Environment" (New Mexico Conference of Catholic Bishops), 214–15
normalcy, cult of, 31–32, 33
Nostra Aetate (Vatican II), 10, 12, 14
    dialogue in, scriptural support for, 107
    encouraging dialogue and collaboration with other religions, 100–101
    prophetic value of, 15
    tradition of, 106

O'Connor, John, 198–99
O'Malley, John, 151
O'Meara, Thomas F., 71
One Church, 112–13
openness, 144
Optatam Totius (Vatican II), 72, 75, 152
ordered church ministry, 80
ordination, 54–55, 57, 75
    as new status in church life, 90–91
    new ways of imagining and living, 81–82
Ordinatio Sacerdotalis (John Paul II), 78
Orientalium Ecclesiarum, 13
Osheim, Amanda, 177–78
other, religious, 12
other faithful, the, 54, 57
    as governors in the church, 60
    human rights of, limiting authority, 63

Pacem in Terris (John XXIII), 62
parish, level of activity at, 25

participation, 144
Pastor Aeternus (Vatican I), 196
pastoral constitution, 129
Pastores Dabo Vobis (John Paul II), 76, 77
Pastores Gregis (John Paul II), 54–55
Paul VI, 8, 12, 55, 60, 83n8, 87, 93n4, 123, 134
Pawlikowski, John, 100, 102
Pax Romana Sudan, 124–25
PCID. See Pontifical Council for Interreligious Dialogue of the Holy See
PCPCU. See Pontifical Council for Promoting Christian Unity
peacebuilding, 124, 126
Peace Unit Program (IMCS), 126
Pentecost, 194, 200–201, 208
people of God
    Catholic Church as, 54
    charged with the mission of the church, 72
    recovering the concept of, 111
    two categories of, 90
performance
    importance of, to the body, 43, 44
    subverting meaning, 44
perichoresis, 142
permanent deacons. See permanent diaconate
permanent diaconate, 49–50, 90
    formation for, 91
    marriage in, 85, 86, 91
    ministry topics related to, 86
    numbers in, increasing, 92
    ordination into, 91

reestablishment of, 87
theological context for,
    87–90
value of, 86–87
personalism, 146
personalist anthropology,
    136–38
personhood, trinitarian aspects
    of, 130
Petrolino, E., 87, 88
Philippines, Catholic bishops of,
    216
pilgrim church, 228
Pius IX, 135
Pius XII, 22, 40–41, 47n6
pluralism, 158
plurality, 117
pneumatology, 228
political theology, 153
Pontifical Council for Inter-
    religious Dialogue of the
    Holy See, 97, 99, 102–7,
    123
Pontifical Council for Promot-
    ing Christian Unity, 97,
    103–4
pope
    authority of, 196, 197
    infallibility of, 196
    ministry of, 195, 204–5
Porter, Jean, 61
pragmatic agreement, 61
preaching, sanctioned, 75
presbyteral councils, 184
presbyterate, 87
Presbyterorum Ordinis (Vatican
    II), 72, 73
presence
    idol of, 226
    metaphysics of, 220–21
presidency, sacramental, 75

priesthood. See also priests
    necessity of, 75
    theology of, 81
    types of, 80, 85
Priestly Fraternity of St. Pius X,
    16
priests. See also priesthood
    celibacy of, 77–78
    decreasing number of, 79
    friendships of, with women,
        81
    as men of communion, 76–77
    men only, 78
    ministry of, 75–78
    relations with deacons, 88
primatial churches, 194, 195
Program of Priestly Formation
    (PPF), 75, 76–77
Protestants, U.S., and public
    theology, 153–54
public philosophy, 155
public theology, 131
    defined, 153–54
    elements of, 154
    new contexts for, 158–61
    radical response to, 157
    rediscovery of, 157
    in the United States, 153–57

racism
    in the church, addressing,
        172–73
    culture of, 169–70
    in the educational setting,
        addressing, 172–73
    systemic, 131, 168, 169–70
Rahner, Karl, 30, 139–40
rapprochement, 10
Ratzinger, Joseph, 7, 16, 178,
    191, 200–201. See also
    Benedict XVI

Rausch, Thomas, 201, 204, 206
reality, integrity of, 152–53
reception, 74
   embodiment of, 185
   orthopraxis of, 178, 182, 187
   of others in the church, 177
Redemptoris Missio (John Paul
   II), 101–2
relational anthropology, 146
relationality, 137
religion
   engaging culture, 124
   privatization of, 153, 157
religious movements, spirituality
   of, 147
religious pluralism, 105, 158
respect, 237
ressourcement, 9, 10
Reynolds, Chris, 31, 32
Reynolds, Thomas, 26, 31–32,
   33, 35n6
rights-talk, criticism of, 61
rights theories, incompatibility
   of, with Catholic doc-
   trine, 62
Rome
   exercising its ministry of
      unity, 204
   growing influence of, 195,
      199
   power coalescing in, 195–96,
      198
   primacy of, 194–95, 204
   reconciliation with, 205
Romero, Pablo Solón, 218
Rubens, Heather Miller, 98
Ruddy, Christopher, 194,
   197–98, 202–7
Ruiz de la Peña, Juan Luis, 152
Rush, Ormond, 182
Russett, Bruce, 66n10

Sacrae Disciplinae Leges (John
   Paul II), 85
sacramental theology, 26, 30
sacraments
   necessity of, 29
   organically related to the
      church, 40
   participation in, 25
   reason needed for receiving
      of, 36n19
   resistance to, 29
sacrifice, Christian, 22
Sacrosanctum Concilium (Vatican II), 9–10, 12–14, 197,
   207
   ableist understandings of,
      28–29
   on agency, deriving from the
      body's united and orderly
      quality, 41
   allowing for bodily engage-
      ment and silence in
      liturgy, 31
   allowing contextual reason-
      ing regarding laity, 30
   on central commitment of
      Christianity, 28
   church as mystical body of
      Christ in, 40
   encouraging active participa-
      tion in the Sacraments, 25
   on liturgy as greatest action
      of the church, 45
   positive vision of, 27–28
   reimagining of, 26
   vision of, 32
Sacrum Diaconatus Ordinem
   (Paul VI), 83n8, 87
salvation, 225, 229–30
Schatz, Klaus, 194
Schillebeeckx, Edward, 203, 230

Schineller, Peter, 203
Schneiders, Sandra, 77–78
scripture, centrality of, 9, 235
Second Vatican Council. *See*
    Vatican II
Secretariat for Non-Christians,
    97
secularism, post-Christian,
    130–31
sensus fidei, applying to all
    Christians, 117–18
sensus fidelium, 109–10, 178
    character of, 181
    discerning, 181–83
    doctrine of, 110–11, 115
    ecumenical debate on, 116
    leading to *consensus eccle-
        siarum*, 116
    operation of, 118
    outside of Roman Catholi-
        cism, 115–16
Sesboüé, Bernard, 79–80
sexual-abuse crisis
    affecting authority relation-
        ships in the church, 64
    church authority and, 53–54
    requiring review of church
        governance, 59–60
    victim-survivors' advocacy
        in, 61
Shepherd of Hermas, 199
signs of the times, discerning,
    85, 131, 135, 136, 170
Sobrino, Jon, 224, 225
social-contract theories, 56
socialization, negative, 131
social pluralism, 153, 154
solidarity, 144, 162n15, 172–73,
    229
South Sudan, conflict in, 124–25
Spirit. *See* Holy Spirit
spirituality

communal character of,
    140–41
in dialogical consultation,
    186
diversity in, necessity of, 187
ecclesial, 186
spiritual practices, sharing of,
    187
Stevens, Krista, 131
structural injustice, 217–18,
    238–39
structure, 70–71
structures, 70–71
subsidiarity, 144
subsistit in, doctrine of, 114
Suenens, Léon Joseph, 2–3, 110
suffering, reality of, 230
Sullivan, Francis, 181
Syllabus Errorum (Pius IX), 135
synodality, new forms of, 11
Synod of Bishops (1965), 11

Terra Nova (TV series), 222–23
Tettamazzi, Dionigi, 86
theologians, dialogue lacking
    among, 3
theological anthropology, 130
    rise of, 139–40
    trinitarian, 133–34
theological ethics, 129, 159
theology
    comparative, 97
    doing, from the cracks of the
        future, 226
    liberation, 153
    liturgical, 22, 236
    moral, 152
    political, 153
    public, 131, 160. *See also*
        public theology
    sacramental, 26, 30
    situationless, 223–24

Theology of the World (Metz), 220

Thijssen, Frans, 113

Thils, Gustave, 112, 113

Thomas Aquinas, 136

Thomism, neo-Scholastic, retrieval of, 135, 136

Tierney, Brian, 62

Tillard, Jean-Marie Roger, 116–17, 194, 202–8

time, understanding of, changing, 219–20

timelessness
internalization of, 222
lived experience of, 223
spell of, 220–23

Tracy, David, 131, 155–56, 159–60, 223, 226

trinitarian anthropology, 133–34
foundations of, 139
practical implications of, 141–44
rediscovery of, 140
relevance of, for Catholic social thought, 146–47
spirituality of unity and, 141

trinitarian relations
applications of, 144–45
principles of, 144

Trinity
identity of, 139
immanent and economic, 139–40
relevance of, recovering, 141

True and False Reform in the Church (Congar), 70

truth, presence of, in other churches, 113

Twiss, Sumner, 61

Unitatis Redintegratio (Vatican II), 10, 11, 13, 109, 114

United Nations, 126
Alliance for Civilizations, 125
Intergovernmental Panel on Climate Change (IPCC), 215

United States, public theology in, 153–57

United States Conference of Catholic Bishops (USCCB), 27, 75, 79, 156–57, 168–69, 183

unity
in diversity, 142–43
spirituality of, 134, 140

universal church
diversity in communion of, 202
existing from local churches, 197
local churches within, sharing bonds with each other, 195
mystery of, 199
overemphasis on, 208
prioritizing, 199–201
reality of, 200
relations of, with local churches, 191, 202

universalistic ecclesiology, 196

U.S. Bishops' Committee on Black Catholics, 168

U.S. Catholic Church
addressing racism in the church, 172–73
increasing number of members in, 79
insufficient response to systemic racism, 131, 168–69
social thought coming from, 154–57

USCCB. *See* U.S. Conference of
Catholic Bishops
Ut Unum Sint (John Paul II),
204

Valadier, Paul, 157
Van Stichel, Ellen, 130
Vatican I (First Vatican Council),
197
Vatican II (Second Vatican
Council), 1, 2, 8, 167
christology of, 152
on the church as the mystical
body of Christ, 39–40
on the church's mission, 72
context for, 135
debate about, reopening,
15–17
decades following, division
of, 19n16
on the diaconate, 87–88
dialogue and, 97–98
differing theological interpretations of, 2
ecclesiology of, 9–11, 13, 85,
117, 191, 197–99
echoing changes in secular
political theory, 56
emphasizing bishops' dual
role, 205
emphasizing communion and
jurisdiction, 202
empowering the church with
a stronger public voice,
154
endorsing liturgical inculturation, 207
ethical vision of, 130
eucharistic ecclesiology of,
207
fresh insight into, from new
theologians, 2

greater understanding of, as
an event, 17
hope of, 14, 17
interpretation of, external
framework for, 16
John Paul II's reception of,
16
literary style of documents
from, 151
liturgical reform resulting
from, 9–10, 21–22
message of, 8
on ministry, 71–74
openness of, toward the
world, 151
participatory governing
structures following, 59
presenting no definition of
Catholicism, 14
reception of, 7–8, 212–13,
223, 227, 230
reiterating Rome's role as
center of communion,
204
relevance of, 3–4, 7–8
renewing the permanent diaconate, 49, 50
shifting from classicist to historical worldview, 135–36
as source of hope, 235
special nature of, 8–9
talking to humanity, 12
theology of, 9
turning point in relationship
between local and univer-
sal churches, 197
value of, 12
vestigial, 113
vestigial elementa, 112–13
victims
communion of, 224
future world of, 225–27

Villagrán, Gonzalo, 130, 131
vocations
    elements of, 86
    promotion of, 236
Vulnerable Communion: A Theology of Disability and Hospitality (Reynolds), 26

Ward, Peter D., 216, 217
WCC. *See* World Council of Churches
WEA. *See* World Evangelical Alliance
Weakland, Rembert, 198–99, 201
Weigel, George, 55
"What Is Happening to Our Beautiful Land?" (Philippine Catholic bishops), 216
White Like Me (Wise), 174
white privilege, 168, 169
Wilfred, Felix, 158
Willebrands, Johannes, 112, 113, 114

Wills, Garry, 167
Wilson, Edward O., 215–17
Wise, Tim, 174
witness
    Christian, biblical foundation for, 104
    ecumenical statement on, Catholic response to, 99–100
Witte, Johannes, 112
women
    as lay ecclesial ministers, 81
    non-ordination of, 78
World Council of Churches, 99, 113, 116
World Evangelical Alliance, 99

youth
    protection of, 61
    transformational potential of, 127

Žižek, Slavoj, 222